The Hedonist

The

Hedonist

World Vacation Guide For Sex Tourism

BRETT TATE

TPB Publishing, Inc.
Dallas, Texas

Travel guides contain information that frequently changes over time. For obvious legal reasons, the author and publisher assume no responsibility for the accuracy of the contents of this book, no responsibility for how you utilize the information in this book, nor do we have any recollection of actually writing it. Use the enclosed information to provide you with an overall understanding of each vacation city, and take advantage of the local web sites provided for any updates that may occur.

Published by
The Professional Bachelor Publishing
Suite 600491
Dallas, Texas 75205
www.theprofessionalbachelor.com

ISBN 0-9752640-0-1
Printed in the United States of America

Contents

THE HEDONIST

" I believe that sex is one of the most beautiful,
natural, wholesome things that money can buy. "

TOM CLANCY, **American** *novelist*

No risk, no reward. Safe and sound in the confines of our simple, efficient western culture world. Carefully settling for the path of least resistance. It's what people strive for, a distinct concrete outcome in life. All meticulously structured, and painfully achieved over a fixed predictable course spanning several decades. The prestigious school, well respected career, 2 ½ kids and a dog, in the classiest neighborhood in Bumfuck, California. Suit yourself, what is one man's paradise, is another man's hell.

Risk takers. The fine line between brilliant and mentally unstable. We've all met them. They're ambitious, spontaneous, shrewd, and innovative. They're wildly passionate about whatever endeavor is currently driving them. They revel in the chaotic. The outcome can bring indescribable success, or catastrophic defeat. Yet regardless of the result, their character remains virtually unchanged. Is it madness? No. It's the thrill of the chase. It's the brazen uncertainty, the sheer recklessness that creates the moment when the hairs on the back of your neck tingle.

Vacations should be like this. Bold, exotic and irresponsible on the surface, but intelligently controlling the risks underneath. If exploring the world's hottest sexual paradises and being smothered by young, uninhibited women sounds intriguing, this guide is for you. The Hedonist was written by a team of motivated, impulsive individuals who share a passion for exotic Sex Tourism Vacations. We've traveled the world extensively and accumulated a bible of information, advice, stories, tricks and tips that we've decided to share. The Hedonist is a turnkey manual, a fast access roadmap to the vital information you'll need in organizing your trip, so that when you arrive, you can hit the ground running. Inside is comprehensive up-to-date data concerning airports, taxis, local customs, hotels, transportation, maps, pricing, and most important, where to find the hottest single women. Inside you'll find the top twenty Ultimate Vacation spots, each is packed with hundreds of single, exotic women who are easily approachable and available in a matter of minutes. We direct you to the hottest locals clubs for getting either part-time girlfriends, or having wild orgies with a buffet of freelancing erotic pros.

We happily dive in headfirst to give you our personal inside scoop of the raunchy darker side of life, as we peer into the heart of the World's Brothels, Red Light Districts, Massage Parlors, Termas, Escort Services, and Go Go Bars with Exotic Shows. Damn, field research can be so difficult.

In addition, in each city we detail the weekend warrior sporting options, as well as sightseeing and local entertainment. Our trips are designed to maximize your fun while keeping it economically feasible for most anyone. Let's face it; itineraries on vacations are generally works of hopeful fiction. The enclosed contents are meticulously detailed, vulgar, and hilarious...soon you'll become an expert on your own World Sex Tours. From the sun soaked topless beaches of Rio de Janeiro, the insanity of Bangkok Go Go's and massage parlors, to the Amsterdam red light district...it's all here for the taking.

There are many do's and don'ts you must memorize before you travel abroad. We provide the quick lessons and insights on how to avoid the tourist traps, rip offs and scams. More importantly, we explain the traits of the girls you want to pursue, and the telltale signs of spotting disaster girls to avoid at all costs. You'll quickly absorb the lessons and insights, saving you from making expensive and stupid mistakes. The clock's ticking, you'll want to make the most of your vacation time. Of course the most important info is how to approach and exploit the mind-boggling chica opportunities. We put you in ground zero of the action in the fastest, and most affordable method possible.

Our criterion for selecting each location has several requirements. **First**, there must be a buffet of insatiable young women available, in an easy access, friendly environment. **Second**, it has to be a tropical climate. There are many desirable locations that could have been included, but weather and price eliminate them. For example, Russia is an oasis of supermodels, but with sub zero freezing temperatures and gold plated women, we're gonna have to pass.

Third, we want cities with a superior local sports scene, including gorgeous world ranked golf courses, Big Game Sport Fishing, jet skiing, scuba diving, casinos, as well as jogging on nude beaches. We include any interesting sightseeing jaunts to entertain you a few hours in each locale. After all, we're not just porn stars, it's nice to venture out to experience a little bit of the country and its culture. For sightseeing tours, we recommend the hottest, young female you can find, and we'll give you the tips and tricks on how to arrange this with little effort and plenty of reward.

Is it worth traveling across the globe for women? Let's do a quick test. Go to your favorite nightclub in America, walk up to the hottest 18 year girl you can find, and offer her $50.

The Hedonist shows you how to enjoy unforgettable adventures with Asian and Latin American women at some of wildest places on the planet. These aren't just vacations, they're life changing experiences. You will be seeing and doing things that will be impossible to explain. So enjoy your research, grab a beer, and book your flight. It's time for you to live the life of a rock star, and fulfill every erotic fantasy you can imagine.

The women are ready and waiting. Don't disappoint them…

WHY WE DO IT

**" Instead of getting married again, I'm going to find a woman
I don't like and just give her a house. "**

ROD STEWART, British *singer*

Imagine someone approaches you with a business offer that has no potential financial return, and proposes a fifty percent chance of losing half your net worth in a few years. This is what every man faces when getting married. It's Russian roulette. The Western culture has adapted to an onslaught of feminism, lawyers, and the divorce industry, creating a new breed of women. Instead of being seductive and feminine, the women have adopted a personality that's impetuous, opinionated, and blatantly arrogant. Western women want all the benefits of being equal, without sharing equal responsibility. The essence of being a woman has left the culture. The hottest ladies have become cash registers with legs. Sex is a negotiating tool to be used in direct proportion to whatever material goods or status they receive in return. Kind of like a call girl who refuses to put out. Not to mention all the drama and baggage they carry around. Married men are reduced to being a slave, psychologist, and a bottomless ATM machine. Like Sam Kinison said, "women are one imaginary crisis away from a complete nervous breakdown, and just looking for a guy to blame it on."

While there's no such thing as romance without finance, it's become a school of female piranha feeding off a bleeding man and his wallet. Fortunately there are alternative solutions. In reality, there is no truth to the power of the pussy theory. The wallet is the life support system of the pussy. How you use it and control it decides the outcome.

Think of those moments when you're bored out of your mind, and dating has become a regrettable chore. We all know the feeling…when you try to rationalize all the whining, worthless gold diggers you tolerate for marginal return. What you should be doing is contemplating your sanity.

It only takes one trip abroad for your eyes to be opened to an alternate universe full of aggressive, young girls. This reality is petrifying to the old crone at home. Western women have a significant interest in keeping "their" men and their wallets at home. They have reason to be jealous, as they simply cannot and will not compete. That would require being nice, putting out, and not chasing money. The Sex Tourism women overseas are a superior female species. Hop on a plane to one of our meticulously planned vacations, and you'll realize you are not the problem; it's the women in your life.

Darwinism is the natural ability to evolve and adapt to the environment for survival. The result here is no surprise. Marriage rates have plunged, and experienced bachelors laugh at loud at the thought of giving an American woman a ring.

In Asia and South America, the essence of being a woman is a cherished quality. They are seductive, exotic, and erotic without moral boundaries. In their culture, there's no greater insult than to lose a man over bedroom performance. They compete for your attention, hold on to you for dear life, and consider it normal behavior to be insatiable nymphos. Sex is one of the most rewarding and mutually fulfilling things to share with a man. Whether out of love or as a client, if it's consensual it is worth every minute. There's nothing degrading at all about satisfying a man, and they look forward to doing it every day with a smile. A few trips under your belt will change your life…many guys say it's so gratifying, it **ruins their life**. There can be a rather severe recovery period upon returning home. Many quit dating all together and just take trips every few months.

Coming from the Land of Opportunity, we take for granted our freedom, money, material luxuries, and how fortunate we are. What we don't take for granted is how passionate, aggressive, and sensual women in other countries are. Complete role reversal. Wherever you go, girls stare you down like sexual stalkers, even when they are sitting with their man. You can approach almost any girl and interview like a champion.

"Would you like to get together some time?"
"Yes"
"Are you available tomorrow night? "
"Yes"
"Can I have your phone number?"
" What's wrong with right now, where are you staying? "

"Can I buy you dinner, get no sex, and you whine to me nonstop…? "
"This ain't America big boy, let's just go to your room now. "

" Will you still respect me in the morning? "
" No, I'll have sex with you in the morning. "

" I hope you're not threatened by an exceedingly endowed billionaire. "
"Let me guess, Motel 6 Mr. Jones?
Love your cologne, is that Budweiser?

6

THE ART OF SEX TOURISM

**" You know, it really doesn't matter what people think,
as long as you've got a young and beautiful piece of ass. "**

DONALD TRUMP, *1991*

Sex Tourism is an Olympic Sport practiced worldwide. The goals are simple...enjoying gorgeous young girls without attitudes, paying rock bottom prices, exploring sights around the world, and returning home alive, with great memories. The men participating are either pros who play the game for all it's worth...or amateurs who are screwed over and eaten alive. Most girls in the sex industry have little education, but are armed with street smarts and experience. Many are nothing more than hardcore con artists. To them it's a game to see how much they can extort from you, and how fast. This is their business. The trick is to be one step ahead of them. Anticipating the scams and ignoring the demands, dumping bad girls, and choosing the sweethearts. Your attitude and approach should be self confident and firm, be charming, have a cutting sense of humor, and bargain like a used car salesman. They have the goods, but we have all the gold. Your goal is to become a Pro when it comes to spending it, and enjoying the fruits of being King around the globe.

When you travel, keep a perspective of how impoverished the country and it's people are. Most girls spend their days in a crowded one-bedroom shack with no AC, watching soap operas. The average monthly income for college graduates is barely $500. Accountants in Cuba make $10 a week. For us, in western culture we take women to dinner, movies, concerts, shows, buy them gifts, open their doors, and are gentlemen. When your abroad, NONE of these things will ever happen in the girls' lives without meeting a gringo. Latin men are poor, women are treated like their property, and they interact with an iron fist.

Don't be a pussy. If you spend any time with a girl, all the little things we normally do for a woman should be a fantasy date to them. From the moment you meet and interact, take inventory of her reactions. Star struck and oozing affection should be the natural response. The good girls all dream of leaving their country and living like this, and should be overwhelmed you are being so nice to little old her. Smiling, stroking, and a lot of crotch grabbing...the girls should be doing that as well. These are the women you should spend time with on your vacation. There's great satisfaction in mildly spoiling a young angel who truly appreciates the thought you put into it. She recognizes your stature as a humble World Charity leader, and she will smother you with her top performance in the

7

bedroom, hoping at the very least for a repeat date with you every night you're in town. Hey, we all have a dream.

Then there are the sharks, the hardcore pros, who like children, will try to push you to see how far they can go. If she gets the slightest whiff that you're content being a servant and a walking ATM machine, you may as well put your head between your knees and grab your ankles. It'll start with buying her friends' drinks, or grabbing your change. She'll ask to be taken to dinner, and then order the most expensive entrée. If you're on Main Street or in a mall, suddenly she needs a new purse, dress, swimsuit, or two pairs of shoes…things you know she would never buy herself. Succumbing to her wishes will only escalate the demands in ever increasing proportions. Sharks never settle for a large piece of meat, they keep on attacking the bleeding wallet until there's nothing left. If she doesn't get what she wants, she'll whine like a bratty child.

For the grand finale, the minute the hotel room door closes, the sweet cuddly personality turns into a raging bitch. She races to your room phone for long distance calls, drains the room bar, starts barking demands, rushes you, refuses most every sexual trick, and then doubles the agreed price. And then she wants cab fare ten times the actual cost for all the trouble YOU caused her. You end up paying like a fool, not getting a nut, and then she slams the door on you….how did you let that happen?

Here's how to avoid this situation before it gets out of hand. In retrospect, it's easy. **NO**. Practice saying it. All you have to do is be firm right from the beginning. Here's the golden rule. If you're not offering it and she's demanding it, the answer is **NO**…with a smile of course. No explanation is necessary. Most girls will back down, if she won't, remind her there are plenty of girls available for you in town, and she is easily replaced. They love testing you, but women respect a man in charge. The cards are entirely in our favor, since we know how to be a gentleman, and we can afford it. Don't let that become your downfall. That doesn't mean a girl can peek into your wallet and take whatever she wants.

Instinctively, sharks travel in packs. They tend to regroup and plot prior to the impending kill. If you leave for your hotel room with one shark, she's in constant cell phone contact with the other sharks, discussing the attack, i.e., the size and rate of the money exchanges, and whether there's more action to be had back at the snake pit.

We all can get initially fooled and fail to recognize our prey. If you're talking in a dark corner with a girl and she's seems like the perfect one, here's a test. Look up quick. In whore clubs, most of the other girls know the status of your potential negotiation. They realize if you've reached this point and she leaves, your wallet is going to be in play. Look to see if your girl has friends who are eyeballing you, knee deep in a scouting report revolving around you, like private investigators. If you're about to exit with your babe and a pack of sharks move in to discuss something with her, it's about their visual impression of how easy you look to be taken, and how much money to go for. It's a pickpocket's football huddle. There are things being said behind the scenes, and most of them involve you parting with all your money. Even the bouncers, bartenders and cabbies can be in on it. Just by being a gringo, you're treated to twice the market rate. In this unexpected situation when the shark circle appears, play along...scratch your nuts, pick your nose, giggle stupidly...then excuse yourself to the bathroom and leave the club. Game over, you won that one.

Be like a lion when choosing your catch. You patiently wait, and wait, and wait, without wasting one ounce of energy, until the perfect catch...the gorgeous little fawn who's lost her way walks in, looking so lost and innocent, like she doesn't belong in the field. They're easy to spot on the beach, and to the trained eye the same applies in nightclubs. Look for a shy young freelancer venturing out, alone, and unashamed to take chances and meet some mysterious men. She dealing with the rotten hand life has dealt her in the only way she knows, and plans on having a little fun in the process.

When you approach her and talk, seek a personality that is self-assured, curious, playful, mischievous, energetic, and sensual. You want a girl who takes an interest in spending time with you, and would be flattered by the minimal wining and dining. She would never think to ask for it. Fascinate her with the differences in your cultures and that kind of stupid crap. Get the topic far away from the obvious pending business deal...ask if she'd like to have breakfast tomorrow morning with you and lay out at the beach. Set up the whole boyfriend aura, and of course compliment her on how she's the only girl you lust for at Club Snatch.

Master the delivery of the speech like it's for an Emmy Award, after all, you'll be using it on a different girl tomorrow night. Remember, if she is having a real good time now, later on you're going to be having a great time. With a sigh, get the negotiations done fast, like they are an annoying interference into your newfound relationship. Then scoop up your grand prize and leave. Assuming she's spunky, has a permanent smile, and an ass that men would go to war over, the deal is as good as done. Next!

Escort Agencies

There are numerous approaches you can take when traveling the world to enjoy the company of women for an afternoon, night, or multiple days. The **first technique**, and obviously the easiest, is Escort Agencies. There are several kinds to choose from, freelance girls from small ads in the newspaper, freelancers advertising on websites, or actual agency girls. The first type will cost next to nothing, maybe 25% of the others, but you are bound to be disappointed in the looks department. There is an easy trick, inquire about the age, and go for nothing over 20. You don't want a bad experience with a seasoned pro who is long past her photograph marketability. Seek out young college girls who are just looking to make ends meet, or some extra money to play with.

Next, independent escorts on websites. The girls pay to run these ads to create business. The sites make considerable money without actual involvement, so it's in their best interests to airbrush the photos to create impulse clients for the girls. The girls tend to charge half of what an agency would, and are rated the highest in performance, since they want repeat customers.

Last, actual agency girls. They tend to be cold professionals, pissed off at their employer and the rules, they rush you, they're clock watchers, and cost twice as much. (If all the phone numbers are the same on the website, you're looking at an agency.)

Whichever you choose, clarify precisely what it is you want. Yes, you have to be sexually explicit on the phone. Know exactly what it is you're going to get and the price before you spend one dime. Also, if there's a photo involved, determine if it is recent shot, and explain if it is not the same girl, you are going to send her back (with cab fare). Generally, the photos are retouched and maybe at best 75% accurate. When looking at the photos, if she appears from the waist up only, or is twisting in a strange fashion, assume she's overweight, or has baby stretch marks, and make another choice. Gauge her personality, if she's a cold fish on camera, guess what she'll be in your room. Negotiate the taxi fares in advance.

Independent escorts can be an extremely efficient and enjoyable experience for the afternoon quickie. Remember, when you remove the night's heavy bar tabs, it's more cost effective than you realize. In Buenos Aires, and Caracas Venezuela, it could actually be the best alternative...as the girls are often knock dead gorgeous. We recommend the girls with photos on house websites that are not an agency.

Nightclub Girls

The **second technique** is a quick session with girl from a club. Everything is done on a business level. You're the employer, she's the employee. A popular strategy, you simply agree on everything upfront, i.e., time limits, do's and don't, photos, or whatever. The advantage over the escorts is you get to see the package before unwrapping it. Get your negotiations done early in the evening. Then take her to another club, dancing, a casino, restaurant...anything to get out of her center of comfort. A new environment puts you more in charge, and makes the interaction easier. Become her friend, and go as long as you possibly can without actually making payment. If you've made a mistake, you can send her on her way. If all is well, after an hour or so of lightening her up, race on back to your love castle where the gods of testosterone take over. Stay in complete control of the situation. If she tries to change the rules at some point, you simply open the door and tell her **You're fired**. (Here the pay later rule shows its value). She will usually change her mind and become the cuddly sweetheart again.

In many cases, the business approach is the only method available due to the language barrier. Most of our vacation spots are in Latin America or Asia. In South America maybe 5 percent speak English, and Asia is barely better.) Often you will find almost no one in the whole damn country speaks English, other than your fellow gringos. If you already know some Spanish, it would help to get Pimsleur tapes to listen to in your car to increase your level of the language. The lazy man's technique is using Spanish closed caption on your TV, or a pocket translator in person. This will give you a decided head start. Columbians, Venezuelans, and Costa Ricans all speak Spanish, and in Brazil most girls understand our broken attempts at Spanish, since Portuguese has a lot of Spanish commonality in its verbiage.

Local Freelancers and Non-Pros

The **third technique** to women on your vacation requires a little work on your part. This is for the guy who wants a short time girlfriend, or perhaps one to keep in touch with and revisit some day in the future. If you going to be in a town for a while, buy a cell phone at the mall. They cost maybe $50, or in some cities you can rent one for $5 a day. Then buy a pre-paid calling card..you want to be available, as overseas it's the girls who do the calling and beg for sex. As you stroll around town, ask the hottest girls you observe for lunch dates...girls in the malls, bank tellers, secretaries,

1 1

a girl walking down the street. If you plan on returning to the city soon, get her email address. Of course, have a special email account set-up in advance specifically for this activity only. You can lead a split lifestyle with quality non-pros during the day and Rock Star threesomes with working girls at night.

Again, if you want to be a pro at this, before you travel on your vacation, do a fair amount of research on some of the cultural things of the country you're visiting. If you want to have a chica's attention, show her you're interested in more than just her pussy. After all, any girl can get laid anytime she wants, the object here is to make yourself intriguing to her. Don't sit there and talk about how rich and important you are. Ask about her, her family, and her life. Ask about her favorite places to go. A lot of the girls are supporting kids without a father, hence the career. Ask about her little one once in a while.

We're not entitled to anything just by being here, but just a minimal effort goes a long way. Treat her like a lady, tell a joke, and give compliments with a smile and you'll own the keys to her heart. Show a sincere interest in her country. Know the names of some of the more famous sights, landmarks, restaurants, beaches, their style of music, and so forth. Rent a documentary video about the country, or perhaps watch a popular film shot there. If you don't know any of their language, your fun will be dramatically reduced. Buy a pocket translator, and learn at least some of their language. Ask your girl what sights you should visit. Steer away from any of her attempts to take you to the nearest mall and drop a fortune on her. Brush that idea aside, "I can do that at home any day, I wanna see more of your beautiful country."

If your plan is simply a beach friend, be forewarned that they always forget their swimsuit, and they'll hit you up to buy a new one. If you're OK with that, make it a pink dental floss bottom and hand her 2 matching pink band-aids for a top. Or, make sure you say ten times "remember your swimsuit". If you plan to travel somewhere far the next day, make her spend the night. They have no alarm clocks, and are 99% of the time will be at least 1 to 2 hours late.

If you want to experience some culture, ask her to be your tour guide for the day, with the agreed price of you paying all entrances fees, food, and drinks. Establish up front there will be **no cell phones**. Otherwise, she'll spend half the day on her phone with her babysitter, her sister, her girlfriends, or suddenly have an imaginary crisis she has to return home to immediately. If she doesn't have a good babysitter, she shouldn't agree to come with you for the day. Settle this upfront. If at any time during the day they start whining, get too drunk, or demand expensive shopping excursions, put them in a cab immediately. If money *is involved*, agree on the exact amount upfront, and write it down on a piece of paper in front of her. Tip for good company and service only.

If there are no issues, a few days of the tour guide routine will be an enjoyable girlfriend experience, and you'll see some sights you wouldn't normally view. Get her to do the talking. Be a good listener. Have no strong opinions about anything, and agree with whatever nonsense she has to say. This doesn't mean you become some limp wrist liberal fag and waste your whole trip in museums. Just put in a few quality hours with her. Buy her some cheap romantic crap like a rose towards the end of the day. Suck it up, and you'll be rewarded in spades later on. Generally the sex gets better and better with the same girl. However, if unsuccessful, hit the nearest brothel the minute you dump her. As fate would have it, Men can be even greater sharks.

Try to understand the women and culture of where you are traveling. This will dramatically increase the fruits of your travel. For example, in South American, a girl still lives at home until she is married, even if she is in her 30's. If she gets married and it doesn't work out, she moves back in with her parents. The family unit is very intact, regardless of the career they have chosen. They are strong willed, hold their heads high, and she will always have her family behind her. The hidden meaning here is to treat them well. If you're a shady character and shell out abuse, they can make one phone call to a brother or friend and you will be living in a world of hurt.

Latin women are in the full time in the business of attracting men. They spend a fortune on clothes, workout religiously, are impeccably clean, and even smell sexy. They'll get boob jobs, dance like they're in Vegas Revues, and will learn anything to give them giving an advantage in snaring a man. Why? In most South American countries there is such a high murder rate amongst young men, that in the popular nightclubs women outnumber the men often 5 to 1. The bottom line is that you are not a threat to women here, you are a treat. They are not afraid to be feminine and will compete with other women to get to you. They are masters at seduction, and will provide the illusion of a girlfriend without a thought. As long as you are paying them, or taking them out, this will continue. A perfect relationship, since paid sex is always cheaper than free sex back home. However, always bear in mind the minute you leave town you will be replaced.

When traveling to Asia, you will be happy to find the bar girls are not like their US women counterparts you're getting away from back home. Thailand citizens are so overwhelmingly polite you find yourself blushing. For every thank you they say, they often bow towards you with their hands clasped together. If they knew you and your mission better, this tradition would fly out the window and wipe out a few generations of history.

In the time you spend with Thai girls, you'll find they are sensuous, compassionate and submissive companions. For the world's most experienced Sex Tourists, Thailand is always the place that is mentioned first as **simply the best**. Upon arriving, you're confronted with a sea of neon lights, screaming loud music, and pure hormonal overload. Every fantasy you've ever had can be fulfilled within minutes, as you're surrounded by a thousands of gorgeous young sexy girls, all seducing you with uncontrollable emotion and desire. Every preconceived notion you had about women is shattered instantly.

When experiencing Thai girls, there seems nothing wrong or immoral about prostitution. The feeling is quite the opposite, more like renting a short-term long distance relationship with a girl. Whether fake or not, they offer up sensuality, happiness, and attention unlike any you've ever experienced. Sure they are doing it for money, but what *you* get out of it is so much more than that. Many a hardened warrior has visited The Land of Smiles, only to return home to a land of tears.

Thailand is the world's largest producer of rice, with almost 50 percent of the population working on the farms. The typical female spends her first 17 years toiling 14 hours a day on the farm for no pay. However, there is a common Thai belief that children must take care of the parents at the onset of their old age, sometimes before their old age. So what happens? The Thai teenage girl feels this burden, and she knows only one way to solve it. Like a lot of farm and village girls she has stars in her eyes. She finds herself with a choice of farm slave labor, or traveling with her girlfriends to the bright lights, pulsating line dances, and fascinating interaction with men from around the world...men who can literally change her life, as well as her family's fortunes.

The Red Light District. Some girls say they love the sex, some despise it. The truth is, though, an evening with a sex tourist will provide her and her family with a week to a month's worth of income. Some girls go there for the dream of leaving their country, while some men go there for the dream of having a sweet untarnished young girl as his future wife. In reality, each party involved is using the other, with both enjoying the benefits of the situation.

On a side note, make sure your girl was actually born one. There's a large bizarre community of lady boys in Asia that can easily fool you. (www.asian-ts.com/preview/preview.html)

The saying goes you can take the girl out of the bar, but you can't take the bar out of the girl. Studies have shown that many of the Thai girls actually love the life they lead in the red light district. Compared to the destitute poor life on the farm, they work with their best friends, dance all night, and earn a living comparable to a millionaire. They are completely independent, can buy anything they want, and meet new and interesting people every night.

These are not hard-nosed hookers, and you should not treat them as if they were. Your interaction time cycle is up to you. You can spend a few hours (short-time), overnight (long-time) or several days. It's up to you Pimp Daddy. Once you agree to go with a girl, she will consider herself your girlfriend until the arrangement ends, and if you act accordingly the payback will be considerable.

Wherever your sex tourism travels take you, we recommend you visit different clubs every couple of nights to meet women. If you keep returning to the same place, you open the door to drama and BS. The girls can become very possessive of you, your manhood and your wallet. Not necessarily in that order. Is it because you're the hottest man on the planet? Is it because they want material things from you? Is it to get a passport to the US? Maybe. The most obvious reason is she is an independent business operator, you are her paying client, and any other girl showing attention to you is cutting into her business cash flow.

These girls get real jealous. When you're new to the game, by the third day you'll walk into the same club and see all your previous night's girlfriends lined up in a row, tugging at you saying *"**Baby please, why you cheat on me? I'm you're girlfriend, let's go now**.*" While it is great to get all the attention, who wants all the headaches and problems? The truth is, just like the strippers at home, they're all great actresses. They will say or act any way necessary, and tell you whatever you want to hear in order to hook your cash and your ego.

When it comes to women on your trips, a reality check is absolutely necessary. You have to keep your head on your shoulders and recognize you're being provided fantasy treatment. The girls are professionals, they know everything about the sex tourist and his methods, and for the most part men don't know a damn thing about them or their methods. The girls know exactly what you want to hear and feel, and will smother you with it for an agreed price. Remember, they're working when they are with you,

you are their client, and the minute you leave town you will be replaced. Unfortunately, men 75% of the time ignore that little piece of advice. Just look around and you'll see some old guy grinning ear to ear with a girl 35 years younger than him, grinding in his lap. If you ask, he will swear up and down that she is in love with him. Comically pathetic. Younger inexperienced guys are just as gullible.

Then again, it gets somewhat difficult analyzing the situation when every time you blink the most beautiful woman you've ever seen has your rod in her mouth. Get a grip. Keep it light, or these predators will eat you alive financially and emotionally. The girls are providing a sexual illusion for you, as well as supporting themselves. Keep it reasonable and straightforward, be interesting, and have a great time. Pretty simple.

" Direct thought is not an attribute of femininity.
In this, woman is now centuries...behind man. "

THOMAS ALVA EDISON
in Good Housekeeping 1912

It's a Performance Art

> " The perfect woman has a brilliant brain, wants to
> make love until four in the morning—then turns into a pizza. "
> **DAVID LEE ROTH** *in 1988*

Road training and mental preparation are essential to any great Olympian, if he expects to perform above and beyond the call of duty. After all, when you're on a sex tour, everywhere you turn aggressive young women will sexually assault you, and it gets quite difficult trying to defend yourself.

When you return, porn stars will be banging on your door asking for your trade secrets. Your buddies will corner you in dark rooms; speak in hushed tones, begging for mere crumbs of your stories…*and pictures*. "You gotta tell me man, what's is like out there….how do you do it?" Like a humble self-made billionaire, you just chuckle, looking off into the distance, and say….

" It's a performance art "

Arriving at the battle scene for the first time (at the most popular club in that vacation city), you should be prepared for complete shock and awe. The walls are lined with gorgeous women eyeing you up and down, licking their lips like sexual predators. Each girl is on a quest to lure you in, and whisper in your ear her overwhelming desire of seducing you multiple times. You feel like a Swedish Supermodel walking thru a fraternity house.

Deep down you know exactly what the situation is. The girls are here for one reason…to exploit you for money. They are using you. Treating you like a piece of meat. When it's all said and done, they'll even demand an entire evening of marathon sex with you. If you're not careful, they'll get their girlfriends or their sisters to join in as well. To make it even more humiliating, the girls will leave in the morning, never to return. No whining, no complaining, no imaginary problems, no bitching and moaning, there isn't even any quality time… the nerve of these girls. It makes you want to fake the orgasm just to get even.

Suddenly, your mind drifts off into a fog, and you imagine yourself back at home, married, and at an all-you-can-eat buffet. In front of you is your 250 lb. American wife. She's droning on and on endlessly about how you never listen to her, or something like that, who knows, you weren't paying attention anyway. Then you look hard at her. *Real hard*. Nothing like witnessing an angry cow stuffing her grotesque face full of cottage cheese and ice cream. She's devouring dessert like a frenzied hyena at the last supper. It makes you sick to even glance at her. Try to envision the weekly trough bill. Imagine the grunts, sounds and smells after her third and fourth flush.

You wake up screaming.

Welcome back from hell, let's return to your vacation plans. Planning for battle takes training and strict discipline. You better be prepared, or you'll be a flash in the pan in a day or two. Because, the inevitable happens to the best of us in the beginning. You arrive, and in the first 48 hours devour 6 different women, drink 6 cases of booze, and get friggin' 6 minutes sleep. By the third day of your trip you've already become irrelevant. You'll be sitting alone in a sports bar at 10 am, shit faced, watching the same ESPN highlights for the sixth time. You're repeating the lines by now, making perfect imaginary wagers on each game's outcome to no one in particular.

And then it happens. An 18 year old Latina goddess saunters on up to the bar, bats her green eyes at you, licks her lips and starts stroking your thigh. She's the girl you've always dreamed of having since high school. She's purring in your ear, and begging you to hit the sack with her, and all you can do is to blurt out in a heavy slur **no thankssssshhh.**

Why? Because….

- IT'S A PERFORMANCE ART ... -

You've gone down in flames. You've had your last hard on. You're package is shooting blanks. No wood, no leche, you're done. You might as well Bobbitt yourself. What a spectacle. You've transformed into the angry sailor in the corner. And there's still four more days left in your vacation. Damn. "How could I do this to myself?" Not even a wingman can help you.

Let's get down to business here. Plan ahead. In the week prior to leaving, you need to get in fighting shape. Cut back on the booze for starters. Remember, shake it more than twice and you're playing with it. Slam multi vitamins like candy. Our bodies are machines, and very few are well oiled. If you're partaking in this sport, chances are your machine needs a major overhaul year round. Chances are your engine blew up years ago.

Back to the basics. Again, this is the week before your trip to paradise. Since drinking dilutes most of the zinc from your body, take extra zinc every day. Take DHEA twice a day to build up your testosterone levels. Add in large daily doses of Vitamins B, E, Iron, Magnesium, and also increase your level of exercising. Like marathoners do, flush your system with twice the water you normally drink. This makes your body *over hydrated*, which helps take care of the dehydration issue in the first few days of tropical weather. Drink a lot of coconut juice to build up for your Peter North blasting. If you can find some juice during your trip, grab it. For food, overload on protein, as in large steak and fish meals. Get some protein bars to eat at your vacation spot.

Last but not least, it's time for your ancient Chinese secrets, as you're transforming into a world-class fuck warrior. We recommend you start taking ginseng, fo-ti, and Yohimbe root. Ginseng is fairly well known in most parts of the world. Fo-ti, or traditionally called he-shou-wu by the Chinese, is an all-natural root that is used to relax the bowels and detoxify and strengthen the blood. Processed fo-ti is one of the more widely used tonics in traditional Chinese medicine, which employs it to enhance longevity, increase vigor, promote fertility, and supplement vital energy (qi). Yohimbe bark comes from the bark of a tree that grows exclusively in remote parts of Africa. *What a transition in life, you're now eating tree bark, and flying across the world and bonking a dozen girls in a week.*

Yohimbe is a sensual stimulant for healthy men and women. Yohimbe's energizing effects stem from its ability to increase blood flow to the genitals. It stimulates the pelvic nerve ganglia and thus is improves a man's erection. In fact, a prescription drug, yohimbine hydrochloride, is an FDA approved drug for impotence. Effects can include increased libido, increased sensation and increased stamina. Women have also reported similar effects and increased sensations, although that could just be a result of being on the recipient end of your porn star talents.

When you're traveling, you have to watch what you eat and drink. If you've ever felt the Mexican Montezuma in your butt, or you're basic water poisoning, you know what we mean. You do not want to spend half your vacation sitting on the toilet, and walking around bow legged with brown racing striped boxers. The rules on drinking their water are pretty well known. No ice, and little to no tap water. Get in the habit of buying a 12 pack of bottled water as one of your first priorities when you land. If you don't, you'll be avoiding water and soon be dehydrated in a day or so. Also, put one bottle in the bathroom; use it for brushing your teeth and so forth.

For meals, find food that has been thoroughly cooked and hasn't been sitting around. Avoid the street food vendors; avoid all lettuce (water based). No raw vegetables or fish. Eat at crowded restaurants that have a high turnover, no stagnant food. Make sure your utensils are clean, as they can carry bacteria.

For an upset stomach, bring along the product called A*ctivated Charcoal.* Found in any vitamin shop, this product soaks up all the toxins in food and alcohol. It's great for an upset stomach as well as for hangovers.

It's rare to get much sleep during vacation due to the pedal to the metal attitude. It's not just the sparse hours you sleep, but the restlessness, insomnia, and lack of REM deep sleep. The solution: buy some *Valerian Root*, another vitamin available at any store. Valerian is widely used as a mild nerve sedative and sleep aid for insomnia, excitability, and exhaustion. It puts you into a deep REM sleep, the quality is increased, and the time taken to fall asleep is reduced. Of course, should you wake up unexpectedly and find some cute young bubble butt laying next to you, don't expect it to keep you from mounting her.

Last but not least is the most important part of the Performance Art. **PACE YOURSELF** !! It is very easy to lose your mind at the sheer quality and quantity of girls who demand sex from you, but you gotta keep your game plan tight. If your trip is gonna be close to a week, limit yourself to maybe 2 sessions a day. Plan an afternoon threesome and a good single session at night. Try to avoid the sleepovers in the beginning, because you'll wake up and do multiple sessions in the morning, which spoils your afternoon romp, which spoils your evening romp. Pace yourself. Also, NO binge drinking. Get shitfaced at home, you're down here to screw, not puke. It's kind of like running a race. It's better to have something left and pick up the pace at the end, then sprinting the first leg and having NOTHING LEFT for the finish. Until you've been through this problem once, you won't recognize the value of the advice. One more thing while we're at it, pick the hottest chicks you can find. This is no time for settling for a 6 because she's nice and talks a good game. Be patient, and when you make your move, go for the 8's, 9's, and tens.

Remember, fat and old chicks are gross.

The end.

THE RULES OF THE CHASE

Memorize these rules to live by:

1)   DON'T fall in love.

We pay them to leave. Leave your emotions out of it. No matter how sweet and innocent they seem, they are professionals. They know exactly what you want to hear and feel, and will smother you with it for an agreed price. You're buying a fantasy. Lust is fine; love for a hoe is ridiculous. Treat everything they say as an exaggeration or a lie and you'll do just fine. Remember, you're on vacation, and in a couple of hours an even hotter girl will be begging to sleep with you. If you start to get weak over one, move up to two girls at a time. Rinse and repeat.

2)   NEVER PAY in dollars

If the girl immediately negotiates in dollars, you've got a seasoned pro....move on. All your offers should be in their currency, and should be in the proximity of the market rates. This shows you have a clue to what you're doing, and gets you a better price in your transaction, and better performance. DO NOT overpay, it raises the cost for everyone else. If you pay too much she'll know you're a fool and the service will be worse and the scams will increase.

3)   NEVER send them money.

If she ever mentions Western Union, she's a hardcore pro full of BS. Her sweet old grandma isn't blind, her buffalo isn't in the hospital, her baby doesn't need medicine, and they're not shutting off the electricity.

If you hit the internet cafes, you'll see girls writing these stupid love letters asking for men to send her Western Union money, with cc lists of 50 names they'll attach one by one. It's a whole side business for some girls.

It's bad enough they lied the first night: "But kumchowchow, I thought you said were in love with me?". If she needs money for din din, shove her head into your lap. "This one's free, honey."

4)   Your word is King.

If she suddenly changes the rules, tries to give you any lip or commands, or refuses to do what you discussed, open the door and tell her to get out. No drama allowed, we can get that any day at home with the old lady. You'll be surprised how fun this can be. Nine times out of ten they'll suddenly have a change of heart and it's business as usual. In this scenario, call room service and have them deliver you a golden throne on a pedestal. Put on a huge pinky ring, chew a cigar, and demand the hummer of a lifetime. BUT, if the girl stays a bitch, a psycho, or is on drugs, take out the garbage.

That's why *you pay later*, to control the situation.

5)   Don't scam them.

Don't say you're in love or want to get married or want to bring them home. Don't refuse to pay. Be honest. If your ego tells you that shouldn't have to pay, or you offer petty fees to girls, the word will spread literally over night. There are certain rules implied in this game, and all the girls talk. They know your prices, your vices, and every position you've done with the previous girl. Do this beggar approach twice at any one club, and no one will approach you. You will need to take your cheap act elsewhere. In countries like Columbia and Brazil the girls know some very bad people who will correct the problems you create. Just one exception here is the girl doesn't need to know if you're married or what your real name is.

6)   "Your girl" is not different from all the rest.

> "Look man, she may have done 12 guys yesterday,
> but she said I'm her favorite."

7)   Be patient.

Sharpen your skills, learn to spot the clues that pinpoint a seasoned pro, and avoid her like the plague. No clock-watchers, you want a young fantasy date. Wait as long as it takes till you find a girl you are really into. You'll be in shock when you look around and see guys settling for some fattie just because she schmoozed him better than the others. If you are going to pay for a chica, make sure you lust for her. Pick something way out of your league that you'll remember forever. Not some perfect 10 cocky looking pro, pick a cute young one who looks shy and new to the game.

8) Trust your instincts.

If you have a feeling she's a little too crafty, or you just smell a problem, dump her. Your instincts are always right. These instincts were given to you from the days of the caveman. You may not be unable to pinpoint why you feel uncomfortable, or have a bad feeling, but trust your instincts and realize they are warning you of trouble ahead.

9) Take safety precautions.

In your hotel room, if it isn't bolted down, it goes in the safe. Keep virtually nothing in the bathroom or on the desk. When a girl is in the bathroom with the door closed, if she's not in the shower, she may be shopping. Say goodbye to all your toiletries. Never leave your toothbrush alone in there either, put it elsewhere. Be very suspicious if you have two dates in your room; keep your eye on the one who's unattended. She's also shopping. NEVER let a girl talk you into taking a shower before her.

Keep your money divided up in a number of hidden places, hide credit card receipts or shred them, and never gulp a drink handed to you. It's safer to drink a bottled beer that never leaves your hand. Some of these girls will hand you a drink that gives new meaning to the term "mind eraser." Unless you really trust them, sleep alone at night. Tell them to come back for breakfast and get another round then.

10) When a girl asks...

Tell her you have been to _____ many times, you are staying for another week, as well as returning again in a few weeks for business. Even if your flight is in 4 hours, swear up and down you're planning on relocating here. In fact tomorrow, the mayor is dedicating a park in your name, and giving you the key to the city in a big ribbon cutting ceremony. This will avoid the girl trying to scam you with an uninspired quickie. If you're perceived a regular, her performance will be her best. This is her business, and the hope is her new meal ticket, (you), will be a repeat customer. Also, you will be much more convincing while saying this nonsense if you are able to hide your raging hard on. Be smooth, confident, and don't drool.

11) Don't take her shopping...
This can easily cost twice as much as having her for the night.

12) When renting an apartment...

You'll be asked to pay in full by the broker. Never do this. Offer to pay for one day in advance, and then if the apartment appears satisfactory, pay for the rest. Pay in full and you'll never get a refund. More importantly, inspect the room with the broker like you're buying it. Check the bathroom for hot water, soap, towels, and toilet paper. *They will skimp you blind.* Check the AC, operation of the safe; look for bugs and cockroaches in kitchen and cupboards, test out the bed. Be patient and thorough. Ask for a different room if you're at all not happy. The broker will pretend he doesn't speak English and then demand the full week paid in full (in perfectly good English). Tell him another room, or it's just a one-day rental. Be Firm. Worst case, grab a hotel and ask around for another apartment broker.

13) Your attitude is everything ...

Smiling and how you act in general towards women is what matters most to the girls. They're used to being treated like crap by the locals. You don't have to dazzle them with money, since just by being a foreigner they assume you are rich. But treating them like a potential girlfriend will pay off no matter how much time you spend together.

14) No credit cards...

Never give someone your credit card in a faraway country. No bar tabs, brothel bills, nothing. Pay cash. Use the ATM for your daily supply of play money.

15) Never underestimate...

Yes, even in a foreign country, never underestimate how conniving a woman can be. Be prepared to watch in awe as that gorgeous, cuddly, innocent chica turns into a scammer or a bitch the minute the door closes in your hotel room. Even worse are the ones who suddenly demand 3x the agreed rate in the morning. Return the favor, don't accommodate, open the door and slam it on her stupid ass. Next!

16) Be a chameleon.

Blend into the culture you are visiting. Notice how the locals dress in public and clubs. If everyone is GQ, with dress pants and shiny shoes, adjust. Don't prance around in the Ugly American tourist kit. If you're older, this would mean the baggy shorts, screaming loud Hawaiian shirt, sneakers,

300-gallon sombrero hat, and Elvis glitter shades. If you're younger, this would be ghetto shorts with exposed butt cleavage, Lakers Jerseys, a dozen gold chains, and the backwards cap. Not only are you laughed at by all the girls, but also you set yourself to be an easy target for thieves.

Some of you will get all-defensive here and say *I'll do whatever I want*. A few years back in Rio a guy like this, an experienced black belt no less, was jumped by a 13 year old boy trying to pickpocket him. The guy grabbed him and threw him. The boy's 14 year old buddy appeared and shot him for his gold chains.

Blend into the scenery. If it's a beach town like Pattaya, shorts, T-shirts, sneakers, and a vicious hangover are perfect attire. Just be aware of your surroundings. Of course, the rule of thumb is dressing classy will get you further with a women. Even in dirt-poor countries like Columbia, a girl can glance at you and tell you what designer label shirt you're wearing.

17) DON'T get caught.

No strip club matchbooks, no woman's hair on your shirts, no lipstick stains, and no Viagra pharmacy receipts or condoms. Hell, burn your suitcase at the airport if necessary.

18) TAKE health precautions.

Bottled water and cooked food are your friends. No ice in mixed drinks, and never drink something handed to you unless you opened it. Use bottled water when brushing your teeth. The street food carts or delivered meals on the beach are very convenient, right up to the point where you spend a week hugging the toilet and walking like you just got off a horse. AVOID THEM. The only beach food should be fruit that you peel, or something you brought from the local convenience store.

19) Check Reservations

Never trust your travel agent, check, check, and reconfirm all your hotel and air reservations. Don't get stranded at Bumfuck Airport.

20)   NEVER NEVER NEVER EVER pay upfront.

When paid later, the girl has an incentive to be great in the sack.

21)   Keep it Quiet.

The information contained in this book should be considered top secret. You are now an elite member of an underground world. Guard this book with your life, as women who find it, destroy it. The less people know about the real world of aggressive, insatiable women out there the better...don't ruin it for everyone else. Feminists have already destroyed Western culture for men; don't think they won't go beyond the borders if it means maintaining access to your wallet. Only share stories with single guys who will actually partake in the adventures. Married guys tend to be jealous, get weak, and spill the beans to their wives. Suddenly, the whole town knows overnight. When you return from vacation, all your discussions should involve either golfing or fishing.

Rio de Janeiro, Brazil

About :

As a tropical resort, Rio de Janeiro is a magnificent site to behold, with its dazzling wide beaches and magnificent bay on one side, and surrounded by the abruptly rising Sugarloaf Mountain ridges and tropical forest on the other. An incomparable hedonist beach colony, the *cidade maravilhosa* (marvelous city) is one of the most densely populated places on earth, and home to the world's most famous beach, **Copacabana Beach.** Jam packed with stunning views of thongs, topless nymphos, and overlooked by the infamous open armed Christ statue looking down with tears in his eyes (and binoculars).

The 3-mile Copacabana beach on weekends has some 7 million Cariocas enjoying fun in the sun, beach sports, and socializing about the upcoming evening's festivities. Your entire vacation itinerary can be fulfilled within walking distance of this location, with its restaurants and cafes, movie theatres, bars, massage parlors, chicas, chicas, and more chicas. This is a 24/7 sin city, and possibly the most satisfying stop on your tour.

Rio is renowned for two colossal events, the infamous **Carnaval,** which begins midnight the Friday before Ash Wednesday and lasts five days. (The next year's starting date is Feb 5 2005). The legendary **New Year's Eve & Festa de Iemanjá** is the second most important event on the city's calendar. Nowhere else in the world can you observe two million white-clad people gathering in a setting as breathtaking as Copacabana beach. The velvety summer sky is the backdrop to one of the world's most spectacular fireworks displays, with hours of fireworks exploding in the glittering sky. On the sand, white-robed believers light thousands of candles and toss flowers as offerings to Iemanjá, queen of the waters, all to an irresistible Brazilian beat. December 31 at midnight on Copacabana Beach is a magical moment every year. Thrilling, unforgettable and incomparable, it truly reflects all the facets of Rio.

Climate :

Rio is in the tropics; heavy rains come quick and hard. Opposite seasons of the US, summer is Dec-Mar, a range from 75 to 105 degrees...rain season is in the summer. Winter temperature is mild...65-85 degrees.

ENTRY REQUIREMENTS :

From the US, passport and temporary visa are required. The visas are 1 to 5 years long, get the longer. There's an office in Houston and NYC, obtainable by mail, takes about 2 weeks. After acquiring the visa you must enter Brazil within 90 days for the visa to be validated. $100+ Here's the Brazil link for info.

(www.brasilemb.org)

The airport departure tax in Brazil is currently $36.00 USD. It can be paid in US dollars or the equivalent in local currency.(Real)

AIRPORT TO HOTEL-TAXIS :

After immigration and customs, it's time for your taxi. Like most airports, the scammer cab touts will immediately attack you. Here, they have uniforms and look real official. Pass them up, they charge double. You have two choices, negotiate a cab for a slightly lesser cost, which may not have AC, or take the radio cab with AC. The drivers of both do not speak English; a good rule of thumb is to write the hotel name on some paper. The cheapest choice is a yellow cab with a meter waiting in the streets. The Copacabana ride is about $30 reais. AC in cab is more. If you hate hassles, the fastest choice is to look for the radio cab booths, of which there are 5...look for women flagging you down. You pre-pay about $45 reais for a one-way trip, you can buy round trip now as well. All of these cabs have AC. These cabs accept US dollars as well. It's $5 more, but why start a trip with a nightmare cabbie. Depending on the time you arrive and the traffic, your travel time to Copacabana or Ipanema should be about 45 minutes. Buses called frescao run by Empresa Real are parked curbside outside customs at the airport and make the same trip for about $5 US. They are an hour long+ trip into the city. The buses follow the beachfront drives and stop at all the hotels along the way. If your Hotel is inland, the bus driver will let you off at the nearest corner. Around the beach, some taxis charge by the meter, others charge flat rates. Ask for all details first.

ELECTRICITY :

The Electricity is 110 V and 60 Hz. You may need an adapter. The outlets take round or flat plugs, not the flat plug with 1 prong wider than the other. Computer outlets are normal, but modem connections could pose a problem.

Money Matters :

Real is the local currency. REAL, pronounced (hey·ALL), or the plural REAIS, pronounced (hey·ICE), Bill denominations are R$100, R$50, R$10, R$5 and R$1 bills. Currently around 3.00 to $1. This is a huge value, as it was worth just 2 years ago around 2-$1. (the Real was floated back in the beginning of 1999.) Cabs only take reais. Banks tend to give lousy conversion rates; the best conversion is ATM's. In Copacabana, next to the Blockbuster is one on Ave. Copacabana. AMEX has offices at the airport and or Avenida Atlantica, which handle traveler's checks, but expect a lousy exchange rate. For late night cash, Help Disco on the beach will exchange US $100 a day. Make sure you have plenty of $R10's and $R5's. On weekends it's very hard to find anyone to make change, or convert money to Reais. Hand a taxi a $50R and he won't be able to break it.

Recommended Restaurants :

Since this info can change weekly, we can't recommend enough the "**Zagat Survey**." Pick up their travel book, or signup online. Worldwide reviews, menus, and pricing.

(www.zagat.com)

Tipping :

At restaurants a 10% tip is usually included. Give a little more only if service was especially good. Taxi drivers do not expect big tips, and extra R$1 is fine. Bellboys and hotel maids expect to get at least R$1. Tips to bartenders are zero to whatever.

Hotels :

To be in the center of the convenient action, it's best to stay in the Copacabana area. The bulk of the tourist hotels in Rio are located here. Most hotels either charge for overnight guests or don't allow them. Hotels run approx. $65 and up to $200 at the Marriott. They also charge 16% taxes on top of that, da bastards.

Recommended for lower cost and on the corner of the busiest block from the action is **Hotel Debret**. It features a rooftop restaurant, a popular nightclub, easy access to everything, and a complimentary breakfast. It's located right in front of the Copa beach, also known as hooker beach. Guest charge of R$35 per night. The club **Help** and many of the best daytime cafes are walking distance.

Atlantic Copacabana is another popular choice, just $48 a night, no chica fee; it has AC, refrigerator and a dining area. Located closer to the Copa/Ipanema border.

Hotel Debret
Av. Atlântica, 3564 - Copacabana
Rio de Janeiro, RJ 22070-001 Brasil
Tel: 55-21-2522-0132
(www.debret.com)

Another option is to stay in Ipanema. This is a not as much a tourist area. Copa beaches are very overcrowded, and are home to a lot more scammers, touts, and crime. The beaches in Ipanema are cleaner, and much more relaxing. Just a $5 reais taxi to all the action as well. Ipanema Inn and the Arpoador Inn are clean and allow guests. The latter is located right on the beach as well. For more upscale, try the Marina Palace Hotel, also guest friendly.

APARTMENTS :
An alternate option, an apartment offers several advantages. Most have security guards, there is no chica visitor fee, and are located close to the action and quite safe. It's also more personal and less embarrassing for the girls, assuming anything could embarrass them at this point. You're missing the maid, but you gain a refrigerator.
For furnished apartments, contact
Ken at :
(www.ez-riorentals.com)
David at:
(www.gringomanagement.com)
Don or Rhonda at :
(www.riotrips.com)
(Don@riotrips.com)
Use this link for an updated feel and inside scoop on hotels.
(http://ipanema.com/rio/hotels/e/hotcopa.htm)

CELL PHONES :
Can be rented for about $5 a day, local calls are 33 cents a minute, US calls are 45 cents. If you plan on spending a few weeks, you should consider one. Most girls give out their numbers. Get one.

GETTING AROUND :

Everywhere you turn there are taxis, they cost $2.50 to start and charge from there. Only get in metered cabs. They don't speak English. Write down your destination on paper if all else fails.

You can also travel quickly in the Metro subway system. It works like clockwork, is very efficient, and heads down into the Centro area near the termas. From Copa, the Metro pickup point is Praca Cardeal Arcoverde. A round trip ticket is around 3 reais, a $1. Like a sore dick, you can't beat it. Check for a metro map for upgrades and new locations for pickup.

You should be aware there is a beautiful non-tourist beach about 30 minutes from Ipanema/Copa area called Barra da Tijuca. To get here, they have small minivans running up and down the main drag. At just 3 reais, it's a true bargain, since a cab could cost you closer to 25 reais. There's also the very popular Barra Shopping mall or Rio Sul here.

CRIME AND SCAMS :

Druggies, TV's, and thieves down to 12 years old abound. After all, Rio is a huge city, and there are a million tourist targets. For the most part you'll find your garden-variety pickpockets. If you don't know by now, no wallets in the back pocket, only carry what you plan on spending at that given moment, and only what you can afford to lose. Get yourself some pants with zippered or buttoned pockets. Always carry around a photocopy of your passport and it's smart to carry written info concerning your hotel. Often the pickpockets will work in groups, you'll see a pack of 6 kids 10-13 years old, a guy jumps in out of nowhere with a knife and the kids do the stealing. Worst spot is early AM on the corner of Miguel Lemos and Atlantica between **HELP** and **Meia Pattaca**. Take a cab.

Most of the violent crime happens in the non-tourist areas that you have no business wandering into. Violent meaning shootings and death. Stay local, take cabs, and move quickly and confidently.

For pickpockets, here's another common scam. Up will walk what will *appear to be* a stunning scantily clad woman (transvestite), she/it will give you a hug and grab your crotch, another one will appear, put your hands on it's chest, suddenly your distracted, your hands are occupied, and then bam, a third one will sneak up and steal away with your wallet. You won't even know it for a few blocks.

For the funniest and grossest scam, watch out for the infamous *shit flickers* in the daytime, near the **Meia Pattaca** café. If you love to wear open toe sandals, there's a very high percentage you'll get hit. The deal is, the shoeshine guys sitting down here will flick shit onto your shoes or toes, profess someone else did it, and then offer to clean it off for a fee. Whatever it is they shoot at you, it's some nasty smelly stuff that you don't want to get hit by.

Another safety tip, if you love the gangsta look with tons of gold necklaces around the neck, Rio isn't for you. It's only a matter of time before a team'll swipe them. The cops will watch and turn the other way. Leave the bling bling at home or in the safe.

Stay away from the beach at night no matter what. Never walk on the beach side of Avenida Atlantica late at night. Leaving **Help** in the early AM can be dangerous. Thugs have been known to hide behind cars a block away and jump you. The cabs at the door charge a few bucks more, but it's worth it. Within one block you're often confronted if alone. Cops are corrupt and look the other way. There is a high crime rate at 2 am, just like any bad part of any major US city. Again, the most dangerous place to be is walking between Help and Meia Pattaca after 2 AM.

Stay away from the buses at night. When going to the beach, leave all valuables in your room. Do not try and hide your money in any clothing and go swimming, it will be gone. Fall asleep on the beach and your stuff is gone. If someone is trying to hard sell you into buying something, a little kid will sneak up from behind to steal your stuff on the beach towel. The streetwalkers in the daytime are mostly stunning transvestites, who double as thieves and robbers.

THE GAME PLAN :
First up is the beach layout…remember SP40, the sun is brutal here, so go real easy on the first day, limit yourself to only one 3 sum.

BEACHES :
Copacabana Beach
Stretching 3 miles long and just 3 blocks deep, Copacabana is the center of Rio's most dynamic activities, and is home to over 160,000 residents. Avenue Atlantica is the long windy main street, known for its famous mosaic boardwalk. Copa is vibrant with action 24/7, from the fishermen yanking in their nets in the wee hours, early am joggers getting rid of the hangover, to sun worshippers in the day, to the non-stop partying at night. Copa never sleeps.

Start your day at the Copacabana beach. Try the beach area in front of Rio Othon Palace Hotel to Meridian Hotel. Many of the hottest chicks from the late night HELP disco can be found here. There are muchas chicas looking for action, and if you can't tell which ones, there are touts hustling chicks, towels, and umbrellas everywhere, just ask one which girls are available. He'll point them out and for a small fee introduce you. Pricing is roughly half in the day at 100R.

Ipanema Beach

Five minutes from Copa, the renowned hotspot has a bit younger group, is less crowded, cleaner and safer, and features the tiniest thongs on the planet. Here you can watch numerous sports; beach soccer and volleyball, foot volleyball, surfing, wake boarding, and jogging. Or, you can pull up a rental chair and binoculars and get bloody shitfaced and rent yourself an afternoon chica.

Arpoador Beach

Just southwest of Copa is home to the best surfing. Here you'll find few tourists, and you'll see where the local wealthy and pretty people hang, i.e., people who can't stand watching shit faced Gringos pick up gorgeous hookers for sport.

Outdoor Cafes

After your beach and daytime action, its time to move on to the late afternoon outdoor beach cafes. There are a number of them to choose from, in the area in front of the major hotels Othon, Meridian, and Rio Palace. Just go for a stroll, you can't miss them. The most well known spot on Avenue Atlantica is **Meia Pattaca**, with another choices called **Mabs**. Further down the beach is **The Balcony**. The line of restaurants is seemingly endless.

Here's the routine, grab a beer or 10, some delicious steak and seafood, and wait for the show to begin. Around 4 pm you'll find two sets of opportunities, either the local or semi pro girls coming from the beach, or the late afternoon dressed up girls looking for men, money, drinks, or all of the above. It's very obvious who's looking for action, if you see one you like, smile....and she'll be at your table quicker than you can say Ultra Sensitive Magnum XL. No matter how hopeless you look or how bad your Portuguese, you can get a rendezvous till the evening for around $50. (If you're into that kinda stuff.) We would recommend you try for a local or semi-pro, as the chance of getting a friend and/or repeat action here is very high. If all you want is a quickie twosome or threesome, the hardcore girls are ready when you are. Be smart, avoid the hassles of the

Hotel Mgt., and potential theft, and ask the "ladies" to take you to the closest short time hotel for the excursion, it's usually right around the corner.

Red Light District
Rio has an excellent red light district, found in the center of the South Side. Head to Lido Square area, near the border of Copacabana and Leme. This home to numerous exotic bars and nightclubs which featuring erotic performances, and burlesque shows with nude dancers. The clubs have the standard neon signs outside, and the featured dancers are usually showed in picture window displays. This is actually a residential area with hotels, restaurants, and the Drugstore Farmácia do Leme, which is open 24 hours.

The kingpin for talent here is **Barbarella**. There's a 50R cover, which includes 2 drinks. The club has a bar fine to take out the girls, in addition to her fee. Expect a rate of $200-300R for the girls. A little pricey, but the samba strip shows and caliber of talent is an incredible sight. Other clubs to visit in this area are **Boite Holiday, Don Juan's, Frank's Bar, La Cicciolina, Pussycat, The New Scotch Bar, Niko's,** and **Baccara.** Drinks are very expensive, and you should pay cash for each one. Credit card tabs have been known to rival the cost of your kids first year in college, as they pad them relentlessly.

The girls are here to dance, gulp whatever drinks you buy them, and many will go home with you. These clubs are for the guys who don't like the terma brothel atmosphere and want to pretend they're not getting a hooker for the night. **Help Disco** (see nightclubs) has more girls, and costs way less. However, the environment reeks of being a cheesy tourist hangout, and the music is techno and played at deafening volumes. Women consider it too disrespectful for a good local girl to attend. The Boites offer a better chance to meet a local girl.

Barbarella (50R entrance, includes 2 drinks)
Ruao Ministro Vivieros de Castro,24
2275-7349
Doma
Avenue Prado Junior, 60
2275-4899
Frank's Bar (20R entrance, includes 2 drinks)
Avenue Princesa Isabel, 185B
2275-9398

Holiday
Avenue Atlantica, 1424 ...phone 2542-4347
New Scotch
Avenue Princesa Isabella, #7...phone 2275-5499

NIGHT CLUBS :

Don't forget to check some of the local discos as well. You'll find a lot of times in the local clubs the women outnumber men between 5 to 1 and 8 to 1. If you can dance salsa, you're 90% of the way in.

Down in the El Centro part of town, **Club Six** is the spot on Friday nights. Great looking local chicas in the 19-24 age range, this place is a goldmine for 7's-8.5's. They play a lot of American hip-hop, top 40, house music, drum & bass, jungle, some rock, Brazilian samba, and reggae. It has 4 dance floors on 4 floors, plus a VIP areaway upstairs that's not guarded by security.

Another new club stuffed with hot little 18-year-old locals is called **The Bunker**. Located down on Raul Pompeia #94, a tad before Ipanema. Non-pros abound here, but if you're not Brad Pitt, don't speak Portuguese or dance well, you'll likely just be window-shopping. Who cares, with a view like this?

The top pimpdaddy club for late night is **Help Disco**, billed as South America's largest dance club. Cover charge is $7, but beers are just $3R. Since the club doesn't open until midnight, you can find a spectacular view just hanging out at the entrance area at the **Sobre das Ondas** restaurant next door. Help is dead till at least midnight, so show up here at 10:30-11pm. The eye candy is stunning beyond belief. Many a pro sex tourist come here and chooses their girl for the night without ever going in. The menu is outrageous. Many girls are waiting outside for guys to arrive and pay their admission into the club. Inside, you'll find 150-250 girls dressed in wild provocative outfits, dancing like sex machines, and 99% are available for the evening. You would happily pay $20 at home just to walk in for this sight alone. The girls range from hardcore pros to part timers, mostly the first. Don't expect to find a classy local girl here, they hate the music and the whole tourist feel. The girls at **Help Disco** know exactly what you want, and with reasonable negotiation skills they will fulfill your fantasy, and probably enjoy the sex more than you will. There's no aura of immorality here or anywhere in Rio. You have the gold; she has the goods, and you both want sex.

Game, set, match.

35

This is not a poser bar where you stand there and expect perfect 10's to run to you. The best looking girls know they will find someone without trying, so they will dance for a few hours first. You have to make the move. Approach her, offer a drink or a dance, and if you like her, negotiate your deal. Most likely she will want to keep dancing till the early AM. Don't despair if you hear the $100 US initial quote, counter with $150-200 R. Never negotiate in dollars. Some will take less just to get it over with. If she won't bite on your price, it's no big deal. There is no shortage or girls here, some 200 plus. Some are truly frightening, but on any given night you'll see 50 or more that are in the 8-9 ranges, if not 10's. You'll find that the most aggressive are at the low end of the scale, they will freely grab your Johnson, and follow you around everywhere you turn, trying to coerce you into making a bad drunk decision. Maybe fun once or twice, but it gets annoying unless they're gorgeous.

Here's a tip. The club is two floors, hop on up to the second floor. There's a great bird's eye view from there to pick out your trophy girl, without getting hassled a thousand times by girls begging to have sex with you. Ah, the problems of life in Rio.

If your goal is to concentrate on just the local girls, a girlfriend, or to try for freebies, Help is not your place. The club is definitely frowned upon by the proud Brazilian locals, who correctly claim it's nothing but a tourist trap for gringos and hookers. For locals, you may need some time, youth, Portuguese, and strong game to move quickly. If you have all of these, you can score on almost any night. Unless you have an extended vacation planned, don't waste your valuable time. Go to the beach at noon, termas around 3:30pm, cafes at 7-10 pm, and Help at midnight. You can't miss at any of these spots.

Brazilian women are all nymphos, and during the sex it is quite common you'll find yourself thinking *who is paying whom?* They truly love to please, or are the greatest fakers on earth. Who cares, you both win in this scenario. The girls come in all shapes, shades, and sizes, and have the best Asses on the planet.

Help Disco
Avenue Atlantica #3432...2522-1296...
(www.discoteca-help.com)

Here's a regularly updated link for the latest hot spots
(www.ipanema.com/rio/nite/e/shows.htm)

Termas

Now, for the professional chicas. The best sex tourist experiences in Rio are found in the Termas. Termas are the Brazilian phrase for spas/ brothels, i.e., a bathhouse. There are hundreds of chicas all over town working in termas, and there's always a new girl to be found night to night at any given club, since there is a very high turnover.

Here's the modus operandi, you pay a cover of $30-40 reais and then change in a locker room into a Hefner robe and slippers. You're given a numbered key pertaining to your individual locker, which all charges will be assigned to. The bartenders ask for your number when ordering drinks, and the girls may want to see the key before entering the luv den. The number comes in the form of a wristband. Wear it on your wrist, don't pocket it. People have been known to swap yours with theirs and run up gigantic tabs. **Don't lose your key.** You get your key, your locker, you take a shower and/or sauna, then head to the bar area. Walk around to survey the place before sitting down, because the minute your down, you're attacked by women. Be very patient. The first few you see will blow you away, but soon you'll realize there are even better to be had. You will need to master smiling and politely getting rid of some girls. An easy way is to say you're waiting for a favorite girl whom you've been with before. There will be times when you have your eye on one chica, and out of nowhere another hot one will appear, have her tongue down your throat and pumping your dick under the robe, and you'll say no thanks. Try explaining that one at home.

You have 3 decisions to make here, which girl(s), how long you want them, and a regular or upgraded rooms. Upgraded rooms have mirrors on the walls, and a huge circular bed with a mirrored ceiling. Often they are positioned like thrones, as you have to climb a few steps to get to it. Careful, when jumping around and changing positions, it's pretty easy to step off the bed, bounce down the stairs on your back, with your dick flopping in the breeze. Cameras in here are not encouraged, but you can slip a small one in your robe, and most girls are more than happy to pose for you. When you pick a girl, she will take your key and go schedule your date, she will also change and come back with a new outfit and look. The effect and minimal time delay is quite effective, when she returns the new look will be twice as hot. What's amazing in the Brazil Termas is how the girls will not stop after the first round; they want 2 or more in 40 minutes. After your session, you hit the shower or sauna and head back to the bar and couch. If the place isn't packed, the girl you just had will come back and resume kissing and stroking, like it never happened. Slow down girl, I'm not that easy.

A short-list of the best Termas in town includes **Quattro X Quattro**, **Monte Carlo, Solarium, Termas 65, L'uomo,** and **Centaurus.**

Monte Carlo,
Also know as Club 19, is conveniently one block from Avenue Atlantica in the heart of Copacabana Beach. After arriving on the first floor, take the elevator to the showers and spa on the 2nd floor, and then the elevator the club and chicas on the 3rd floor. Hours of operation are Mon.-Sat. from 4pm-2am. Cover is 40R and prices are 200R for 40 minutes or 250R for one hour in a suite.

L'uomo
A few blocks from **Monte Carlo**. Located on the second floor of a shopping center, and not that easy to find without help. Same management and setup as Monte Carlo, pricing is the same, and the hours are Mon-Sun 4pm – 2am. If there's no selection at one Terma, head to the other. L'uomo seems to get the nod between the two for quality of girls, although diamonds in the rough are very common at both. Another good feature is that if you're there in the afternoon, they let you return later in the evening without additional cover if you inquire at the front desk.

Quattro X Quattro
Located in El Centro at Rua Buenos Aires 44, Quattro X Quattro has the largest selection of women, from 50 to 100 exotic nymphos…all shapes, sizes, and colors. Lately this has become the home of the Brazilian blondes. This is a downtown businessman's club that gets packed quickly; it's best to time it for the 3-5pm shift. At night the place is almost claustrophobic it's so crowded. The entrance is a narrow hallway, and then you head up stairs to the second floor entrance. Pay the cover, then with your numbered locker key it's off to the lockers. Quick change and shower, back to the stairs and up one more level. Upon entering you'll notice a bar right in the middle of the action, which includes great stripper shows, some live lesbian acts, multiple nude synchro dances, and more. The shows last 40 minutes at a time.

There's also a third floor bar in the back area, which is more intimate for your couch interviews. The bar also serves food. Just plop your happy ass down on the couch, or sit at the bar. Within seconds, some girls will recognize you're a famous wealthy and well-hung stud, and will come up and jump in your lap, make out and stroke you, until you can't wait any longer. This can be so much fun, groups of locals come in just for this foreplay for an hour or two, and then leave. Pricing for **4X4**, a $30R entrance, beers are $ 5R, and one hour in a suite with your date is just

$160R. Rooms are on premises, complete with bed, shower, and mirrors for your porn star experience. Finish before 5pm and they waive the entrance fee. You pay your tab when you leave. Drinks for you and the girls are same price, and cheap. The girls are in bikinis or lingerie, and often dancing salsa.

There's also a bar on the first floor below **4X4**, where you can go before or after your session. A lot of the Terma girls hang out in here to drink and dance. Here you can get the girls' phone numbers, and arrange for the two of you to meet up later that night or have her come over the next day for a quickie and hit the beach. They all freely offer up their phone numbers unless you're some a cheap Charlie or an ugly rude troll.

Termas 65
This spa is the second most expensive next to Centaurus, entrance fee is $40R and the girl is $210R, and they have a restaurant and a great masseuse. There's a pleasant professional atmosphere here, as opposed to the balls to the wall frat party schtick at **4X4**. The exotic shows, stripping and nude dances here are tantalizing. Most important are the girls, as there are many young stunning, fun, classy girls who take real pride in making you sweat 10 pounds and walk like you just got off a horse. Don't be surprised if you leave here faking your manly composure, and then end up at the hotel taking a 6-hour nap.

Termas Solarium is roughly 15 minutes from Copa in the Jardim Botanico side of town; address Rua JJ Seabra, 21, Jardim Botanica. A sexy club located in a restaurant row as well, about a $2 cab ride from Ipanema. Entrance is $40R, a session is $120R. The upgraded hour in the Jacuzzi suite is $260R. A nice crew of hotties here, and a local manager who will point out ones he recommends. The bonus is they are open on Sundays.
(www.solarium.com.br)

Centaurus is the granddaddy of them all. The highest class, and highest dollar club as well, located in Ipanema. A slightly different setup, you pay an entrance fee up front of $290 reais, which includes a 40 minute session. A second round with any girl is $215R. Upon entering, an available hostess will show you around the club and try to get you to choose her. The answer is no, you want to hit the sauna first. There's so many girls here you want to wait as long as humanly possible before you decide. Similar Terma arrangement, in that you change and shower in the locker room, and then waltz around in your Playboy robe and flip-flops. The club itself is 5 stars immaculate. When strutting thru the first time, tilt your head in an aristocratic way, and mumble to yourself about some imaginary billion

39

dollar business deal. This will not only display what an important dignitary you are, it will hopefully stop you from blowing a premature load during your gawking and stupid impersonation.

Talk about eye candy. Centaurus has arguably some of the hottest women in all of Rio. Now, if you like your women thick, morena or with the bigger bubble butts, you may not like the place. If you like a loud Animal House atmosphere, then don't come here. But if you like a Gold Club environment packed with gorgeous, classy petite college students mostly in the range of 8 and up, this is your place. You could spend your kid's entire education fund here and feel it was entirely worth it. "Looks like community college, sorry kids, you were so close."

There's a huge sports bar area with TV's playing the numerous sporting events of Rio. That would be soccer, soccer and soccer. Try not to mimic the announcer if there's a goal scored. They also feature live music on certain nights, as well as girls on stage doing some sexy stripping acts. Throughout the club there are countless girls roaming and attacking you. The upgrades are 2 girls, or the mirror suite for 1 hour. In the suite there's a gigantic round bed with mirrors on all the walls and the ceiling! Practice Mr. Universe flexes while slamming your trophy hoe. **Centaurus** is a once in a lifetime experience. Or, if you're at all like us, it actually happens quite often. You're safe paying here with a credit card.

Here's the Termas Locations :

Quattro x Quattro
Centro district, downtown
Ave. Buenos Aires #44. The sign say Whiskeria.
Mon-Fri 2pm - 1AM.

Centaurus
Rua Canning 44 in Ipanema
Open 4-2am Mon-Fri, 4-12pm Saturday
2523-4088

L'uomo
(Copacabana District   )
Mon-Fri 3-2am, Sat-Sun 3-midnight.
2549-4113   **(www.luomo.com.br/english/eindex.htm)**

Monte Carlo (Club 19) in the Copacabana District
Mon-Saturday 4-2pm...phone# 2255-4489

Solarium
Rua JJ Seabra 21, Jardim Botanico
2274-2741 **(www.solarium.com.br)**

Termas 65
Rua do Rosario 65
one block from 4X4
Mon-Fri 2pm-midnight.
(www.termas65.com.br/index.asp)

Termas Rio Antigua
Rua Joaquim Silva, 2
2224-9591
(www.rioantigo.com.br)

Escort sites :
Barra Vips - **(** www.barravips.com.br **)**
Chantily – **(**www.chantily.com.br**)**
CIA Plus - **(** www.ciaplus.com **)**
ClassiSex - **(** www.classisex.com.br **)**
Company Girl - **(** www.companygirl.com.br **)**
Contatos – **(** www.contatos.com.br **)**
DeStack Girls - **(** www.destackgirls.com.br **)**
Escort Girl - **(** www.escortgirl.com.br **)**
Karla's Models - **(** www.karlamodels.com.br **)**
Malicia – **(** www.malicia.com.br**)**
Mclass – **(** www.mclass.com.br**)**
Paraiso Escort - **(** www.paraisoescort.com.br/ **)**
Rio Vip's - **(** www.riovips.com.br **)**
Scort Show - **(** www.scortshow.com.br **)**
Sexy Dreams – **(** www.sexydreams.com.br **)**
Sexy Hall - **(** www.sexyhall.com **)**

Vacation Stuff :
Tell the old lady you went to Rio to see the parakeet zoo in the mountains.
Here are the other things you did in Brazil.

Sightseeing :
You have to make sure you do some Mountaintop Viewing while you are
down here. Sugar Loaf is home to the infamous Christ statue overlooking

Rio you've seen in the postcards, and the sight from the top is extraordinary. Take the train up to the top of Corcovado, two cable cars lift you 1300ft above Rio and the Baía de Guanabara, offering a view of Rio that is like none in the world. Choose a clear day at sunset for your journey. The two-stage cable cars leave about every 30 minutes from Praça General Tibúrcio in Urca. If you're a climber, there are some 50 clear routes to take here, starting up the backside of Pão de Açúcar.

The infamous statue Cristo Redentor. From the city going up 2330 feet is the mountaintop. By the way, don't be disappointed when you get up there, the statue is only about 28 feet tall, it looks 200 feet in photos. The mountain offers magnificent panoramas of Rio and surrounding areas. Sunset up here with a girl is worth its price in gold, and we'll spot you bonus points if she's wearing no panties and backs up into you on the trolley on the way down. At night, the brightly lit statue is visible from all over the city. Make sure it's clear out if you travel up it, the storms come in a hurry, and there are monsoons with lightning that you don't want to experience up there.

The streets along the ocean are closed on Sunday, rent yourself a bike and cruise for the day, the view on the beaches will scar you for life, or at least until your next visit back here.

Carnaval

The Carnaval in Rio began it's tradition from pagan festivals long before the middle ages and was developed over the years in Brazil as the Catholics decided to let loose before Lent. Traditionally during Lent, Catholics gave up certain pleasures such as eating red meat and drinking alcohol for 40 days, starting Ash Wednesday the last day of Carnival. The five day long celebration begins with a ceremonial handing over of the keys of the city from the city Mayor to Rei Momo, the king of carnival and Lord of Misrule.

Famous for its Samba music, partying, and packed beaches. There are parties in the streets with bands, private clubs and hotels around the city offer Carnival Balls, ranging from chic sophisticated to scandalous parties with scantily clad, or practically nude women. There are also the amazing world famous Parades in the Sambadromo. Remember, for the tourist, during the Carnaval the prices double, the density of people is worse than Mardi Gras, and crime escalates. If you're OK with this, it's located right on the beach and certainly will be a moment for the record books.

GOLF :

Golden Green Golf , Av. Canal de Marapendi, 2901
Phone: 434.0696....Opening Hours: Tuesday to Sunday, from 7am.

São ConradoGávea Golf Clube
Estrada da Gávea, 800 Phone: 322.4141, Tuesday to Sunday, from 7am to 6pm, 18 hole course open to members and non-members.

DIVING :

Barra Squalo
Av. Armando Lombardi, 949, shop D Phone: 493.3022
Mon-Fri, from 11am to 8pm; Saturday, from 10am to 3pm
Underwater photography and diving expeditions with equipment.
Jardim Botânico Diver's Quest
Rua Maria Angélica, Phone: 286.2513 Mon to Friday, from 10am to 8pm; Saturday, 12-6pm (www.diverquest.com) Standard PADI courses. Equipment hire and maintenance. Diving expeditions.

SOCCER :

Maracanã (Mário Filho Stadium) Phone: 567.7676, Daily 9 to 5 pm Built in 1950, the Maracanã stadium is still the biggest in the world, with 150,000 capacity. Home to massive rock concerts.

Amsterdam, Netherlands

About :

The Netherlands neighbors are Germany to the east, Belgium to the south, and the North Sea to the north and the west. The population of the country is 16 million, with the capital Amsterdam being home to 750,000 people. Amsterdam is one of the largest trade ports in the world, yet architecturally it still appears to be living in the 17th century. It is also most visually stunning cities in the world, where you can delve through centuries of history aboard a canal boat or explore the array of excellent museums.

Numerous canals encircle the old city. In the canals beneath the stigma of orgies and weed, young Internet entrepreneurs strike deals across Europe from their houseboats. Besides the quaint canal boats, the city's waterways are home to massive cargo vessels from around the world, as well as cruise ships. Practically everywhere you turn in Amsterdam there are canals, as at last count there were 165. In addition, there are countless smelly yellow canals next to passed out drunks in the streets, but these tend to disappear quickly.

Amsterdam is pretty much the ultimate hippy city, as anything goes here. Drugs and prostitution are legal and one of the city's main sources of attractions for tourists. The streets are picturesque 17th and 18th-century architecture, traveled by fleets of bicycles to exotic cars; all mixed amongst tree-lined canals and numerous parks and museums and live sex shows.

We've all heard about the world famous **Red Light Districts** of Amsterdam. Day and night, strolling the streets you'll see hundreds of "ladies"(?) sitting in display windows like department store mannequins, wearing next to nothing. They offer discrete paid interludes in these rooms behind curtains. It's not only legal; the government now forces the girls to pay taxes. Amsterdam's Red Light District, known locally as the Walletjes, or Wallen (little walls), is located along and around two of the city's oldest canals, the Oudezijds Achterburgwal, the Oudezijds Voorburgwal.

Entry Requirements :

Passport required, and must be valid for at least 3 months after the last day of the intended visit. Visas are required if your stay exceeds 3 months. A uniform type of visa, the Schengen visa, is issued free of charge for tourist, business and private visits. Short-stay, Multiple-entry and Transit visas are available for between £17-35, although prices can fluctuate. All visas are subject to a handling charge of between £7-£35, depending on the type of visa and the exchange rate.

AIRPORT INFO :

Amsterdam Airport is called Schiphol, its code is (AMS), website is: **(www.schiphol.nl)** Schiphol International airport is located 11 miles southwest of the main city. Your entry is an expensive 30-minute cab, an expensive KLM bus, or the inexpensive train, which leaves every 15 minutes for its 20-minute ride. The direct rail link between the airport and Amsterdam Centraal Station has trains every 15 minutes from 0600-0000 and every hour through the night.

The Netherlands' national airline is KLM-Royal Dutch Airlines (KL). KLM flies direct to all major European, North American and Asia-Pacific cities. From Amsterdam to New York is 7 hours, including a stopover in London. Distance to London is 1 hour 20 minutes; to Manchester is 1 hour 15 minutes.

CLIMATE :

Mild, maritime climate. Summers can be described as mild to hot, nothing excessive. Winters can freeze your butt off, and large snowfall is not unusual. It rains very often in Amsterdam, as the heavens are unsuccessfully attempting to wash away all the filth and sin in the town.

MONEY MATTERS :

The Euro is now the official currency. The first Euro coins and notes were introduced in January 2002; £Euro = 100 cents. Notes are in denominations of £500, 200, 100, 50, 20, 10 and 5. Coins are in denominations of £2 and 1, and 50, 20, 10, 5, 2 and 1 cent.

Currency exchange :

The letters GWK ·indicates Exchange offices. GWK is a national organization with currency exchange offices at major railway stations, at Schiphol Airport and at the border crossings with Germany and Belgium. Hotels tend to charge high commissions. Verkoopt means sell, while Koopt means buy.

Credit & debit cards: MasterCard, American Express, Diners Club and Visa are accepted, as well as Eurocheque cards. As always, call your credit card company for what is available. As of our last trip, the friendly girls of the Red Light district still don't have the electronic *swipe the crack with your credit card* payment feature.

Get with the program girls.

GETTING AROUND :

Easiest and by far cheapest transportation are the trams around the city. To board, go the *rear*, and push the button, and the door opens. You buy a ticket good for one hour here…good for as many trams as you'd like in that hour. To get off, push the red STOP button. Tram tickets are much cheaper if you buy in advance at the station or the post office, and they never expire.

To pass yourself off as a local in Amsterdam, get a trench coat, looked stoned and scowl a lot. Try to appear like you've been sleeping under bridges, or attending Nirvana concerts. If people talk to you, invent a brand new slurring language and mumble it quietly. Practice bizarre cadences and voice inflections.

RECOMMENDED RESTAURANTS :

Since this info can change weekly, we can't recommend enough the "**Zagat Survey.**" Pick up their travel book, or signup online. Worldwide reviews, menus, and pricing.

(**www.zagat.com**)

CRIME :

Ignore any guy hanging out aimlessly. They're either drug dealers or thieves. They tend to pretend to be the local expert guy who knows everything, everyone, and who specializes in changing currency. Kind of like a New York politician, only a little more trustworthy. Pickpockets are out in full force, so be prepared. Walk tall and quickly, like you're a man on a mission 1500 miles from home, in town to rent pussy from whores in windows. In other words, look stressed out and married.

For police, or other emergencies, dial 112 anywhere in the country.

HOTELS :

There are some 350 Hotels in downtown Amsterdam. Make your weekend reservations well in advance. Despite the numerous hotels, availability can be slim and prices rise.

Here's a short list of cheaper local joints.

France Hotel
Oudezijdskolk 11, tel: 020-422-3925
Just one minute from the RLD. 3 star canal hotel, TV, shower, and Internet in lobby. (www.francehotel.nl/francehotel.html)

Hotel Centrum
Warmoestraat 15, tel: 020-624-3535

Hotel Old Quarter
Warmoestraat 22, tel: 020-626-6429
StableMaster
Warmoestraat 23, tel: 020-625-0148
Kabul Budget
Warmoestraat 42, tel: 020-623-7158

For complete listings and pricing :
(www.bookings.nl)
(www.hotelres.nl)

THE GAME PLAN :

Ground zero is the **Red Light District**, the most famous district in the world. You need to aim for the Oedekerk canal near Casa Rosso. Look for the big red light, no joke. What you'll find are several blocks containing hundreds of women in picture glass windows, with private curtained rooms for sex behind them. The mannequins in the window are exotic women from around the world. Every look, size, race, and color is represented here. The occasional hedgehog and uberslut, but what can you do.

Just take a stroll inspecting windows until you find a girl you like. There are roughly 150 girls to choose, as well as ones whistling to you in the alleys between buildings. Most people have a mental picture of this red light district as a dirty sleazy area. On the contrary, Amsterdam is immaculate; you won't find one cigarette butt in the streets. Also, when you pop into one of their large pubs in between rounds, you'll find them to be the nicest ones you've ever been in.

Make sure to convert your money to euros prior to arriving here. The girl's rates are 50 euro for 20-30 minutes. They have some games they play that you need to be aware of. First off, make sure the 20 minutes starts when you're naked and on the bed. Second, no cell phone interruptions allowed by her. Third, the ridiculous up sells. It's like you're at a car dealership. Get everything clear in advance or you'll dislike the whole event. If you request her shirt off during sex…up sell, touching breasts…up sell, various positions…up sell…you get the picture. Try to negotiate for a longer date upfront to allow for these games. Very little English is spoken. Bring your own condom and lube. BYOCL. Make sure you have a girl who's been a girl her whole life.

Here's a complete map and walking tour of the RLD.
(www.rld-info.com/MapRLDWallen.htm)

There are plenty of bars in the area for the booze and food in between, and they'll hand you a hashish menu if that's your thing. It's all perfectly legal. In some of the bars you rent your beer mug by the hour, with unlimited refills! There's also some great old school heavy metal clubs there as well, check out Excalibur for some great headbanger tunes. Hit the brothel, hit the hash bar, and hit the metal bar. Rinse and repeat.

For picking up locals or semi-pros late night, check out the Jazz band at Bimhuis or the disco at Escape. If you bore of the quickie red light district routine, there are also houses that are less expensive, a little more private, and charge around 70 Euro for the hour. Since the names can change quickly, here's a website with directions, pictures, maps, and the lowdown on each.

(www.sex-world.nl)

Next place to visit in the Netherlands is the **Almaar Red Light district**. Located maybe 20 minutes northwest of Amsterdam by tram. Travel north on the A9 from Amsterdam. Find the train schedules here: **(www.ns.nl)**

The red light district is in an area called **Achterdam**, another home to a high concentration of the some 120 Dutch window prostitution babes. The women are allowed to display themselves at the Achterdam only. Street prostitution is prohibited in Alkmaar. Gotta have some standards dammit. The Achterdam is a small craft street in the monumental inner city of Alkmaar, about 300 feet from the renowned cheese market.

Pricing varies per girl at 35E for 20 minutes to 60E for a half hour, and the girls don't do the up sell crap so much. All in all, it's a more pleasant experience than Amsterdam. Here's a website for directions and the street layout.

(www.rld-info.com/Alkmaar1.htm)

Another city to visit in the Netherlands if you're feeling adventurous is **The Hague**, located southwest on the North Seaport. Here also is a large red light district, as well as the same house arrangement with complete listings again at the same website.

(www.sex-world.nl)

Most feel the quality is higher in Amsterdam. Remember, the Netherlands borders Germany... make sure you read about our vacation chapter review of **Frankfurt**, Germany. It's a world-class experience at the **FKK Atlantis** and **Oases** clubs, without any of the seediness feel of Amsterdam. Worth a visit. Good sites for more info:

(www.rld-info.com)
(www.ignatzmice.com/Adam/)

VACATION STUFF :
Tell the old lady how it's your life's mission to see the Van Gogh Museum. Tourism website is: **(www.visitamsterdam.nl)**

CASINOS :
There are a total of 12 casinos in the Netherlands, the largest being the Holland Casino in Amsterdam.

Holland Casino Amsterdam
The 92,664 square foot casino features 576 slots and fifty-five table games, open 1:30pm-3am daily.
Address :
Max Euweplein 62, Hirsch Passage 7, Amsterdam
Telephones +31 20 521 1111

Table Games – 55 total
American Roulette-13 tables-NLG 5/100 to NLG 6,000/20,000 bets
Blackjack- 9 tables- NLG 10/500 to NLG 200/10,000 bets
Caribbean Stud Poker- 4 tables- NLG 20/50 to NLG 400/750 bets
French Roulette
Poker – 5 tables- NLG 10/20 to NLG 100/200 bets
Punto Banco – 5 tables- NLG 100 to NLG 20,000 bets
Sic Bo – 1 table- NLG 5 to NLG 3,600 bets
Slot Machines – 576 total
Video Slots – 191 machines
Dress Code (Proper Dress)
Entrance Fee (NLG 7,5)
ID/Passport Required (ID/Passport Required)

The website is **(www.hollandcasino.nl)**

GOLF COURSES :
The exclusive reputation golf used to have in Holland is fading. These days, courses are crowded with players, especially weekends. A safety certification is required for professional courses, but public courses are open to everyone, with many courses also offering driving ranges. You can play at a private club if introduced by a member, or if you belong to a British club; otherwise, go for the public courses open to everyone. See the Amsterdam Yellow Pages, or contact the Amsterdam Golf Club (497 7866).

De Hoge Dijk
Public 18-hole course on the edge of Amsterdam. Reservations required.
AmEx, DC, MC, V. +31 (0)294 281241/285313
Abcouderstraatweg 46, Amsterdam
+31 (0)294 281241/285313
Metro Nieuw Gein; from Holendrecht- take bus 120, 126 to Abcoude

Golfpark Spaarnwoude
An 18-hole course, with two short courses and a pitch and putt.
Reservations can be made up to three days ahead. Open summer 6.30am-
8.30pm daily. Winter 8.30am-3.30pm daily. No credit cards.
Het Hogeland 2, Velsen-Zuid, Spaarnwoude
Phone: +31 (0)23 538 5599

Golf Centre Amstelborgh
Borchlandweg 6 , 1099CT Amsterdam

Golfclub Amsterdam Old Course
Zwartelaantje 4 , 1099 CE Amsterdam

Amsterdamse Golfclub
Bauduinlaan 35 , 1165 NE Halfweg nh

MUSEUMS :
The **Van Gogh Museum** is home to over 200 paintings by Vincent, one of
the world's most visited museums. Hey, you gotta kill time somehow
between sessions. Japanese prints, which influenced the old ear-slicer, are
also on display. Next-door is the home of **The Stedelijk Museum**, covering
1850 to the present. Considered one of the world's leading museums of
modern art, quite a diverse, confrontational collection. *It's hard to even type
this nonsense with a straight face.*

CANAL SIGHTSEEING :
Don't forget to do the canal tourist trip, nothing like cruising around town in
filthy piss canal water. You can even do a solo pedal boat deal, or ride in a
tourist boat. The canals freeze in the winter, watch the old lady's expression
when you pull out some skates and suggest your going to Amsterdam to
skate. The ice is not that thick, try not to bring your window dates here.

CYCLING :
The Netherlands is rightly known as 'the land of bicycles', as some 15
million Dutch people regularly travel by bicycle. It's a huge social sport,

and one of the easiest ways to get around, as well as the easiest way to *get a bike stolen* if that's your gig. Bikes are available to rent at the train stations. A popular site for cycling is **Vondelpark**, west of Leidseplein. Detailed cycling maps (recommended) can be obtained for every province from local tourist information offices; as well as indicating cycling routes and tracks, the maps provide route descriptions and guides. Cycling lanes are recognizable by a round blue sign with a white bicycle in the middle. There's a public planted forest called The Amsterdams Bos, which is great for jogging and hiking. Another great bike route is along the Amstel River, going south to Oude Kerk.

Angeles City, Philippines

About :
Nestled in South-East Asia, the Philippines are comprised of over 7000 islands, with just 2000 of them inhabited. Most are less than ½ mile long. To the north is Taiwan, with Eastern Malaysia and Brunei to the southwest, and Indonesia is south. Filipinas appearance is unique amongst the Asian women, as they are a mixture of both Asian and Spanish. Combine that with the gorgeous long black hair, dark tan, contagious personality, and nympho traits and you've got yourself one of our top 20 spots to visit on your sex tour.

There's a danger element to traveling at times due to the current political environment, not to mention the typhoons, earthquakes, volcanoes, floods and the terrorists. You would never know it when you meet the women here. Filipinas are always smiling, sweet, and subservient. In other words, the exact opposite of American women, who also tend to be a huge danger element concerning your wallet and sanity.

The economy is largely farming, mining, and fishing, with coconuts being the largest produced crop. The rainfall can be massive, and with its location and poor infrastructure, roads are flooded out with little effort. Transportation is third world.

The ideal time for travel here is December to May, as that's the off-season for typhoons. The food here is delicious, the accommodations are dirt cheap, and English is spoken almost everywhere.

(www.tourism.gov.ph)

Climate :
Angeles City is hot and very humid all year round. Filipina women are also hot and humid year-round, especially inside the strip clubs on **Field Street**. The weather pattern across the archipelago is roughly divided into the dry season (January to June) and the wet season (July to December). The average annual temperature is 25°C (77°F). The best time to visit is between December and May.

Entry Requirements :
Passport required, visas are not needed for stays up to 21 days. Three-month visas cost $35US. Departing the country will cost you $55P.

AIRLINES:

The Philippines' national airline is Philippine Airlines (PR). Other airlines serving the Philippines include Air France, British Airways, Cathay Pacific, Gulf Air, Kuwait Airways, Northwest Airways, Royal Brunei Airlines, Silk Air, Qatar Airways, Singapore Airlines and Malaysia Airlines.

APPROXIMATE FLIGHT TIMES :

From London to Manila is 20 hours; from Los Angeles is 14 ½ hours; from New York is 17 hours; from Singapore is 3 hours 40 minutes; from Hong Kong is 2 ½ hours; from Bangkok is 2 ½ hours; and from Sydney is 8 hours. **From Airport**: Taxis to Angeles City are about P1,800, and take from 30-60 minutes.

COUNTRY DIALING CODE: 63.

TIME ZONE: GMT plus 8 hours.

MONEY MATTERS :

Philippine Peso (P) = 100 centavos. Notes are in denominations of P1000, 500, 100, 50, 20, 10 and 5. Coins are in denominations of P5, 2 and 1, and 50, 25 and 10 centavos.

For the current exchange rate:

(www.oanda.com)

ELECTRICITY :

The outlets are 220-240 volts, but most hotels offer outlets for 110-120 voltages. Try to research this first before you blow up the building.

RECOMMENDED RESTAURANTS :

Since this info can change weekly, we can't recommend enough the "**Zagat Survey**." Pick up their travel book, or signup online. Worldwide reviews, menus, and pricing. **(www.zagat.com)**

CRIME :

Like any poverty stricken country, crime and hustlers flourish. Common sense should keep you out of trouble. There are scams involving guys pretending to be pimps trying to lure you to private parties full of girls. Avoid free rides to anywhere. Avoid walking around at night. Avoid guys knowing the best place to convert money. If you take a taxi, make sure the driver turns on the meter. If he gives you a story that it is broken, get out and take another taxi. Some restaurants try to sweet talk you into their *specialty meal* and get you to order it without an upfront price, then they hit you with a $60-75 bill. Always get the price up front. Avoid the jeepneys and trikes, they are full of pickpockets. Pay the extra buck for a taxi.

Take nightclubs or girls advice from Americans or tourists only, the locals are only looking the scam you with a smile. (think your wife).

ATMS in daylight are very much subject to high street crime in the Philippines. Pay cash for your drinks in the bar, no tabs

Note: you have to be careful moving around because the streets, if you can call them that, are like a video game to walk through. There are no sidewalks, and every 2 seconds you're almost run over by a jeep, taxi, or bicycle.

Skip the clubs on the north side of Fields Avenue, west of Papillion Bar. DO NOT go into **"Why Not Music Box"** or **"Sky Trax Disco"**. These businesses are for the local Filipinos. There are periodic reports of violence against foreigners who venture into areas full of drunk, single Filipino men. DO NOT drink the water, make sure all your food is cooked…skip all the street food vendors, and all unknown drinks handed to you.

HOTELS :
Here are a few choices close to the action. Get in good with the doorman, most of them can provide you with girls within minutes.

Oasis Hotel :
126 rooms off Don Juico Avenue in Clarkview. Once a favorite of visiting air force officers, this quiet, respectable hotel is located within a secure residential compound. The hotel has all the services you will need including 24-hour room service, 24-hour foreign currency exchange, 24-hour high security and dual-key safe deposit boxes, laundry service, internet access, gift shop, swimming pool etc. The hotel restaurant, Maranao Grill, is open 24 hours and there is an English pub. Standard and deluxe rooms are offered, but if you're going to stay here, take a P2700 junior suite (ask for a discount). The suites are the largest rooms in Angeles and your best option if you like to have two or more girls for the night. Telephone Nos.: 322-3301 to 03, 625-8301 to 03, 893-3301 to 03.

Orchid Inn :
The economy player's choice, across the street from the action, many regard this as the best choice as it's smack in the middle of 100 clubs, but still reasonably quiet. It also has 24 hr. room service, and a great pool at roughly $35 a night. Book well in advance. Tel (63)(45) 322-0370.
e-mail: orchid@datelnet.net

Kokomoz :

All rooms have queen size beds, hot water shower, marble floors, refrigerator, cable TV, and Internet connection, complete with a computer. Rooms facing Santos Street have been insulated to reduce noise. Introductory rate is P1,250/night including an American breakfast, which is 3 eggs, your choice of bacon, sausage or ham, toast, potato and coffee or tea. e-mail: rooms@kokomoz.com

Apartelle Royal :

Kitchen, a Jacuzzi, and walking distance from the action on Field Street. Rooms are priced from US $23 - $36.
Tel (63)(45) 625-6032.
e-mail: apartelleroyal@digitelone.com

For local listings of other hotels:
(www.angeles2.com)
(www.angelescitysexguide.com)
(http://travelsexguide.tv/main_nation3.htm)
(www.margarita-station.com/hotels.html)

TRANSPORTATION :

Buses for all long distance inter city travel, as there's only one railway. For between islands, there are plenty of ferries and boats. Car rentals available. In the city, taxis, jeeps, and mototricycles are found everywhere. At night, the jeepneys can be dangerous if you have a bad freelance driver, also pickpockets ride with you and you'll never see it coming. Ask the club to arrange a ride for you, or better yet, take a cab.

THE GAME PLAN :

Filipinas are an exotic combo of both Oriental and Spanish descent, with gorgeous long black hair, tight little bodies and beautiful dark bronze skin. While intelligent, confident and friendly, the residents are famously poor and are dealt a lousy hand in life. There are many local girls desperate for an American boyfriend or husband. Very often the locals are more than happy to go out for short time dates, just as long as you keep the payment terminology expressed in the terms *helping her out*, or simply saying you'd like her company and *will take care of her*. They still have a lot of pride. It's probably the best situation, because they're sweethearts and squeaky clean, and for the most part honest…well as honest as you can expect of a woman.

55

Hardened pros or overweight girls are nonexistent. The Filipinas girls all have permanent smiles, that innocent girl next-door look, and are very anxious to get naked with you. Don't be a prude, help them out. The Philippines is Americanized and most speak English. The rates are cheap, as the average monthly salary in the Philippines is $80 American. Hell, my bar tab last night was higher than that.

In Angeles City, you have some 100 bars all in a row in the red light district. All good things point you to **Fields Avenue**, with about 9 side streets containing clubs connected to it. It's orgy central for every man in the world. Regardless of your age, weight, appearance, wealth, or social skills, you can have as many young good looking girls as you want, 24 hours a day. Whether a regular bar or strip club, all the girls including waitresses are available for take out, with bar fines of around 1000p ($18), which the girls split with the clubs. Payment is made to the mamasan in the club. A small tip for good service is appreciated, but not mandatory. There is some pressure to buy "lady drinks", which the girls make $ on, but not too bad. There are so many bars you will run out of time on your vacation before you hit them all. Each one is packed with 18-year-old girls begging for you. Some clubs have over 50 girls in various bikini or schoolgirl outfits. Pretend you're the evil principal.

Remember that the clubs constantly change girls, names, owners and reputations. What is lousy one afternoon could be the best another evening. Unlike most strip clubs around the world, the girls dance in groups of 5 to 10 at a time, and a new group appears every 30 minutes. Be patient with each place you enter. The girls outnumber the men 10 to 1, but a girl doesn't have to leave with you. So make sure she likes you first, then be smooth, buy her a drink, loosen her up first and make your move. A little compliment and attention goes a long way here. She may end up giving you a reason not to take her, and all you've lost is a drink. (100-150P).

First stop, try **The Blue Nile**. An exceptionally elaborate club, meticulously designed, where no expense was spared in creation. Interior design is in Egyptian motif, with mummies and golf leaf. The lighting system consists of some 400 spotlights, smoke machines and special effects, with an equally amazing sound system. Many feel it is the premier club in Asia in this aspect. A bevy of hot young dancers in their matching schoolgirl outfits with thigh high boots, appear on a two-tier stage, powered by a hydraulic system which rises 10 feet in the air, with 20 go-go dancers on the top tier and another 20 down below. Like many clubs, this is not a camera friendly place. Nero's Bar is found next door, also a Vegas like club with a center stage, girls, girls, and more girls.

Similar setups are at each club, with a barrage of young dancers all doing the Solid Gold Dancer routines at the same time, kind of an overload feeling the first time you witness it. Clubs to also visit are **The Bunny Ranch, Treasure Island** (great private shower shows), **Roadhouse, Confetti's, Champagne Bar, Brown Sugar, Gecko's, Camelot, Blue Fox.** Daytime club with the best selection is **Dirty Duck.**

For afternoon fun, check out "**Blow Row**", with it's real name being Santos Street. Here there are 14 open-air clubs in a row, about as low budget as they come. The names are irrelevant, although **Black Pearl** has the most girls and routinely gets the thumbs up. No AC, cheap sound system and lighting, BUT, for P500, about $10 gets you two hours with a young girl who can suck a golf ball through a garden hose. Forget 2 hours, you're lucky if you'll last 5 minutes with these girls. Each club has 4-20 girls, forget looking for a model here. The girls on Santos Street have doctorates in sucking, see if you can try to negotiate down to $9 bucks with a straight face, you cheap Charlie. Beers are 30P, ladies drink 80P, there's no shower, and you may not want to sit on the bed. Stand there and bark orders, they may not understand English here.

In call massage girls are readily available as well. Be forewarned, Filipina girls will latch on tightly. If your vacation plan is establishing a whole posse, you gotta be slippery. They tend to hang around your hotel in the wee am hours waiting for your return.

One of the hottest new spots in Fields Avenue is the brand new **Pick Up Disco,** gorgeous and upscale decorated disco. The girls are dressed to the hilt and strutting their stuff with a group of equally gorgeous friends. No expense was spared in the planning of the three-story structure, from the raised central dancing stage, to the gold-trimmed balconies and railings that surround the band stand and upper floor ramparts, all the way to the 3rd floor VIP area. The 30-foot high ceiling -- painted like an open-air desert night complete with stars – combined with state-of-the-art lasers and concert lighting resembles Las Vegas rather than Angeles City.

If you plan on staying a week or longer, pick up a cell phone and pre-paid cards at the local mall. All the girls carry cell's and will come by your hotel any hour.

Local phone service providers.

(**www.globe.com.ph/**)   (**www.smart.com.ph/**)

To get a feel of the area, and a quick bite to eat, head to **Margarita Station**. There will be many regulars, expats, and tourists here who can give the latest and greatest things to do in town. They also have Internet service, bar, and pool tables. Great Thai food, make this your first stop in town. For a great local map, go this link…maps.

(www.cyber-sisters.com/Member/Main.aspx)

Print out this **Field Street** map for the bar layout.
(www.acmap.com/fields_complete.asp)

Clubs :
(www.roadhouseclub.com)
(www.insomniagroup.com)
(www.champagne-angeles.com/brownsugar/default.htm)

CASINOS :
Casino Filipino Angeles is a 6,811 square foot casino featuring 287 slots and thirty-nine table games. The property has one restaurant and a hotel with fifty-six rooms, open 24 hours.
Address :
Century Resort Hotel Complex
MacArthur Highway, Angeles City, Pampanga, Central Luzon 2009
(www.newpagcor.com/cf_angeles.htm)

Slot Machines - 287 total
Table Games - 39 total
Baccarat , Blackjack, Casino War, Craps , Pai Gow Poker, Stud Poker

Casino Filipino Mimosa is in Angeles City and is open 12noon-6am weekdays; 24 hours weekends. The casino features 109 slots and twenty-four table games. The property has a hotel with 337 rooms.

Address :
2059 Mimosa Drive
Mimosa Leisure Estate, Clark Field
Angeles City, Pampanga, Central Luzon 2009
+63 (45) 599-6020 General Information
Slot Machines - 109 machines
Table Games - 24 total

VACATION STUFF :
And now for the cover story for the old lady.

GOLF COURSES :
There are approximately 70 courses, unfortunately good golf courses can be difficult to access: all private clubs have armed guards with instructions to refuse entry to non-members. Courses that admit visitors tend to be expensive. Some of the best courses open to non-members include: **El Club Intramuros** (at the Grand Boulevard Hotel, central Manila); **Forbes Park** (in southeastern Manila, where two of three courses are open to visitors); **Canlubang** (one of many spectacular courses in southern Luzon and the only one open to non-members). A Nicklaus course design.
(www.manilasouthwoods.com)

DIVING AND SNORKELING :
The Philippines has a wealth of opportunities for diving and snorkeling. Favored spots are Boracay, Alona Beach (Bohol), Puerto Princesa (Palawan) and the island of Apo. Canoeists can shoot the rapids in Pagsanjan, 70km (43mi) southeast of Manila. For dive resort hotels, try Lalaguna Beach and Dive Resort or Big Apple Dive Resort.

FISHING :
The Philippines' warm waters, incorporating almost 750,000 sq miles of fishing grounds, rank 12th in worldwide fish production. These grounds are inhabited by some 2400 fish species. For deep-sea fishing, your catches will include game fish such as **giant tuna, tanguingue, king mackerel, great barracuda, swordfish** and **marlin**. Local tour operators in Manila will help arrange trips. As a rule of thumb, the big game fishing is best from December to August.

GYMNASIUM :
Best in town is AC1 Gym on Friendship. $150P per day.

KAYAKING:
Boating enthusiasts can rent traditional canoes (bancas) on most beaches. For kayaking, try this highly recommended company.
Tribal Adventure Tours
2772 Daan Hari St.,United Hills
Paranaque,Metro Manila.
Tel/Fax:(2)8232725,8216706; tribal@mnl.sequel.net

SURFING :

Right now, the most exciting surfing destination in the world is the Philippines. This is not only because of the great waves - like **Cloud 9, Tuason Point, Majesties** and **Cement** - which rank up there with the best in the world, because they're virtually undiscovered and not crowded. And it's not only because of the variety of the breaks: everything from easy beach breaks that are ideal for beginners to adrenalin-inducing barrels that challenge top international surfers.

BOARDSAILING :

The Philippines is the kind of destination board sailors dream about. When the northeast monsoon (called the arnihan by the locals) blows in, it brings clear, blue skies, warm weather and steady winds of 15-25 knots. If your idea of great sailing is to hook in, sheet in and plane effortlessly along a spectacular coastline, you can't do much better than the top boardsailing areas in the Philippines.

CURACAO
Lesser Antilles, Caribbean Islands

ABOUT :

On a clear day in Curaçao – and that means most days – you can see Venezuela a few miles across the sea in South America. When you hear salsa and merengue on the buses and glimpse the Latin style and verve of the islanders, you'll know you're not very far from South America.

Sunbathers by the dozens are gorgeous and topless Dutch women, spread out amongst some 38 popular beaches, from large strands to secluded sun-traps cut into the rocks on the craggy coast. The **Curaçao Underwater Park** is a haven for divers and snorkelers – a 12-mile reef with coral beds, walls and shallow wrecks. Water sports such as fishing, windsurfing and water-skiing are major island activities, as is ocean-lined golf.

Curaçao has a population of 130,000 and is made up of 55 nationalities. Willemstad is the island's capital and only city. It's an island of salsa, jazz and tumba – a local specialty. Curaçao's annual Salsa Festival and Jazz Festival are among the highlights of events each year. During February's Carnival Week the streets and beaches really are alive with the sound of music and bootie shaking. Even the binge drinking gringo tourists get in the act, displaying their horrid attempts at looking cool dancing, while sporting hideous bitter beer faces and farting off tempo.

Curaçao is located in the southwestern Caribbean. The largest of the Netherlands Antilles, it is 38 miles long and varies from 2 to 7.5 miles wide. Curaçao, along with neighboring Bonaire and three islands in the north eastern Caribbean (St. Maarten, St. Eustatius and Saba), form the Netherlands Antilles. Located just 35 miles north of Venezuela, it's only 2 1/2 hours by air from Miami, and just 1-½ hours from Montego Bay. Dutch is the official language, but Curaçaoans also speak English and Spanish.

There are a number of cruise liners that service the island. Air Tours/Sun Cruise, Carnival Cruises, Holland America, Princess Cruises, Norwegian Cruise Line, and Royal Caribbean Cruise Line. How nice of them to drop off fat angry housewives on our private hooker island.

CLIMATE :

Located in the tropics, just 12° north of the Equator -- and outside of the hurricane belt -- Curacao has a warm, sunny climate year round. The average temperature is about 27° C (mid 80s F). The average temperature of the bootie is about 150° C. Trade winds blow constantly from the east, picking up in the spring months. The whores blow constantly in a north to south movement. The rainy season, October to February, is marked by short, occasional showers, usually at night, and continued sunny weather by day. Total annual rainfall averages only 570 mm (22 inches).

AIRLINES :
DCA, American Airlines, Avianca Airlines, KLM Royal Dutch Airlines, Servivensa Airlines, Aeropostal and Air Jamaica.
Miami: 2-1/2 hours, Caracas, Venezuela: 45 minutes and Montego Bay is 1-1/2 hours away.

ENTRY REQUIREMENTS :
Canadian citizens and US need either a valid passport, or proof of citizenship in the form of an original birth certificate accompanied by photo ID, and an onward or return ticket. Most other nationals need only a passport. You will need to apply for a resident permit if you plan to stay for longer than three months. You are not allowed to work or live on Curacao without a work permit.

DEPARTURE TAX :
An airport tax of U.S.$ 22.00 per person for international flights and flights to Aruba, or U.S. $7.00 per person for inter-island flights is payable when leaving the island.

TAXIS :
Taxi's are easy to recognize by their signs and the TX on their registration plates. The prices are based for 1-4 people from 6 am-11pm. A fifth person costs 25% more. After 11pm there is 25% surcharge. Agree on price before traveling. There are taxi stands at the airport, hotels.

Taxi Main Office: tel: 869-0747 Complaints: 869-0747. In every direction they rob you blind, 6 miles from airport to hotel is $15. Trips to Campo are $20 each way. Rent a car.

TELEPHONE :
Good IDD service to Europe. Country code: 599. Outgoing international code: 00.

Mobile telephone: TDMA network exists. GSM 900 network operated by Setel NV has just been established. Others include GSM 900/1900 network operated by Curaçao Telecom NV.

(www.curacaotelecom.com)

Handset rentals at the airport post office. There is a 5 per cent tax.

MONEY MATTERS :

U.S. currency is King of course, and since you're on vacation, you're temporarily King as well. When you drop the last of your cash in some titty dancers thong, you are no longer King, and it is time to get your happy ass off our island, you broke fool. Travelers Checks and CC are fine. Debit Cards are accepted at a few large shops and supermarkets. Prices are quoted in the national currency, the Netherlands Antillean guilder (also called the florin), abbreviated NAFl. or ANG. It is currently pegged to the US dollar at a stable rate of US$ 1 = NAFl. 1.77 for cash, 1.78 for traveler's checks. Exchange rates may vary slightly at stores and hotels. Bills of US $50 and US$100 can be hard to cash. The larger denominations of guilder bills (100 and 250) are hard to cash for small purchases. There are no restrictions on how much money you can bring.

For the current exchange rate:

(www.oanda.com)

BANKING HOURS :

Banks are open Monday through Friday 8:00 a.m. to 3:30 p.m. The airport bank is open Monday through Saturday 8:00 a.m. to 8:00 p.m. and on Sunday from 9:00 a.m. to 4:00 p.m. Selected bank branches have ATMs that spit out US dollars. International credit cards are accepted at most major commercial establishments.

ELECTRICITY :

Electricity is 110 - 130 volts/50 cycles, similar but not identical to the US standard. Most 60 cycle electrical appliances from the United States will function properly. Dual voltage appliances from Europe and South America will need an adapter plug, readily available on the island.

Vibrators will operate on the standard American batteries.

WHAT TO WEAR :

Casual tropical wear is in order. Supersentive condoms are casual and in order as well. Use extra suntan lotion down here in the tropics. Most indoor establishments are air conditioned, however, from experience let us tell you it's really hot and humid in Curacao. The AC really does not make that much a difference when you're doing the horizontal sledgehammer.

Locals dress fashionably, particularly for indoor evening events; dress for the outdoor festivals is decidedly casual. The strong trade winds may make wraparound and billowing skirts a problem, that is if you're the kind of guy that wears skirts. Dropping a lot of cash in brothels will remove all need for woman's clothing. Some restaurants prohibit shorts or sandals; (does that mean Speedo's are OK?), some casinos will require jackets for men. Overly revealing clothes and bathing suits are not appropriate on their hotsy totsy upscale beach. We recommend you rent a scorching hard body chica for the day, and make sure she wears next to nothing and parade her thru all the scowling fat wives, just out of principle. Actually, the beach is full of hot young topless Dutch girls. They probably won't notice her, but they'll scowl at your fat belly, shit eating grin, and raging hard on.

TIPPING :
Tip porters NAFl. 1 per bag, and taxi drivers 10% of the fare. Restaurants usually add a 10% service charge to the bill; you can leave a couple more guilders change if you like. All this beside the 5% Government sales tax.

RECOMMENDED RESTAURANTS :
Since this info can change weekly, we can't recommend enough the "**Zagat Survey**." Pick up their travel book, or signup online. Worldwide reviews, menus, and pricing.

(www.zagat.com)

HOTELS :
This is a tiny resort island, thus you'll find several large 5 star resort hotels available at a healthy rate, and a number at lesser-known locations. All rates are subject to change during the year. A surcharge of 7% government tax and 12% service charge usually prevails. Mafia skimming Netherlands style. Pricing at the Marriott and Hilton Casino hotels $150 and up.

Curaçao Marriott Beach Resort and Emerald Casino
The Marriott on Sunday has $20 all you can eat brunch including Champagne/Wine and lots of great food. Scuba diving centers on the premises. 599-9-736-8800 for a direct line.
(www.marriot.com)

Hilton Curaçao Resort
196 Rooms, +599-9-462-5000 Hotel Reservations
(www.hiltoncaribbean.com/Curacao/Home.htm)

Here's a link to all price ranges on the island:
(www.curacao-tourism.com/accommodation.htm)

Breezes Resort & Princess Casino
+599-9-736-7888 General Information
(www.breezescuracao.com/curacao_info.asp)

In addition to the expensive hotels, there are an abundance of short time apartment complexes with a kitchen in the range of $50 a night when you book several days in advance. To rephrase, there are a bunch cheap ass dumps available as well. Websites:
(www.apartmentscuracao.com)
Also here: (www.Curacao-Tourism.com) (www.Curacao.com)

Keep in mind that the girls at Campo Alegre will hang out with you at the hotel beach in the daytime, but they're probably not going to hang out at Motel 1/6th, there's no romance without finance.

CAR RENTAL :
Although the island is tiny, the cabs are ridiculously expensive, up to $3 a mile. Definitely rent a car if you are staying several days, since you'll be making 1 or 2 daily trips to El Campo. From the Marriott, it's a $20 cab ride each way to the brothel. The girls are just $29, so you're paying more for cabs than pussy! What a sick world! Screw the bastards, rent a car. Available are Avis, Budget, Hertz, National and Thrifty. Gas is $6 a gallon!

THE GAME PLAN :
There's only one place you need to go on the island. **Campo Alegre**, also called Le Mirage. This is possibly the best all-inclusive brothel in the world. It's located at the end of the island away from all the major hotels. Campo Alegre was converted from an army barracks into a state sponsored Brothel, with 10-foot high walls and armed security to keep the jealous wives out. Inside it looks like it looks like an apartment complex, with over 100 one-story air conditioned units where the girls live. Rooms are extra clean, with mirrors on the walls, a bath, and even cold beer. The resort has multiple facilities, including an open-air sports bar with nude pole dancers, as well as exotic show events on weekends at midnight. Every other night, they pull a volunteer out of the crowd and he does a chick in front of everyone. In the bar are billiard tables, big screen TV's, and 150 chicas. You can hang out here between rounds and make a whole evening of it.

For your dates, if you don't see a potential girlfriend in the bar area, just stroll around the entire grounds and check out the girls standing near their units wearing practically nothing. They really like you a lot, think you're dashing, gorgeous and funny, and can't wait to tell you all about it in their apartment. Pricing for your date is $29 per half hour. The girls want local currency (Netherlands Antilles guilders), so change your money with the cashier at the entrance first. You can have multiple girls at the same time, but it's not discounted. What nerve. You can stay in her place as long as you want by the way. The cover is just $3, beers are $3.75, drinks a bit more. The grounds are meticulously maintained, and so is the Latina coochie. No cameras, booze or weapons are allowed, and you're frisked at the entrance. A large friendly security staff is very visible.

The girls are flown in mostly from Columbia and the Dominican Republic. They mail their photos and health test results in advance. If hired, upon arrival is another checkup, and they're tested weekly for HIV and STD while living on the grounds. Fail the test once and they're removed from the brothel campus. They pay $40 a day to work and live here, so there's a healthy income for them compared to their poverty stricken countries. The age range is from 20-35 tops. Some dogs, some average, but most overall from 6-8 with a fair amount of 9's. They are only allowed a 90-day visa for work, and only two terms a year, so there's always new blood. They tend to wait for you to make the move there. The policy is they have to be at work between 6 PM and 6 AM. You can take one out of there during their off hours, but get her back by 6pm or it's a $40 fine. A lot of them like to hang out on the beach at the Hilton and Marriott. Be forewarned, these hotels are very strict at night, so she will need to be well dressed to get in then. Many girls are looking for American boyfriends and husbands, so make sure you try for daytime fun.

Campo is slow during the day with a lot less selection. (open 24/7). Not to say you should avoid the day. The hottest girls are busy all night and you may never see them EXCEPT maybe the daytime. And of course, in the day your session tends to be less rushed. You'll need some Spanish, as virtually no English is spoken by the girls.

If you must go elsewhere, you'll be disappointed, but here's the scoop. As far as titty bars, across the street from the Holiday Beach Hotel is Club Havana. Don't expect to see any diamonds in here. The girls are South American and Dominican, and will leave the club after the 2am closing time and return to your hotel for a large fee. The only benefit of doing this over Campo is that you'll have a girl all night. A change of pace, but you can have 2 higher caliber girls for the price of 1 at Campo.

Also, since there are Casinos on the island, expect to see girls loitering around 1am on for the guy who just won a little. You'll be able to spot them easily, and if not, staple a hundred to your forehead and stand near the hotel elevator. It's amazing how perceptive a woman can be sometimes.

As far as regular clubs, try **Mambo Beach**, ironically located on the friggin' beach. It's great Thursday thru Saturday, often times Sunday is an even bigger night. Remember, this is an upper income Dutch Resort Island, so there are tons of Scandinavian blue-eyed blondes on vacation here, as well as the Latina hotties. This club is huge, holds around 800 people, and has a massive sound system with speakers everywhere, and stages and salsa dancing all around.

For a more upscale club, try **The Living Room** on Fridays. There's also an after hours club called **Zenzurro** that's good on Fridays and Saturdays, with some pros in attendance as well. Other choices include **Ole! Ole!** on Friday and Saturday nights (tel. 599/9-461-7707), offering live music. The beach club **Hook's Hut** also, located at Piscadera Bay (tel. 599/9-462-6575). Hook's is a mainstay for Jazz music on the island, with great live entertainment booked regularly.

There have been numerous streetwalkers sightings in the downtown area. The girls seem to have lost their hotel key, and they'll search your crotch for it in your back seat of your rental car if your pants are down and your twenties are up.

VACATION STUFF :
Tell the old lady you flew across the world to take advantage of the fabulous duty free cooking spices they sell. If she asks twice, smack her around a little bit...who's got time for that shit.

GOLFING :
At the **Blue Bay Golf & Beach Resort**, the sand, trade winds and spectacular natural environment challenge the golfer right through to the last hole. This stunning 18-hole championship course will require not only that you bring a sound game, but that you bring a good camera as well. In the event that you totally suck at golf, bring a hot Columbian stripper from El Campo along for the cart ride. She should preferably suck as well...and often. As far as equipment, you carry a bag for the clubs, she carries a bag for booze and condoms. Another hole-in-one, that's three today.

SNORKELING & SCUBA DIVING :
Curacao's more than 100 dive sites are famous all over the world with visibility ranging from 60 to 150 feet, with water temperatures a comfortable 70 to 85 degrees Fahrenheit. Curacao has some of the best snorkeling and diving in the Caribbean. The Curacao Underwater Park is a 12.5 mile coral reef that has been protected as a National Park. Divers and snorkelers will find an underwater paradise of "Mushroom Forests" and "Car Piles". Guides are available for hire, and lessons are offered for beginners. Hookers are also available for hire throughout the island, but for diving are strictly a bring your own status. **BYOH**

DEEP SEA FISHING :
Private boats are always available for charter. Curacao is one of the better Big Game sport fishing locations in the world. You will find yourself reeling in an assortment of the trophy fish, including **Blue Marlin, Dolphin, Sailfish, Tuna, Wahoo, Barracuda,** and **Snapper.** Arrangements can be made through the major hotels for the charters and marina information. The fishing is in nearby waters, and provides an exciting challenge even for accomplished fishermen. It also provides a little sideshow after that psychotic threesome you had the previous night. A Multi language crew is ready to help you with any request you may need.
Pricing range: Half Day(6 people max) $300. Full day(6 People max) $450.

CASINOS :
There are 8-10 casinos on the island, all located in the 5 star major hotel chains spread out along the ocean drive. We list the three larger ones here.
Curaçao Marriott Beach Resort and Emerald Casino
Open 11am-4am daily. The 5,000 square foot casino features 135 slots and twelve table games. The property has five restaurants and a hotel with 257 rooms. **(www.marriot.com)**
Address:
Piscadera Bay, Willemstad, Curaçao..Telephone +599-9-736-8800
Slot Machines - 135 machines
Table Games
American Roulette- 1 table- USD 5.00 to USD 500 bets
Baccarat- 1 table- USD 5.00 to USD 1,000 bets
Blackjack- 6 tables- USD 5.00 to USD 500 bets
Caribbean Stud Poker- 2 tables- USD 5.00 to USD $5,000
Craps- 1 table- USD 5.00 to USD 500 bets
Mini-Baccarat- 1 table- USD 5.00 to USD 500 bets
Roulette

Hilton Curaçao Resort

Open 10am-4am. The 5,000 square foot casino features 170 slots and seven table games. The property has five restaurants and a hotel with 196 rooms.

(www.hiltoncaribbean.com/Curacao/Home.htm)

John F. Kennedy Boulevard

Piscadera Bay, Curaçao Netherlands Antilles

Telephone +599-9-462-5000 Hotel Reservations

Slot Machines - 170 machines

Table Games – Blackjack, Caribbean Stud Poker , Craps, Mini-Baccarat, Poker, and Roulette.

Breezes Resort & Princess Casino

Open daily 11:00am - 4:00am. The 15,000 square foot casino features 300 slots and nine table games. The property has seven restaurants and a hotel with 347 rooms.

Dr. Martin Luther King Boulevard 78, Willemstad, Curaçao

Telephone +599-9-736-7888 General Information

Slot Machines - 300 machines

Table Games

Blackjack, Caribbean Stud Poker, Poker, Roulette.

(www.breezescuracao.com/curacao_info.asp)

SAN JOSE, COSTA RICA

ABOUT :
Costa Rica is located in Central America, between Nicaragua and Panama. The country has a population of 3.8 million, with the capital **San Jose** coming in at 340,000. The people are 96% Spanish descent. CR hosts more than one million tourists each year. National parks cover almost 12% of the country, and forest reserves and reservations boost the protected land area to 27%. Rugged highlands are found throughout most of the country, and range from approximately 3,000 to 12,000 feet above sea level. Beautiful beaches on the west coast, and there are several active volcanoes (Volcán Arenal, Volcán Irazú). The country has a relatively long coastline in both the Atlantic and Pacific oceans, as well as a number of rivers and streams that attract expert kayakers and rafters.

Costa Rica is a tropical paradise, with exotic jungles, gorgeous beaches, world-class sport fishing, volcanoes, and some of the finest Latina chicas in Central America. CR is so popular for sex tourist industry, chicas fly in from Columbia, Panama, Dominican Republican, even Europe, to handle the overflow of US men and their money. In addition to a sea of local discos, vacation resorts, and nightclubs, San Jose has some **100 massage parlors** and **brothels** for you to choose from. The local girls are gorgeous and dress to kill, hip huggers, midriffs, waist length black hair. They take great pride in looking like sexy mattress monsters. You're head will be sore from constantly turning around and staring. Fortunately there are no parking meters in town, or you'd be walking into them.

Here's are links to the local papers.

(www.insidecostarica.com)
(www.amcostarica.com)
(www.ticotimes.net)

CLIMATE :
Costa Rica's year round climate is pleasant with naturally occurring breezes cooling down most of the coastal areas. The rain season if from May to November. We're talking rainstorms that resemble rivers pouring down from the sky, and then ten minutes later they're gone; the streets get flooded above your shoes easily. The Caribbean coast tends to be wet all year. The women in the country are nymphos and tend to only have wet seasons. The 'warm' dry season is December to May, though temperature differences between summer and winter are slight. San Jose is your basic hot and humid hellhole slum. The average annual temperatures range from 31.7°C (89°F) on the coast to 16.7°C (62°F) inland. Expect 250 days a year of rain.

70

ENTRY AND DEPARTURE :

From the US, a valid passport gets you 90 days there without a visa. You need a pre-paid airline ticket to exit Costa Rica or proof of financial resources ($400 - $1,000.00 in cash, traveler checks) either to return to your home country or to go to another country. Your passport cannot expire earlier than 90 days from the date that you arrive in Costa Rica. For example, if you are going to fly to Costa Rica on January 1st, your passport cannot expire before April 1st of the same year. If staying for more than 90 days, a valid passport will be required and you must file for a stay extension at the Immigration Department of Costa Rica. Or, you may exit Costa Rica and re-enter. Most tourists visit Nicaragua or Panama - Costa Rica's neighbor countries - for a day and come back into Costa Rica. A $20 U.S. dollar fine will be charged upon departure from Costa Rica if you overstayed your permitted length in the country.

(www.costarica.com/travel/visas/uscitizens.html)

Once there, put the visa in your hotel safe and carry around a copy of your passport. *Departure tax* is tax of U.S. $26.00 per person for international flights. The tax payment portion takes only a few minutes though, but the international flight check in can take hours.

AIRLINES :

The Costa Rican national airline is Taca International Airlines (TA) Taca International flies direct to Costa Rica from Miami, New Orleans, Los Angeles, New York, Mexico and other destinations in Central and South America. The Visit Central America Pass is available from Grupo Taca and is an economical way to travel to Costa Rica from the USA and from Costa Rica to other Central American countries. Major US carriers are American Airlines, Delta, and Continental. Flight times: from Houston is 2 ½ hours, NY is 7 hours, Los Angeles is 11 hours, and London is 12 hours.

MONEY MATTERS :

U.S. currency is King of course. Bring crisp new bills, avoid $100 bills. The local currency is colones, around 415 to 1 dollar. Best place to transfer money is the hotels, the Morazon in San Jose pays slightly higher than the others. Forget the banks, the line can be hours. Airport currency exchange is likewise a rip off. Never use a credit card to buy colones, there are huge hidden charges. Negotiate all your dates in colones. "this is Costa Rica, honey, not the US."

TAXIS :

The airport is 20 miles from San Jose, i.e., Sin City, and it's only a $12 cab ride. Skip the rental car, in town it's a nuisance and a potential liability. Cabs are $1.25 every direction in town, most places are walking distance. The road trips for eco-travel have dirt-cheap transportation included…plus there are no street signs anyway, chances are you'd get lost or maybe end up with your rental car down a cliff the way the rain comes down here. As soon as you come out of the airport there's a huge line of cabs. Buy your ticket at the well-marked ticket booth, don't go direct thru a cabbie.

WHAT TO WEAR :

Skip the typical ugly American clothes, i.e., shorts and Hawaiian shirt. Shorts are rarely seen at all. The girls like a man dressed up with a little class. Or, they like a man in shorts and Hawaiian shirts with a lot of cash to burn. The choice is yours. Costa Rica is real hot and humid. Light shirts are a must. If you travel outside of town, the 5 floor San Pedro Mall has no AC! It's like a sauna mall. Overall, air conditioning is a unique and exciting concept not found in most parts of the city. The rainy season is a joke, runs from March thru December. The rain starts with no warning and is brutal for about 15 minutes. Be prepared to move fast and get stuck under an awning for a while.

CRIME :

Tican criminals are little people, but still creative in their scams. The standard one involves teams while you are walking around town. An older lady will bump into you real hard and someone else will pick your pocket. Keep your money secure elsewhere, don't carry a wallet, and as always, don't carry more than you can afford to lose. If you're winning big in a casino, somebody is probably watching you, and you'll be bumped outside. Hide the money, walk quickly and confidently. Remember, cabs are $1, the town is tiny, and the main hotels are a block or two away. If you won a lot, take a cab.

TIPPING :

Retail establishments add a 10% service charge as well as 15% local tax. Thus, the tips tend to be small, and the tits tend to be large.

RECOMMENDED RESTAURANTS :

Since this info can change weekly, we can't recommend enough the "**Zagat Survey**." Pick up their travel book, or signup online. Worldwide reviews, menus, and pricing. (**www.zagat.com**)

72

HOTELS :

To be in the center of the action in San Jose, there are three main hotels you want to choose from.

Hotel Del Rey

Avenida Primero y Calle 9,

San José, San José 1017, (888) 972-7272 (www.hoteldelrey.com)

Home of the famous **Blue Marlin**, ground zero for the girls, everyone here is available. The girls are checked for ID by security, and the problem girls are not allowed entry. The del Rey is around $65 a night. They charge $10 per guest in the room, but they keep her passport and papers at the front desk and check with you before releasing her (all the hotels do). Across the street is:

Hotel Morazon

Frente al Parque Morazan

San José, San José 1017, Costa Rica

506 219 2470

Located one block from the del Rey, the Morazan, is around $45 a night, not quite as nice, but they have no guest fee.

Hotel Presidente

Avenida Central entre Calle 7 y Calle 9, San Jose1017

#506 221 3832 $60 to $100, including breakfast.

Located a few blocks away from the **del Rey**, the breakfast café has the best view for local chica watching seats. No hotel guest fee, but only 1 guest at a time. They have a Jacuzzi on the roof you can rent. Incredible master suite.

(www.hotel-presidente.com)

THE GAME PLAN :

The main show is the **Hotel del Rey Casino**'s lobby bar. There are very few places in the world where you will walk in and be so overwhelmed with the first site. Indescribable. It's worth going with newbies just to see their initial reaction. OMG Jaw drop. The best way to describe it is a Sports bar brothel. The girls here must all be clairvoyant or something. Every one in there can tell you're a brilliant and special man, and they all want to sleep with you now…a lot will only need an hour or two to appreciate your magic. A lot of them will spend the night. There are about 60 girls in here at any given time, and maybe 10 guys tops. Also, there tend to be a new batch of girls every hour or two. Date gifts of $100 are requested, just laugh and offer $50-75 worth in their currency. The girls are local ticas, Columbians, Dominicans, and other South Americans. Most are all pro, a fair amount of part-timers as well. The hip hugger bootie pants is the style here. A few hogs, age is generally 18-25 years old. If the girl is aloof and mechanical in the bar, that won't change later when it really counts. Also, be very specific on what you want on your date, time(two hours), positions, tricks, etc.

The date is best if you pay afterwards. "Pagar cuando terminar." Tell her this in the bar. A common scam is she agrees, gets back to your room, showers, and when you're both naked, then she asks for money up front again. Just stand up and get dressed and open the door. Usually she'll change her mind, if not tell her to take a hike. Try to be a gentleman and make it a pleasant experience. Most will give phone numbers and you can hook up the next day or the entire trip if you'd like. Remember, all the girls talk to each other at the DR, if you're an ass or a scammer, none of the girls will have anything to do with you after that.

Across the street is **Key Largo**, which has a live band playing closet classics from the US along with salsa. Ten years ago this was the hot spot, and the rate was just $20. Capitalism reared its ugly head. The club is still trying to find a way to make a comeback. Grab a girl at the DR and take her here. It will lighten her up, it's a great place for the girls to dance to live music, and a great place to get drunk. The bartenders here are the hottest girls in town. They have great seafood here also.

Live Sex

For a change, check out the **Park Hotel** lesbian show Friday and Saturday night. At 10 pm, six girls grind each other on top of the bar, using toys, tongues, you name it. The crowd gets oil to rub them down. Non-stop action. Most girls you wouldn't want, but for a show it's a must see once time. If you want a stool at the bar for the closest view, make sure you bring crappy clothes to wear, as you'll be covered in splattered oil from the show.

Discos

For meeting local girls, just north of the downtown Holiday Inn is the **El Pueblo** area, with over 150 bars, clubs, and restaurants. This is a hot spot if you're under 40, and the locals here are great looking. In fact, you won't see one overweight girl your whole trip.

Besides this, the whole city has about 50-100 massage parlors. Here is invaluable map detailing all the hot spots as well as the hotels, clubs, and malls. Make sure you print this out.

(http://adultcostarica.net/index.htm)

Massage Parlors

The preferred spas are **New Fantasy**, **Blue Zone, Idem**, **747, Cha Cha,** and **Oases**. NF is around $18 per 30 min date, $34 for an hour. This includes massage, steam room, shower, and other extras. When you arrive, there's a huge one-way mirror that allows you to look in at the 30+ potential dates sitting on a couch. In Thailand they call this the fishbowl. Its basically a holding pen and quite a sight. Usually peering in will be 10 other guys who haven't got laid in two years in the US, and now suddenly they are picky and have high standards. Get a grip guys. The girls are 18-22 years old, and the bang for the buck is quite a value…some very enthusiastic performances.

Next up is **Idem**, a health spa with a bar. You sit and have a beer or 10, the girls are all hovering near the bar. When you're ready, point to your date. She knows she's lucky for you picking her, and has a special room to take you upstairs to tell you all about it. There's a lot more girls here than NF, 23-35 in age, a little better looking, and the dates run around $55. The boss here is named Roberto, he speaks English and can refer you to the best performers for what you're seeking. Great threesomes can be had.

Strip Clubs

Avoid at all costs, the biggest scam going in CR, they have been known to pad your CC bills three to five hundred dollars.

Ram Luna

For those who spoil themselves, take a girl to this restaurant up in the mountains. In the mountains above Aserrí, south of San José. Directions for Taxi Driver: Del centro de Aserrí, cuatro kilómetros sobre la carretera a Tabarca. Tel: (506) 230-3060 / 230-3489

Recommended Dish: "Lomito Mirador," a beef tenderloin. Dinner entrées range from $6 to $13. Wednesday-night all-inclusive "Tierra Tica" Costa Rican buffet with open bar, live music, typical dancing and festivities costs $28 per person. Fireworks display at night as well.

Escort Sites :

(http://www.costaricaescort.com/indexen.htm **)**
(http://www.guiascostarica.com/guia/e2.html **)**
(http://costaricaescorts.net/index2.htm **)**

VACATION STUFF :

Tell the old lady you flew to Central America to buy a 200-gallon sombrero and some coffee. While you're down there, grow a handlebar mustache and practice twirling your cap gun.

Eco-Sporting :

Costa Rica is an adrenaline junkie hot spot. That's why you went there, remember? There is a fascinating canopy daytrip tour that many people take tour near San Ramon. After climbing several thousand feet up thru dense jungle, you then zip line across a steel rope from one side to the other(100 yards). It's an amazing thrill because you're flying thru the air thousands of feet above the rain forest. This is not designed for those who are afraid of heights, over weight and out of shape. Great for group trips.

On the Pacific Coast is the best surfing in Central America, and for windsurfers go to the **Laguna de Arenal**, located next to the infamous volcano. For snorkeling and diving, try the **Reserva Biologica Isla del Cano**, 12 miles west of Bahía Drake, off the northern part of the Península de Nicoya and in the **Parque Nacional Isla del Coco**.

Another favorite vacation activity here is the violent white-water rafting. Outfitters and guides can arrange trips. The **Reventazón River** (class III) is suitable for beginners, next level up is done at **Pacuare** (class IV) and the **Pascua** (class V) rivers. The best times to go are from May to November.

Río Reventazon, in central Costa Rica, is one of the most exhilarating and scenic rivers in Costa Rica for kayakers and rafting as well.

Windsurfing :

Lake Arenal was recently voted one of the world's top windsurfing spots. Situated at 5580ft (1700m) above sea level, the lake offers its best windsurfing between April and December.

Golfing :

For golf, there are two, 18-hole golf courses near San Jose. First up is **Cariai County Club**, the only catch is you have to stay at Melia Cariai Conference Center. The second 18-hole golf course is **Parque Valle del Sol** in Santa Ana. There are also many golf courses throughout Costa Rica away from San Jose.

On the west coast, at the ritzy **Marriot Los Suenos** there's a third 18-hole course carved out between lush rain forest mountains with great ocean views. Well kept, about $90. Remember, it rains often and hard. For all Costa Rican golf info, go to Costa Golf Adventures. Toll free: 1-877-258-2688 from US. (www.golfcr.com)

Sport Fishing :

Costa Rica coasts offer some of the best Big Game Sport Fishing in the world, with fishing on both the Pacific and Caribbean coasts. Here you

76

can catch **Marlin, Wahoo, Tuna, Tarpon, Dorado, Snook,** and **Sailfish** all year round. Costa Rica currently holds 18 world record catches.

(**www.ticotimes.net/fishing.htm**)
(http://costaricasailfish.com)

Marlin
Caught every month of the year, with mid-November to early March exceptional, then slowing a bit from April into early June when it picks up again, peaking in August and September.

Sailfish
Caught throughout the year, with May through August normally the top season. They may begin to thin out in September and the slowest months are from late August through November.

Tuna
When all else fails, there are always tuna, any time of the year. More often than not when you'd just as soon avoid them to concentrate on billfish. The yellow fin and some big eye tuna are often found well inside the Santa Catalina Islands, 30 minutes or less running time from the beach, while schools of 12 to 20 pounders are usually abundant on the outside. You frequently find concentrations of 40 to 60 pound tuna, and there are plenty of the 200 to 400 pounders caught every year.

Dorado
More properly known as dolphin, these colorful gamesters are most abundant from late May through October when the seasonal rains flood the rivers, carrying out debris that forms trash lines close inshore that they like to lie under. Troll past a floating log and you'll likely hook a dorado.

Wahoo
The first showing begins about the time the rains start in May, peaking in July and August. Most are caught around the rocky points and islands, but you will pick one up offshore.

Roosterfish
Available all year, but there are more caught in the Papagayo Bay area from November through March. That may be because more boats in the northernmost area of this region are fishing inshore during those windy months, and the roosters like the structure of the shoreline and islands where they're found in 50 to 60 feet of water. For the best up to date fishing info and Charter info, go to:

(www.fishcostarica.com/index.html)
(http://centralamerica.com/cr/fish/)

If you're already staying in San Jose, there's a travel agency in the Hotel del Rey where you can arrange charter boats trips and shuttle to the water for ½ day, day, and multi day excursions. Going rate is about $ 500-600 for a full day per boat plus about 50 bucks for transportation.

Jaco Beach is about 2 hours west of San Jose on the Pacific side of Costa Rica. If you prefer the finer things in life, stay at **Las Suenos Marriott Ocean and Golf Resort**. The hotel features magnificent colonial architecture set on the Pacific Coast, (1 hour, 45 minutes from Juan Santamana International Airport) on a 1,100 acre rainforest with an 18-hole championship golf course. Some attractions include: Casino , Spa Services, Tennis Courts, Water Sports, Deep Sea Fishing, and a 250 slip Marina. It's literally jungle territory, with monkeys in the trees, and Amazon hookers in the bars as well. Twelve miles away is a crocodile safari where the beasts jump out of the water and eat out of the guides hand. He even has most of his fingers. Las Suenos is a resort area specifically designed for wealthy Americans. If you're looking for lady company there, you'll have to bring it with you.

Heading out further south is Jaco Beach. For lesser expensive there's the **Hotel Cocal** on the beach, it's got a nice pool decent rooms and is either $59 or $69 a night off-season. Besides the **Beatle bar**, there is **El Centro Disco**, at late night, with pro, semi-pro and non-pros late night. Jaco is definitely a weekend only place for action. Also, there's a few strip clubs, the best being **Club Hollywood.**

The best chica bar is called the **Beatle Bar**. It's pretty much a weekends only club. Jaco is a surfer town, so the bar is full of locals, surfers, and a fair amount of friendly ladies who are dying to hear all your bullshit fishing stories, for a fee of course. The smartest approach is to bring a girl from San Jose with you for an overnight trip with you. She probably has never been to the area and it will greatly enhance your outing. Interview well.

The nicest beach in the area is Manuel Antonio. Best place to stay is the Costa Verde Hotel. By the way, Grey Line Fantasy Tour bus shuttles back and forth from the Best Western Irazu.
(www.bestwesterncostarica.com)

There are two towns that people go to for sport fishing, **Quepos** and **Jaco.** Jaco has average to lousy fishing, with a great hooker bar full of 40 to 50 girls. Quepos is outstanding for fishing and lousy for the chicas. Last trip in 2 days we caught 24 sailfish. The choice is up to what your true goal is.

CASINOS :

There are 5 casinos in downtown San Jose. Forget Vegas, picture your local bar with a couple tables. The Tropical next to the DR is decent. A lot of the shy semi-pros hang out here as the competition for men is fierce at the Hotel Del Rey, where you'll spending most of your trip. Our favorite for layout is the **Colonial**. The main casinos are walking distance from each other. **Hotel del Rey Casino, Hotel Morazon, Binions Horseshoe and Colonial**. Binions and Colonial are the only ones with craps. A quick note, pay close attention if playing craps there, the dealers change every 20 minutes, and they often have little understanding of the payouts or betting rules for that matter. Craps gives the best odds here. And you can bet double odds on the PASS/DON'T PASS and the COME/DON'T COME lines. The Colonial is the only one with real roulette, the rest play canasta, which is the same betting board, but they use a lottery spinning wheel to pick the numbers. As far as the slots go, in CR they can set the machine's payoff to any percentage; there is no minimum as in the States. The local games of Rommy looks like Blackjack, but a natural 21 pays even money rather than 1.5-1; however, you get 3-1 for three of a kind or a 3-card straight flush. Tute is Caribbean Poker. It's a version of 5-card Stud Poker, each player out to beat dealer instead of each other. The Colonial and Horseshoe are the only places that deal from the shoe in blackjack.

Remember, there is no Gaming Commission here, thus nobody to whom you can complain. The owners, managers, and pit bosses may or may not enforce the rules. The games are not regulated nor do government authorities observe them.

The best advise is don't ruin your vacation by playing the casinos right out of the gate. Have a few days of fun and lust, and then give it a shot. At the del Rey, look for the young hotties pretending to play the slots...the kind that are shy and intimidated by the stigma of being a primetime hooker in the snake pit. You'll feel like Jim and Marlon in this discovery zone.....bring you're fake Rolex and feast on the prey with reckless abandon.

Club Colonial Casino
Avenido Noveno y Avenido Undecimo, San José +506 258 2807
Table Games - 7 total.
Roulette, Craps, Let it Ride, Baccarat, Poker, Rommy, Blackjack
See this link for all the Costa Rican Casinos
(http://casinocity.com/CR/cities.html)
There are some decent sports book rooms as well in town. The Morazan on the second floor is a great setup for betting or just kicking back and watching multiple screens.

BANGKOK, THAILAND

ABOUT:

Thailand is a fascinating combination of old traditional eastern culture and frenetic paced Western Capitalism. **Bangkok** is a city of contrasts; you'll be driving in an air-conditioned taxi while an ox drawn cart pulls up besides you. Downtown you'll find dilapidated shacks next to century old temples with exotic gardens, all surrounded by brand new office buildings and 5 star hotels. Traffic is a nightmare, the heat is stifling, and the women are gorgeous. Having supported the US during the Vietnam War, free trade and big business have emerged in force, leaving the monarchy and destitute poverty behind.

Electronics, textiles and tourism are the largest industries here, and Thailand is the world leader in exportation of rice. Not all of the country has adapted to capitalism. Fifty percent of its the citizens still work in the poor climate of rice production, although this represents just 12% of the country's income. Thus, you have a huge disparity of wealth between outer country folks and city people. Overall, Bangkok has evolved into a world business player in just a few short decades.

Bangkok is the neon-lit Southeastern Asian capital of the sex world, full of half million wild, sexy, young available women. The city covers 610 sq. miles, located in the middle of Thailand and it's rice fields, surrounded by a network of natural and artificial canals crisscrossing the city. Bangkok is surprisingly easy to get around with its excellent public transport systems. A new overhead rail system connects the main shopping, entertainment and business areas of the city, while river taxis and express boats link many of the older historic sites. For an easy view of the layout of Bangkok, go the observation deck on the 77th floor of the Baiyoke Sky Hotel, ranked as the second tallest hotel in the world. As far as sightseeing tourist attractions go, there is the Royal Grand Palace, Wat Pho and the National Museum. All are located west of the railway. For the fun stuff, we concentrate on the east side, the Sukhumvit Road area.

Each year, Thailand has become a vacation destination for close to 10 million tourists. This has been the case for the last 25 years or so, as it is one of the world's favorite spots for sex tourism. The origin of this came about due to Thailand being an important US ally. They became home to the US Air Force troops for their R&R breaks over the years during conflicts and wars. When there's a lot of Americans on vacation, there's a lot money to spread around. So as always, capitalism forces took over. The commercial sex industry exploded almost overnight. After the Vietnam War

80

a lot of the US military came back to Thailand, and many of them never left.

Thai girls typically are sweet sexy little spinners when compared to Westerners. A fat, mouthy, opinionated hag is impossible to find in this country. Thai girls have beautiful long shiny dark hair, a sexy tan, gorgeous endless smiles, and a seductive femininity that can be overpowering. Few men are not affected by their shy but incredibly naughty girl next-door persona.

When experiencing Thai girls, there seems nothing wrong or immoral about prostitution. The feeling is quite the opposite, more like renting a short-term long distance relationship with a girl. Whether fake or not, they offer up sensuality, happiness, and attention rarely found in the US. Sure they are doing it for money, but what *you* get out of it is so much more than that. It is this experience that keeps men coming back for more and more. Since the price is almost free, any multi-girl fantasy is easy to purchase. Sure it ruins your life for a while when you return home, but you're an airport ticket away from paradise.

Here's the Local paper in English.

(www.bangkokpost.com)

CLIMATE :
Bangkok features intense heat and stifling humidity; with the evenings cooling off to merely miserable. The best time to visit is between November and February as April is generally the hottest month and October the wettest.

ENTRY REQUIREMENTS :
Passport required, and a $13 departure tax. Passport valid for 6 months beyond intended length of stay required. Anyone intending to stay longer than 30 days must obtain a visa prior to arrival.
(Bangkok is 12 hours ahead of New York time.)
Types of visa and cost: Tourist: £25 (single entry); Non-immigrant: £40 (single entry), £90 (multiple entries valid for 1 year); Transit (single entry): £15. Prices are subject to change.
Validity: All visas are valid for 3 months from the date of application. Tourist visas are for stays of up to 60 days within that period.

AIRPORT TAXIS :
Airport taxi or limousine from inside the arrivals hall. Fares are around 500-600 Baht. If you want a meter taxi (less luxurious, less expensive) join the line outside the arrivals building and get a taxi voucher from the ticket booth outside. Tell them your hotel, payment is upon arrival. Fares vary

depending on the time/distance from around 200Baht upwards. A small tip is always appreciated.

Depending on your hotel location, the driver may ask if you want to take the toll way. There are two main toll roads into central Bangkok, which cost 30-40 baht. This is an extra separate charge from the fare and optional. You should pay the driver direct as you go through the toll way. It can be much quicker to take the toll roads in standard rush hour periods.

Airport limo company site.

(www.thaiair.com/thailand/limousine/fares.htm#Schedule)

GETTING AROUND :

The bus system of Thailand will bring you to anywhere and from anywhere without problems, and in relative comfort. Every travel agent in Thailand is able to sell you a ticket to Bangkok.

The sky train (similar to the underground railways in most major cities only it's above your head) really makes a difference with all the street traffic. You can now go from Silom Road to Sukumvit Road and other parts of the town in a matter of minutes, even on a Friday afternoon. It doesn't solve the chronic traffic congestion since it is too expensive for most Thai workers, but it makes life much easier for tourists and people staying a short while.

Taxi is still the best way to reach parts of the city not covered by the sky train. The old taxis without a meter are a thing of past. Now you don't need to bargain the price of the ride before getting in: just check that the meter is working.

Passenger boats in the river are another way to get around. Even these water taxis are an option worth considering. They are interesting, colorful and sometimes even practical.

MONEY MATTERS :

The baht is divided into 100 satang.

Notes: 10, 20, 50(blue), 100(red), 500 (purple), 1000 (grey)baht.

Coins: 25, 50 satang; 1, 2, 5, 10 baht.

For today's exchange rate, go to here:

(www.oanda.com)

ATM machines

Available at most banks and shopping centers throughout the city. Thai Baht only. ATMs generally have Thai and English language displays and will accept most internationally recognized foreign cards. ATM's accept cards under the CIRRUS, VISA or MasterCard.

Travelers Checks / Credit Cards :
Most traveler's checks can be cashed at banks. Take your passport or ID. MasterCard and VISA are widely accepted by major banks, restaurants and shops. AMEX and Diners and tend to be accepted only at up market venues.

Banks :
Open Mon. - Fri. from 9:30am to 3:30pm. Currency exchange centers operate in most tourist areas from 7.00am to 9.00pm, everyday, including holidays.

Helpful Tips :
The temperature and humidity here is stifling, bring sunscreen and sunglasses everywhere you go. Slam bottles of water down like it's last call. AVOID getting drinks with ice as the source is questionable, meaning your shorts will all have racing stripes quickly. Only accept the ice cubes with holes through them. When you're eating out in the evenings, watch out for mosquitoes. Ask the waiter to put a mosquito coil under the table to discourage them. Wear pale colored slacks and mosquito repellant.

RECOMMENDED RESTAURANTS :
Since this info can change weekly, we can't recommend enough the "**Zagat Survey**." Pick up their travel book, or signup online. Worldwide reviews, menus, and pricing. (**www.zagat.com**)

CRIME AND SCAMS :
Thailand is the land of bartering for everything, and there's plenty of it, as they also specialize in selling knock off versions of Rolexes luggage, and everything under the sun. Thus, stay on top of the currency exchanges, watch for bogus folded bills, and make sure you pay in their currency for everything. The cabbies will constantly try to take you to a buddy's store to get a commission. Give a specific street address when you tell your destination. Don't say I want to go shopping at a mall. In advance, make sure you've either agreed on a clear price, or demand that the meter be running. If they try to scam you and start playing the "no English" game, tell them "tourist police." Suddenly their memory gets much better.

HOTELS :
A gazillion Hotels to choose from. If you have the time, travel agencies in town get you the best deals for cheap quality hotels. If not, walk up rates can be done easily, here are a few to start with.

Baiyoke Suite Hotel Bangkok
All rooms come fully equipped with modern amenities and the upper floors provide splendid views of the city. The property is located in Pratunam, close to department stores and wholesale shops selling a wide variety of merchandise.
209 room(s), Price From Thai Baht 1120 (Approx 28 US$)

Comfort Suites Bangkok Airport Hotel has 150 well-appointed, air-conditioned rooms. All are comfortable, sound proof, and protected with security door locks. $ 1300 BHT, $ 32 a night

Playboy Hotel off Soi 3, 700-800 baht, short time and long time.

Royal Asia Lodge: 91 Sukhumvit Road, Soi 8
Just 2 minutes from the district, with a free shuttle. Right next to the sky train. 890 Baht (US$21) for a king size bed. Recommended highly.
(www. royalasia.co.th)

Nana Hotel ***
Located in the Sukhumvit area, in the heart of one of Bangkok's busiest nightlife districts, ideal for singles looking for the unique entertainment found in the Nana Plaza area. The **Nana Hotel Bangkok** is conveniently placed near the Bangkok Skytrain, so travel around the city is quick and easy, with direct access to Siam Square, Silom, and other popular shopping and sightseeing areas. Although the Nana Hotel Bangkok is not close to Don Muang Airport, the expressway makes access to the hotel relatively easy. One of the most popular discos is in the basement, **Angel Disco**, and picking up a freelancer or local requires simply standing in the lobby. How's that for service.
4 Nana Tai Sukhumvit Road, Bangkok 10110, Thailand
334 rooms $25
(www.nanahotel.co.th/html/index.html **)**
(www.precisionreservations.com **)**

For you rich bastards :
The Hilton Bangkok is a low-rise architectural retreat that merges effortlessly with the magnificent, botanical Nai Lert Park that occupies more than half the property. 338 room(s), Price From Thai Baht 3510 **(**Approx $85 **)**

Marriott on Suk. Soi 2 True 5 star hotel, great location, including breakfast $95 + 17.7% tax. **(** www.marriott.com **)**

84

Complete hotel listings here:
(www. bangkoktonight.com/hotels/)

ELECTRICITY :

Voltage is 220 Volt AC with flat 2 pin plugs. You can buy an adapter for shavers, laptop computers, mobile chargers, etc., on arrival at most department stores.

Most hotels now have Internet either from the room by laptop, or from their business center. Charges vary from around 100 Baht for the first 15 minutes with lower charges afterwards. Additional surcharges times apply, so check first. There are also Internet cafes in most shopping areas which are generally expensive.

Map of Bangkok :
(www. bangkok-maps.com)
(www. royalasia.co.th/map.html)

THE GAME PLAN :

Bangkok Nightlife.
Welcome to Holy Land O Smiles. Unashamed hedonist insanity is the Bangkok sex industry. Everywhere you turn are sex clubs and massage parlors, as well as restaurant and cocktail bars. Bangkok alone is home to dozens of discos, almost a 100 GoGo bars, hundreds of karaoke bars, and literally thousands of pubs and cafes. Packs of people of all types, not just the old horny men you'd expect, but mid 20's guys and girls on vacations all peering into the sea of blatant hookers and naked strippers. The layout is real simple, the main street is **Sukhumvit Road**, and the side streets are called Soi and number in order, odd one side, even the other.

Neon Go Go bars and people bartering goods light up the alleys. Wander on in and discover miles of girls in bikinis or topless grinding to the latest top 40 western hits, a virtual sexual Disneyland. It's an all-round mesmerizing sight to view, and knowing not a lick of the Thai language is not a problem.

The number of prostitutes in Thailand range from 300,000 to one million. (Side note: you have to be very careful about lady boys in Thailand. We're talking a complete sex change. They are taller, w/big feet and big hands. They thrive on fooling you.)

People come to Thailand to see the beautiful architecture, landscaping, and of course, the clubs where girls shoot ping pong balls out of their pussies. Try to wipe that shit eating grin off your face the first time you see the nude line dances by gorgeous Thai girls who look like teenage virgins. One of the strangest act we've seen involved a full beer can placed inward and then with no hands, she turned it around and shot it out.

Olympian talents here.

There are three main sections of the city's strip clubs, and massage parlors. **Soi Cowboy**, **Nana Entertainment Plaza**, and **Patpong**. Keep in mind, the location and layout of the red light district has been a constant for some 30 years now, the names of the clubs may change, but the song remains the same. It's usually the same owners just mixing things up a bit.

Nanaplaza Entertainment Plaza :
Location: Sukhumvit Soi 4, use Sky train to Nana Station.

Nana is a large multi story complex of Go-Go bars consisting of ground floor beer bars, as well as home to three floors of Ripley's believe it or not sleazy nightlife. Many of the clubs here will put on a show that has to be seen, and is better off not repeated. On the first floor we find **Hollywood Rock, Playskool, Rainbow 1 and 2, Voodoo,** and **Buttums Up.**

The second floor is predominately the small little bars that are home to the veteran Thai customers and expats. Best one to check out is **G-Spot**, located in the far right corner

Three huge bars occupy the third floor. Right side is **Carnival**, and the left is **Hollywood Two** and **Hollywood Strip**. A great first stop for the Short-term tourist.

Here's some quick reviews of recommended bars you should visit.

Playskool
Located in the far right corner of Nana, between Hollywood and the 2 Rainbow bars. The traditional setup with a central stripper dance stage. It fits maybe 6 girls, but they pack in about 20 girls, all shuffling aimlessly around looking for their night's partner. Playskool is always packed with customers, and close to 100 dancers. The hottest girls are already *bar fined* and gone for the night by 11 pm, so make your trip here early. Some of the hottest looking Bangkok girls work here. The sexy schoolgirl uniform was the mainstay outfit, but it seems to have disappeared into topless girls in thongs. That doesn't mean you can't take the girls home for some disciplining. Cheap drinks, and indoor bar/outdoor patio.

Angelwitch
Angelwitch is hidden on the second floor of Nana in between all the small bars on the left side, close to the (in)famous Casanova lady boy bar.

Unfortunately, there have been a lot of political crackdowns on the total total nudity here, so it's hit or miss for that aspect. Angelwitch is infamous for it's sexotic shows, and is packed to the gills on weekends. Come here to see their intricate choreographed shows starting after 10 P.M. Highlights include S&M shows as well as exotic Thai dancing.

G-Spot

G-spot is the biggest "A-Go-Go bar" in Bangkok, located on the second floor of Nana Plaza in the far right corner. It features 3 dance stages, the entrance is next to the left stage, and sports the club's dirtiest dancers. Always nude in the past, during crackdown season they are topless. Since the stages are larger and not so packed, you'll get to see real sexy dancing, instead of the stupid stripper shuffle. The girls can really move it here. After your fifteenth beer, feel free to act like you're the choreographer.

Hollywood Strip

Located on the left side of the third floor of Nana is the Hollywood Strip. There's a huge rotating carousel stage on the left and another stage on the right. This place was famous for it's bizarre shows in the past, and the girls were always nude. Previous favorite acts included playing *hide the live frog in the coochie*, and other great family fun. There was no level too low for debauchery here in the good old days. It's toned down currently, but these things pass over quickly and the freak shows reappear.

Voodoo

One of the biggest strip clubs, Voodoo bar is located on the ground floor of Nana Plaza in the far left corner. It features a huge dance stage, with the middle section containing a rotating carousel. You get to lust after close to 100 girls, and there are many top-notch lookers here. Arrive early, the club gets cherry picked before midnight. Outside you'll find a huge bar as well, with sports on the TV's and a ringside view of the action walking in the streets.

Rainbow 2

The latest edition of the Rainbow bars, this club is friggin' huge. Located on the far right corner of the ground floor of Nana Plaza, next to Hollywood Rock, it is home to well over 100 dancers. If you can't find one you like here, you should pack your bags and get on home to your 200-pound nagging wife. Maybe you should try envisioning her if you find yourself having ridiculously high standards. The typical Thai girl's body weight could be a rounding error when calculating the weight of many US women.

Other clubs in Nanaplaza to visit are **Buttums Up, Carnival, Fantasia,** and **Hollywood,** as well as dozens of other smaller ones.

Soi Cowboy :
Soi Cowboy is located just off Sukhumvit Road between Soi Asoke and Soi 23, just a short walk from the Asoke Skytrain station. It covers a 300-yard long street area, and is comprised of close to 50 clubs on both sides of the road. Here a sex tourist can find endless scantily clad Thai girls grinding to loud classic western hits, and enjoy picking up a subservient young honey for a remarkably small date fee. As you pass by each club expect half a dozen girls waving and screaming at you, trying to pull you into their bar. If you're bored, walk up and offer them an autograph if they can give you directions to a good Irish pub in Manhattan.

Some of the namesake bars to visit here are **Long Gun, Tilac, Dollhouse, Baccara, Midnight Bar** and many others. Nestled in between these large clubs are dozens of smaller bars to pop in and out of. Soi Cowboy is known to be somewhat more laid back than the other sections, but they do have their share of exotic shows featuring a buffet of naked dancers slithering up and down acrobatically between the stage's chrome poles.

Most of the bars at Soi Cowboy charge a fee (bar fine) of about 500 baht to take one of their little honeys home with you. The girls are roughly 800-1500 baht for a short liaison of a few hours, or 1500 to 2000 for an entire evening of debauchery. In Cowboy you can move your date and your happy ass on upstairs to a private room in about half the clubs.

Beer costs 60 to 85 baht during happy hour($2) in the smaller bars, a little more at the premium spots, and the girls house drinks they want you to buy run a tad more.

Long Gun :
Most clubs down here come and go, but for years now this one has been a mainstay in Soi. It's not the biggest club, but it's offers up some of the best feature shows in town. Come early if you expect to even get in here. Although they do offer up some great-choreographed strip tease acts, people come here for the down and dirty. Long Gun is the big daddy when it comes to vaginal trick shows. Don't expect to see a dance show when these are going on. The girls are masters of their own domain.

11pm is show time, and the naughtiest of the crew come out in their boots and bikinis and start off their shows with bananas, balloon tricks, and a unique way of opening Heinekens. Soon, the clothes come off, and they put all kind of objects into the coochie. They shoot darts 10 feet out popping balloons, aim table tennis balls into a glass, open soft drink bottles etc. Stand back at the end of the act, they like to spray the bottles over the customers up close. A word of caution, these are real darts they shoot out, try not to get an eye gorged out when they happen to miss. It'd be a little tough to explain to the boss at home. "there I was..."

The Dollhouse Soi Cowboy
The newest location, with its more famous club in Pattaya. The layout on the first floor is a large pageant-like stage, with barstools surrounding it. The second floor has two smaller stages, and more of an US lap dance environment. One of these stages has a clear floor, so the first floor customers can look up and see all the way to...um Bangkok, as the girls wear see thru clothes and no thongs. The Dollhouse has plenty of sports on its 100-inch Big Screen TV, in case 100 girls running around in transparent clothes or butt naked bores you. Get used to the 50-cent tequila shots specials, the girls working here down dozens of them thru the night. How exactly can you tell whether a girl is speaking or slurring in Thai?

(www.thedollhouseagogo.com/index.html)

Suzie Wongs on Cowboy is definitely a Bangkok must. The Suzie Wong girls are now well known as some of the stars of the Bangkok nightlife. Not only does the bar employ some of the best looking girls in Bangkok, but also they have that sexy and drunk attitude that makes for a great time in the bar.

Soi Cowboy has a ton of smaller more intimate bars as well. A few favorites are **Jungle Jims**, and **The Toy Bar**. The girls here drink heavily and realize you're a famous porn star and hope to have a chance to audition in your hotel room. Dates are around $30-40, as well as a bar fine of 500Bt.

Patpong
Location Silom Rd or Suriwong Rd. Use the Skytrain.
Patpong is definitely the top dog of all the Bangkok nightlife, with a huge concentration of exotic bars in a tiny area. At night it's a supermarket of imitation items, such as Rolexes, jewelry, clothing, luggage and so on. Everything is negotiated in the stores and stands, and even their method of bargaining has a Asian traditional feel to it. When its bartering time, the seller will not directly tell you a price, instead he types an amount into a calculator, to which you are invited to respond.

On Patpong 1 as you try to tackle all the endless titty bar row, make sure you check out **King's Castle I** and **King's Castel II**. Patpong 2 has some specialty bars, where girls practice sword swallowing in private or do you right at the bar if you want. Take a photo for the family album! The girls have an assortment of fantasy Costumes and toys, and will perform S&M, BDSM, or virtually any act. You name it basically. Dates are around 1600 baht for 90 minutes. **Star of Light** is another popular one. Avoid going upstairs to the bars with the shows. There have been stories of people being ripped off with huge bar tabs . In fact, try to pay for all drinks at once, no tabs ever.

Thai Soapy Massages

This is a whole other sport in Thailand that you must do at least once in life. For soapy body massages, hop a cab to Ratchadapisek Road. They are all centered here and there are also several **Karaoke Bars** in the area as well. Definitely a great relaxing experience in Bangkok, so here's the lowdown. You go in and view a pack of girls thru a glass gallery, called the fish bowl. The girls all have numbers on their shirts for identification. That way you can tell your friends how hot #217 was last night. Makes for a real personal experience. Drinks are available, you pick out your girl, pay and move to a room. You hop in the hot tub and get a sudsy bath, then onto the massage mat. Best done in a sandwich, i.e., 2 girls. Request the body massage, where they use their whole bodies instead of just their hands. Then it's onto the bed for the last part of your date. The whole thing is around 90 minutes, with the massage fare of 1300-2500 baht. Use this link for the latest up to date locations, addresses, prices, and reviews.

(www.bangkoktonight.com/massage/)

Blow Job Bars

This one friggin' takes the cake. If you don't have the time to take a girl back to your hotel, or upstairs at the local go-go bar, what do you have left that's quickie? **Blow Job Bars**. These bars provide a level of service not normally found in go-go bars, that you may find either disgusting or hilarious. You walk in, sit down and buy a beer, and for less than $10 a girl comes up and blows you right at your stool. Don't spill your beer mate. If you're running low on quality money shots, maybe pour some suds over her head.

Definitely different strokes for different folks, but if you are curious check them out! These are all around the Patpong Soi 2 .

Star of Light Bar   Patpong Soi 2
(on your left hand side if entering Patpong 2 from Surawong Road) Blow jobs in a private room or at the bar counter. Blow Jobs slang in Thai is called "*Smoke*", as in "*Me like smoke you long time!*"

Local Discos :   Here are some local discos with freelancers:
Concept CM2 (basement of Novotel Hotel, Siam Square)
This is a huge Bangkok club full of pros and non-pros. They feature a house band playing band 80's and 90's US music, as well as the typical *Ornamental* fast techno crap. Cover is $6 weekdays and $12 on weekends. Girls are $25-45. A lot of hot talent here, a little expensive comparatively, but more locals and most speak English.
Angel Disco (ground floor of Nana Hotel)
Spasso at the basement of Grand Hyatt, (cabbies call it "Erawan")
Rivas at basement of Sheraton Grande Sukhumvit
QBar at the end of Sukhumvit Soi 11

(**www.bangkoktonight.com/discos/**)

THAILAND ESCORT SITES :
(www.bangkok-escorts.com/girls.html)
(www.escortsinthailand.com)
(www.bkkescorts.com)
(www.bangkoktonight.com/escorts)

VACATION STUFF :
For the cover story to the old lady, tell her you childhood fantasy has been to fly halfway around the globe to play glow in the dark bowling at midnight.

GOLF COURSES :
There are around 35 courses around the greater Bangkok area, with beautiful courses and inexpensive fees. Whether you're in Bangkok for business, a gangbang, or just fancy a game of links, there are great choices here.

The Royal Golf & Country Club
(located southeast of Bangkok, a short taxi)
69 Moo 7, Sukhumvit 17, Bang Sao Thong,   #(02) 738 0133. 18-hole championship course. B800 during week, B1600 weekends.

The Rose Garden Golf Club
(located 20 miles southwest of city)
Tha Talad Sub District, Sampran, Nakhon Pathom
adjacent to National Highway Number 4
(tel: (034) 322 588)
18-hole championship golf course
B700 during week, B1300 (closed Mondays).

If you get to venture out, head to the beach resort of **Pattaya** (see chapter), located Southwest of Bangkok on the Gulf of Thailand. This is home to Thailand's largest beach resort, where there truly is something for everyone, including exotic golf courses, great Sport fishing, and endless bars full of Thai girls screaming "me so horny, me wuv you wong time".

In Pattaya, there's a number of 5 star resort and golf developments with some of the worlds top designers creator a number of great layouts. Te impressive list includes Nicklaus, Pete Dye, Robert Trent-Jones, Gary Player, Dennis Griffith, and Nick Faldo.

Check here for the latest courses and info :

(www.golfasian.com/golfinfo/golfinfobangkok.htm)

(www.thailandgolfholidays.com)

(www.golforient.com/index.html)

OCEAN FISHING :

Thailand takes great pride in it's deep-sea sport fishing. In fact, the most expensive rods in the world are made in Chiangmai, Thailand, which is also the home of 10 trout fly companies. Again, just head southwest of Bangkok down to **Pattaya**. Here you can break out the cigars for the abundance of trophy catches to be made, featuring **sailfish, marlin, Mahi Mahi** (dorado), **tuna**, shaved pussies, and other species. Shallow island reefs are home to many species of light-tackle game fish including **sea bass, barracuda, giant trevally, queenfish** and **mangrove jack**. Pelagic species like **black marlin** and **sailfish**, as well as **king mackerel** and **tiger sharks**. Late November is a good time to go after marlin, tuna and any number of other fighting fish such as larger black marlin, up to 300kg. Also found are **yellow fin tuna** (20kg**), Wahoo** (40kg) and numerous **barracuda, Dorado** and **skipjack tuna**. Sharks like tiger, hammerhead, bull and the occasional **Mako Shark** take the bait during day or night-fishing trips.

Here are some sites to arrange your fishing trip, and where you'll find the least expensive route to take.

(www.asiatradingonline.com/fishing.htm)
(www.asiatradingonline.com/pattayafishing.htm)

CASINOS :

Gambling is illegal in Thailand. Guess they have high standards here. Of course, girls shooting darts 10 feet from their pussies and popping balloons is perfectly acceptable behavior.

HORSERACING :

Horseracing takes place every Sunday in the sweltering heat at the Royal Bangkok Sports Club. Betting in Thailand is illegal, but never mind, supposedly hookers are too.
Location: Henry Dunant Rd, **Open:** Every Sun afternoon.

BOWLING :

Brunswick Bowling transforms into a disco, complete with lasers, music and luminous bowling bowls. 9pm-12pm.
Location: Brunswick Bowling, RCA Bowl
3rd Floor, RCA Plaza off Petchburi Rd
Skytrain: Not available. Go by taxi and drink heavily.

THAI BOXING :

One of the toughest martial arts, Thai boxing uses almost any part of the body; feet, elbows, legs, knees, and shoulders. The contestants undergo a rigorous training schedule from an early age and acquire cult status if they are successful. The big fights happen at the weekend amid much mayhem. Watered down simulation fights can be seen in the RLD streets for tips.)
Main venues: **Lumpini Stadium**, Rama IV Road
Open: every Tuesday and Friday at 6.30 -11: 00p.m. and Saturday at 5.00- 8:00 and 8:30 - midnight. Price 220 - 800 Baht.
Ratchadamnoen Boxing Stadium, Ratchadamnoen Nok Road, (Every Mon and Wed, Thursday at 6.00 p.m.)

For the local up to date info on clubs and bar girls, visit these sites.
(www.bangkokeyes.com) (ww.clubelectricblue.com/links.htm)
(www.bangkokbargirls.info/NanaPlaza/map.htm)

CARTAGENA, COLUMBIA

ABOUT :

Located on the northwest tip of South America, between Venezuela, Brazil, and Panama, Columbia is the fourth-largest country in South America, and the only one with coasts on both the Pacific and Caribbean. The official language is Spanish.

Cartagena faces west towards the Caribbean Sea. To the south is the Bay of Cartagena, which has two entrances: Bocachica in the south, and Bocagrande in the north. During the 16th and 17th centuries, Cartagena was a prime target for English and French pirates. Many of Cartagena's fortifications still stand: the Castle of San Felipe, built between 1536 and 1657; the walls around the Old City (las Murallas); the undersea wall across Bocagrande built between 1771 and 1778; and the forts of San Jose and San Fernando, built between 1751 and 1759 at Bocachica.

Many colonial buildings can be found in the Old City, including the Palace of the Inquisition, a cathedral, the Convent of Santa Clara (now a hotel) and a Jesuit college. St. Peter Claver patron saint of the slaves worked in and from the Jesuit College. Just outside the city walls, you can see the "India Catalina" statue, a local Indian hero. On it's beaches, you can usually find some unconscious binge-drinking Gringos, also resembling stone statues.

If it is beaches and warm Caribbean waters you are after, not far from Cartagena are crystal clear waters and magnificent reefs. Unfortunately, the hidden meaning here is the water and beach is elsewhere. Cartagena's is one of Colombia's major seaports, located next to the major oil pipelines. They can claim whatever they want, but this is not conducive to a gorgeous beach. The sand in Cartagena is dark and nasty, and the water is filthy. Who gives a flying fuck. You're view is fantastic in your beach chair ($2 a day rental), you're slamming your tenth umbrella drink, and girls flock to you looking either to practice their English, or to sleep with some Englishman, or both. If you have problems picking up girls, just tell the beach tout you want one, and in minutes he will have some contestants parading in front of you for your shopping pleasure.

Offshore, there is abundant marine life, perfect for **snorkeling** and **scuba diving** alike. Cartagena is a quaint fishing town, and its Old City is somewhat reminiscent of Cuba, with the beautiful Old Spanish architecture in gorgeous pastel colors, as well as breathtaking cathedrals. The busiest season is Dec-Feb, when Columbians take their vacations. Hotels can fill up so plan ahead. Also, plan ahead and do some research, make sure you don't go on one of Cartagena's 3-day weekend events, as well as during

Christmas time. A large majority of girls go home to visit their family.

(www.cartagenainfo.com/english/index.html)

(www.discovercartagena.com)

CLIMATE :

Both mountainous and spotted with the rainforest, the temperature varies very little year round, it's scorching hot, since it's so close to the equator. Equator=SPF 40+!!

ENTRY REQUIREMENTS :

U.S. Passport must be valid 3 months beyond intended stay, tickets and Documents for return or onward travel. No visa is required for your stay up to three months. Departure tax is $23.

For business travel, you need to get a visa and contact the embassy.

(www.traveldocs.com/co/embassy.htm)

U.S. visa requirements (http://usembassy.state.gov/colombia/) or Colombian visa information that is available through any of the Colombian consulates around the US and the world.

(www.colombiaemb.org/consulados_visas.htm)

AIRLINES :

Colombia's national airline is Avianca (AV). British Airways and Avianca each operate flights, Monday to Saturday, to Bogotá. During the summer season, British Airways only operate flights Wednesday, Friday and Sunday. Other airlines flying to Colombia include American Airlines, Air France, Continental Airlines and Iberia. However, as with Avianca, some may not fly direct there but with other airlines as part of a Code Share agreement. Most visitors fly to Colombia's major international airport in Bogotá; the other international airports include Cartagena and San Andrés. Approximate flight times: From London to Bogotá is 11 hours 45 minutes, from Los Angeles is 10 hours 30 minutes, from New York is 6 hours 30 minutes. Cartagena (Crespo) (CTG) is 2km (1 mile) from the city.

All air tickets purchased in Colombia for destinations outside the country are liable to a total tax of 15 per cent on one-way tickets and 7.5 per cent on return tickets.

RECOMMENDED RESTAURANTS :

Restaurante la Olla Cartagena
AV. San Martin no. 5-100
Bocagrande #Tel 6653861
A great seafood platter for 35K P, consisting of shrimp, fish, lobster, clams and calamari. Located across from the casino.

Restaurante Riquisimo
This is a great outdoor café restaurant near the Las Velas hotel, serving fantastic steak, chicken as well as beans and rice for under $10. You'll keep on returning, nice view, with fresh food arriving daily. Bring a girl here and she'll think you're a millionaire.

Since restaurant info can change weekly, we can't recommend enough the "**Zagat Survey**." Pick up their travel book, or signup online. Worldwide reviews, menus, and pricing.

(www.zagat.com)

TIPPING :
Taxi drivers expect 10 per cent tips. Porters at airports and hotels are usually given 500 pesos per item. Restaurants and bars usually add a 10 per cent service charge to the bill or suggest a 10 per cent tip. Maids and clerks in hotels are also tipped.

CRIME :
The facts are important to remember; Columbia maintains the second highest murder rate in Latin America, it is the home to one of the most powerful drug trafficking rings and remains rife with narcotics-related violence. It is also in a region where guerrilla and right-wing paramilitary forces have become increasingly active in recent years. Security forces are a common everyday sight. Police and security are ever present. Armed security guards are at offices, malls, restaurants, and the streets. Do not be put off by this, it's a natural occurrence. Worst scenario is your cab is pulled over and armed police with machine guns searching the car for drugs. Ironically, people in Columbia think of America as the most violent place in the world. Just stay in the city and you're fine, venture out in the countryside and you may not return. As a whole, Cartagena is not the violent image you hear when people think of Columbia.

It's safe to walk in the day, take taxis at night. One warning, be very careful not to hit on some drug lord's girl, ask her if she has a boyfriend if you're nervous. Also, never take open drinks from strangers. In Columbia they have some mind eraser drug, as in a total eraser drug they put in your drink where you'll forget everything. Also, only use the yellow marked taxis.

MONEY MATTERS :

Currency: Peso ($), around 2800 to the dollar. ATM's often give better exchange rate than the banks, but there's a daily limit.

For today's exchange price, go here:

(www.oanda.com)

HOTELS :

Taxis around town cost $1.50 to almost anywhere, take your time choosing your place.

Calle Las Velas Hotel No. 1-60
This is the place we recommend, directly across the street from the main action, overlooking the beach...great ocean view from the balcony. Guests are fine, across the street from La Perla Casino and Las Dolce Vita.Tel: +57 56 650000 105 Quartos Rates: from $US 29.

Hilton Cartagena
Located on the tip of El Laguito Peninsula, surrounded by water on three sides, hotel grounds include 3.6 pools and Jacuzzis, and lavish tropical gardens. Avenida Almirante Brion Cartagena 57-5-6650666
1-800-774-1500 **(www.hilton.com)**

Hotel Bocagrande del Mar
Bocagrande, Ave.San Martin #7-159, Cartagena, Colombia
PBX:(5) 6654435   Prices $28 single low season,$35 high.
(www.hotelesdelmar.com/english/hbocagrande.htm)

Hotel Internacional
Direccion : Bocagrande, Av. San Martín
No. 4-110 Tel:(+57 5) 665 2675 Cel.: 315 750 1908

Hotel Playa
Direccion : Bocagrande Av. San Martín #4-87
Tel:(+57 5) 665 0552 - 665 0593 $25 + rooms

Hotel Charlotte
located in Boca Grande, stunning $50 suites.
Address: Avenida San Martín N° 7-126
Telephones: (+57 5) 665 9298
(www.hotelescharlotte.com)
For more hotels:
(www.cartagenainfo.com/english/index.html)
There are also plenty of apartments available at very reasonable prices overlooking the bay. Playa Mar and Torre Marina are great locations, from $35-60 a night depending on room size and quantity.

THE GAME PLAN :

What makes **Cartagena** unique as a sex tourist location is that it's virtually undiscovered. The ambiance can be best described as a combination of small scale Rio de Janiero and Havana. The city itself is stunning, with gorgeous pastel buildings full of history, and a party all night atmosphere full of Columbian hotties (**Calenas**). This is not a highly traveled tourist trap, and with less sugar daddy's to be had, the ladies will latch onto you tight and try hard to be your girlfriend for your whole trip. The exact opposite of the typical saturated pro situation, where there are so many dudes the girls will want to dump you after an hour or two and race back for more. The city may be the easiest place in South America to meet local girls in public or on the beach.

The Beach

Daytime action is as easy as it gets, because the beach touts are pimps that would make Heidi Fleiss jealous. Like all touts, they are as annoying as hell, constantly looking for an angle, working you for drinks, shortchanging you, buying girls drinks when you didn't order them, etc. The area to park your happy ass is the beach in front of the Hotel Las Velas near the end of the island. Here's the recommended approach. Use the tout for your $2 chair or two, and maybe the overhead umbrella. Bring bottled water and refuse all other offers. Tell him if you have problems getting girls you will call him over. Cut him off right after the chair, and be firm with a smile. It is real easy to meet girls. You are a curiosity to them, and most will come over if you wave to them. The tout's talent however is substantial, he will literally chase a girl you point at and if available, bring her over, with the deal basically done. He gets a 10,000K cut out of her pay. Her cost for your beach date rendezvous is around $30. That's it.
    The area where you'll be hunting at night is called **Bocagrande**. This is comprised of your standard set of "ocean drive" roads, running

parallel to the ocean for a stretch of 2 miles, full of nightclubs, discos, bars and shopping areas. There is one other section of town you're be bouncing back and forth to..."**the Old City**". This is great for daytime walks and lunches, as well as home to the most popular discos for the local girls. The trip is just a $2 cab ride away.

Cartagena is a great buyer's market. When you venture into the den of the dragon (**LDV**), the women outnumber the men around 5 to 1. Inside are up to 50 working girls in the club and loitering outside, with maybe 5 to 10 gringos. As far as the girls, they are hot hot little spinners, very exotic looking, and they're as uninhibited as Brazilians. You can stroll to the beach and pick one up, or stroll down the street and get a date in minutes. It takes zero talent to be a porn star here. The average monthly income in Columbia is just $500, so this is a very inexpensive and fun stop on your world tour. One that is usually revisited time and time again.

Happy Hour

In Boca Grande at night you want to start your evening at the corner of Carrera 1 and Calle 5, right on the beach. You can't miss the area, there are 2 clubs called **El Castillo Disco** and **La Escollera Disco** next to each other. It's a big party in the street, people watching and hooking up start early here. There is a mix of local girls and semi-pros...there's really not much difference between them, as most will cross over. Just smile at ones you like, and if they return it, call them over. Later in the night at the end of Calle 1 there's another club area, centered around **Disco Banana Rana**. Girls are loitering in the streets waiting to be had.

The popular area in the Old City is located around the street **La Calle del Aresenal**. Girls want to be taken there from BocaGrande to hang in the discos, especially at the club **Mister Babilla**. There are of course the loiterers outside looking for you to pay their $5 cover to get in. Some working girls, some college girls, and definitely a lot of lookers here.

La Dolce Vida

2o Piso - Local 2-4 Telephone: 655-0977. Located in front of the Las Velas Hotel, this is a classy dance club with available dates that run around $80K pesos for short time, and 80K to 150K for all nighters. This range can be considerable, based on your looks, and bargaining skills. The short timers gotten late usually turn into overnighters, just give a propina (tip) in the morning if you'd like. What commonly happens is the night before as you're leaving with the girl, you're thinking to yourself how lucky you'll be spending the next few hours with her. Then in the morning, (these girls sleep forever), you're now thinking how do I get rid of her and meet some new ones. Takes some talent and practice to boot them like a pro. The LDV is very similar in layout and situation to the **Hotel del Rey** in Costa Rica (see chapter), except this is a disco...a little better since they are shaking it like pros when the latest top song cranks out. As far as the actual pickup, you have to make the move. That means you smile and wave her over..takes about 10 seconds. However, if you're a loud mouth arrogant drunk, none of the girls will have anything to do with you. Only Spanish is spoken. Also, it's somewhat dark inside, so take your girl outside and get a better look before taking your walk of shame, or hang outside and do your picking from there. You are in Columbia, the cocaine capital of the world, and if a girl is overly hyper and going to the bathroom every 5 minutes, expect her to be a problem, desperate and going psycho on you....avoid.

Casas
Throughout Columbian cities there are independent houses of ill repute, with no signs on the front door. Utilize the cabbies for the info on the best places if you can't find some gringos to join you. These are well known by all the cabbies. They tend to be less than classy, sometimes in scary parts of town. For safety, have the cabbie wait for you, and/or, have him come inside and buy him ONE beer. Don't let him run up a tab. The casas are a little bit heavy on the currency...but it's a nice change of pace.

Playboy
Bosque Avenue, Del Nilo Dg 21 #48-04 Tel 662-0717
Great looking girls, can be little pricier than LDV.

Penthouse
Bosque Avenue. Buenos Aires # 53-74 Tel 662 2215

Manila House
Bosque Transv. 49 # 21B96 Tel 672-2794

International Bar Disco
El Sena No. 20-100 Diagonal
Antigua lesa. Tel 6622417
Open 24 hours

There's always a new place...mix up your clubs from night to night, otherwise you'll be returning to high drama as multiple girls lay claim to owning you. It's a good feeling, but if you want variety, tour the town for a diverse mixture of girls.

VACATION STUFF :

Tell the old lady you got bored and are popping on down to pick up a couple Kilos of gold for the Christmas holidays.

Rosario Islands

As previously mentioned, the sand and water ashore leave a lot to be desired. Just 20 miles southwest of Cartagena, lies the idyllic coralline archipelago of **Islas de Rosario**. Travel here is arranged at your hotel or through a travel agent, departure is from the Cartagena Harbor. There is a great day event arranged from the Cartagena Harbor out to the azure blue Caribbean waters. This is a great little day trip to do with a chica or two, out to the azure blue Caribbean waters. The Islas del Rosario is a 30-island archipelago, home to a nationally protected park, and what is touted as the Caribbean Basin's most beautiful aquarium, **Acuario San Martin**. The aquarium has a show that features trained dolphins performing tricks, sharks, sea turtles, and stingrays. They have a skit where a shark hops out of the water onto a platform begging to be fed. Be a good sport and throw him your empty Budweiser and some used condoms. You can also make arrangements to swim in the holding tanks with the dolphins.

Interspersed amongst reefs surrounding the anchorage are little islands and islets, each supporting private homes, ranging from small, brightly colored, thatched-roofed huts to impressive weekend villas. Overnight accommodations are available. Excellent spots to snorkel and swim in the crystal clear waters, or have an afternoon meal. There are hidden spots to play doctor with your date, and the total cost of the event is just $25 each for the tour…or $60 per boat. A good diversion, do this.

CASINOS :

Atlantis Casino
Bgde. Cra. 2 No. 5-145 Av. San Martin …Tel.: 655 0932
Casino del Caribe
El Laguito C.C Pierino Gallo
Tel.: 665 0573

Casino El Dorado
Bocagrande Bgde. Av.San Martin 5-35 , Tel.: 665 4693 / 665 0511

Casino La Perla
Parque Comercial Pierino Gallo Laguito …Tel: 6650573

Casino Royal Ltd.
Blgd. Cr. 1 2-87 Hotel Caribe, Tel.: 665 0414

Casinos y Sunministros Ltda.
Mamonal Via Mamonal Km. 8 interior de Atunes de Colombia
Tel.: 668 6529

DEEP SEA FISHING :

The Caribbean Coast is notorious as a haven for **snook** and **tarpon**. Tarpon especially can be found in this area year round with a peak season from Dec-May. Other species found in the area include **calba, Atlantic Sailfish, Billfish, Wahoo, Tripletail, Mackerel,** and **Kingfish**. You will also find **Dorado** present near the mouths of surrounding rivers. Also note that **Barracuda** can be found along the Caribbean Sea close to the shore, careful swimming here.

GOLF COURSES :

Club Campestre de Cali is a large sports complex containing great courses..located in south of the city of Santiago of Cali, set against the Commercial Center Unicentro, diagonal to Holguines Trade Center. A location that's easy access since any point of the city. The most prestigious Universities surround it. Tennis, polo, futbol, squash and spinning, all here as well as the golf course.

(www.campestrecali.com)

Frankfurt, Germany

About :
The fifth biggest city in Germany, **Frankfurt** has attained substantial economic power – both within Germany and abroad – thanks to its position as a key transport hub and its status as a major venue for international trade fairs and other business events. Located in the middle of the highly productive Rhine-Main region in Germany, right at the center of Europe, the city is the financial heart not only of Germany but also of the European Union, pumping Euros into the world economy.

Just in the last 2 decades, Frankford has become quite the cosmopolitan international town, home to the Germany stock exchange and 350+ financial institutions. The architecture and tone is distinctly the American look, like a mini Manhattan. However, don't be confused. Frankfort is still home to more arts and museums than most any European city other than Berlin. The airport is massive, only Heathrow is bigger. Downtown are FKK spas to enjoy if you want, but we're taking you a bit out of town for the cream of the crop.

Climate :
Same as cold US states, winter is from November to February. Bitter cold if you're into that. Summer is June to August.

Entry Requirements :
Passport of course.   Departure tax just $5 right now.
(www.timeanddate.com/worldclock/full.html)

Airport Information :
Flughafen Frankfurt/Main (FRA)
Tel: (069) 6900. (website: www.frankfurt-airport.de)
Frankfurt Main airport is located eight miles southwest of the city center. It is the largest airport in continental Europe, handling more than 40,000 flights from 110 airlines every week and serving over 290 destinations in 109 countries. It is a major European transport hub alongside London, Paris and Amsterdam. Terminals one (concourses A, B and C) and two (D and E) are linked by free Skyline shuttle trains.

Major Airlines:

The national airline is Lufthansa (tel: (069) 6960 (local); (01805) 838 4267 (national); (website:**www.lufthansa.de**) Major airlines include Air France, Alitalia, British Airways, Cathay Pacific, KLM, Qantas, SAS, South African Airways and Turkish Airlines.

MONEY MATTERS :

Euro rules here. In the FKK clubs, they don't accept AMEX, and they pad all Credit card bills 10%…pay cash.

RECOMMENDED RESTAURANTS :

Since this info can change weekly, we can't recommend enough the "**Zagat Survey**." Pick up their travel book, or signup online. Worldwide reviews, menus, and pricing.

(www.zagat.com)

CRIME AND SCAMS :

Typical pickpockets hanging out in Frankfurt, but a lot of police presence makes it little trouble. Avoid the Red Light Districts in downtown, total rip-offs, $5 drinks become $50, girls say one thing and then refuse, arguments, etc. Go to the recommended places below, there isn't one ounce of trouble. Do not try to bring in a camera, they will be confiscated, you doonkoff. Viva Heineken !

HOTELS :

These hotels are out of Frankfurt in the heart of the fun. If you prefer Frankfurt, remember it's a convention town that can book up quick, population is only 650,000.

Zum Goldenen Boden
5 Philipp-Reis-Str.
tel# 985163, 70 beds, 40 euro.
1 minute walk to Atlantis. **Stay here for FKK Atlantis.**
Zum Schwarzen-Adler Hotel
Located Midway between FKK Atlantis and Oases
Nice old fashioned and traditional.
Unlike the hoes you'll be doing.
An outside Beer garden to boot.
Vogelsbergstrasse 2 63674 Altenstadt
Tel. 0 60 47/ 96 47-0 (**www.zum-schwarzen-adler-altenstadt.de**)

Comfort Hotel Stadt Karben
61118 Bad Vilbel
phone (06039) 801-0
Stay here for Oases. 10 minutes from **FKK Oases**
Rooms $50-100 euro here, and in downtown Frankfurt rooms can be down
to 35-50 Euros.

AUTO RENTAL :
National Auto Rentals
Frankfurt Airport T1
TEL: 06969072791 ..Offering free maps, you'll need one.

THE GAME PLAN :
Make sure you fly into Frankfurt Airport, not Haan, which is 75 miles west
of Frankfurt. . From Frankfurt Airport, you're traveling due east to the
northern Frankfurt suburb of **Altenstadt**. Public transportation is 1-2 hours,
and requires bus to train to bus to train 3 times, too much hassle. Get a car
and haul ass, a rental car drive is 1 hour or less. Cars will run around 65-70
euro a day, unlimited miles. A home base should be set up near two specific
recommended places, although there are many more to choose from.

Rent a car, you'll be driving an hour to Altenstadt. Take A3 to A66
to Hanau to A45. A45 to exit 39 which is Altenstadt, left at the end of the
road. Straight for 2-3 miles till the circle. Go left in the direction of Bahnof
for 1 mile, there's a light and a REWE supermarket there. Go left about a
mile, then Helmershauser Strasse, then to Siemenstarsse Road on the right.
Go right and you'll find **FKK Atlantis** at the end on your left.

For an alternate route, when you leave Frankfurt, drive with your
head out the window like Ace Ventura and follow the pussy smell. If the
scent becomes overwhelmingly strong, and you see men limping towards
their cars holding their crotches. You're there.

After you're little tour of Frankfurt, you can catch a train into
Amsterdam for more sex touring. (see chapter). FKK Atlantis and FKK
Oases are the preferred stops for quality, quantity, as well as price. We'll
supply more names later on. The FKK spas in Germany resemble the layout
of *termas* in Brazil. You arrive, pay a 30-65 Euro entrance fee, change in a
locker room, and walk around in robes and slippers. *"Good evening Mr.
Hefner."* The prices for sessions are 50 per half hour, they are fixed, and
there are very few clock-watchers here. In Germany, the FKK's are 90% for
the locals, the occasional tourist is rare. However, a cover story to the girl
about being a repeat business customer should improve your service. Expect

high quality, and an outstanding erotic performance, the girl will usually perform well also. A very good value. And we mean quality. It's damn hard to get out of there. (word to the wise: the German girls' service isn't preferred).

Atlantis is very upscale, and features stunning exotic women from around the world; Africa, Asia, South American, Russians, you name it. There are around 50 girls working there. They know you are an Oil Tycoon, and a well-endowed descendant of 007, so they all want to get naked quickly for you. None seem to have the annoying pro attitude either, AND there are only upscale hotties here.

What's so special about the place, is after your session, you can relax in an awesome pool or Jacuzzi, drop into one of four whirlpool spas, there's a tanning bed, sauna, steam room, massage girls, etc. When you bore of this , you could waste some time drilling a couple more exotic chicas that rate 8 or 9. Hop in the pool with a drink for as long as you want, watch the talent stroll around the place. You'll get company in the pool, don't worry. You can also hang out on the many couches around the bar area and make out till you're ready. Keep in mind, the place gets packed in the early evening and you gotta move quick sometimes for one you see, no posing time here after 8 pm.

Next up is **FKK Oase**. Located north of Frankfurt, it's about a 30 train followed by a 10E cab ride. Take the S5 train on track 104 to friedrichsdorf via bad hombug. Train leaves around every half hour. Warning, last train back leaves at 8pm from OASE area. FKK Oase is an beautiful outdoor setting, larger and more comfortable than Atlantis, however it seems Atlantis has the most girls and better looker ones. Oases has a huge screen porn theatre, outside lawn hangout area with Jacuzzi and whirlpool. Indoor the girls heavily grope you on couches as foreplay to entice you into the rooms, or you can have it right there on the couch(same fee). They even have a disco room with couches against the wall full of lounging naked temptresses. Hit the bar area or the Jacuzzi are and patiently pick out your women. The best time to go is 5-7pm, as the shift change means twice as many women to see. $60e entrance, $50e girl per half hour. FKK Chantel Chevalier Exklusiv is in downtown Frankfurt. Others include FFK Sudbad, Babylon, Bernds, Relax, Wiago, Parksauna, Mondail.

(website: **www.atlantis-therme.de**)
(website: **www.fkk-oase.de**)
(website: **www.f35.de**)

For the local club scene, traditional Kneipen (bars) cluster around the **Alt Sachsenhausen district** (between Brückenstrasse and Dreiechstrasse). Also, most of the top hotels in Frankfurt have busy and popular clubs of their own, as the clientele is often business travelers. Expect to see women loitering around hoping to trade a peek of their body for a chunk of your wallet. In the pop clubs, techno is particularly popular. Many bars in Frankfurt also offer live music, particularly jazz. The best venues are around Kleine Bockenheimer Strasse, otherwise known as Jazzgasse (Jazz Alley).

Local club magazines
Strandgut **(www.strandgut.de)**
Fritz **(www.fritz-frankfurt.de)**
Kultur News **(www.kulturnews.de)**
CityMag **(www.citymag.info/frankfurt)**
Prinze (**www.prinz.de)**
All have information on the nightlife in Frankfurt, with the latest on bars and nightclubs…available at the tourist information center.

Frankfurt Online
An excellent source of information and listings.
(www.rhein-main.net)

Live Music:
The biggest venue in town:
Die Brotfabrik, Bachmannstrasse 2-4
Features live international music. **(www.brotfabrik.de)**

Batschkapp, Maybachstrasse 24
Hosts rock, pop and DJ acts, with guests including German punk rockers Die Toten Hosen and famous names like Tracy Chapman and Napalm Death. **(www.batschkapp.de)**

VACATION STUFF :
Tell the old crone you're doing a research project for National Geographic on the correlation between excessive Heineken's and hairy armpit women.

Horsetrack :

Frankfurt Raceway
Address
Renn-Klub Frankfurt e.V.
Schwarzwald Str. 125
Frankfurt, 60528
+49 69 678 0900

Golf Courses :

Frankfurter Golf Club
Golfstrasse 41
60528 Frankfurt / Main
Tel : (069) 66 62 318
Exquisite, classic parkland course. Traditional German clubhouse. Great 18th hole with the skyscrapers of Frankfurt in the distance. For connoisseurs of the game, German golf at it's finest. Located 6km southwest of downtown. Huge list of others to choose from.
(www.golfeurope.com/euro_clubs/germany-golf-courses.htm)

Casinos :

Bad Homburg Casino is the nearest casino – in the spa town of Bad Homburg, just to the north of Frankfurt, on Im Kurpark. Table gambling is available 1500-0300. It costs €2.50 for a day card and the minimum age is 18 years – ID in the form of a driving license or passport is required. Dress code is smart, with no jeans, sports clothes, sandals or trainers. A jacket and tie is required for men.

108

Aruba

About :
The smallest and westernmost of the Caribbean islands, Aruba lies just 18 miles off the coast of Venezuela and 42 miles west of Curacao. The island is 19.6 miles long, and six miles across at its widest point, with a total area of 70 square miles. Approximately 101,000 people reside here full time, and more than 540,000 visit during the course of a year. You'll find fabulous clean white beaches, perfect mild weather, and great-secluded coves for swimming. Nearly every night there are theme parties, treasure hunts, beachside barbecues, and fish fries with steel bands, limbo or Carnival dancers. Perfect for bringing your imported Columbian dates from San Nicolas red zone. Aruba is home to a whole world of duty-free shopping and many cruise ships visit the shores during their Caribbean itineraries. Holland America Lines, Cunard, Royal Caribbean, Majestic, Sun Line and Princess amongst others sail to Oranjestad. Dutch, English and Spanish spoken.

(www.arubatourism.com)

Climate :
Temperatures year round at 80 degrees. No rainy season, light winds consistently. January, February and March are the most popular times to visit. During Carnival, just before Lent, the island is hopping with parades, festivities and parties.

Entry Requirements :
From the US, a birth certificate and photo ID is required, although a passport is recommended. The Passport must be valid for at least 3 months after intended return to home country. For stays of over 14 days and less than 30 days, the traveler will be issued with a Temporary Certificate of Admission by the Immigration authorities on arrival in Aruba. All visitors require a return or onward ticket. In this case the visa cost for single entry is approximately £16 depending on the exchange rate.

Departure tax: US$34.25 per person for all travelers over two years of age. This is normally included in the ticket price.

Airlines :
Airlines serving Aruba include Air ALM, Avensa (from Venezuela), Avianca (from Colombia), American Airlines, Continental Airlines, KLM, Martinair (from Miami) and VARIG (from Brazil). Land at Hato

International Airport. Approximate flight times: From NY is 4 hours, LA is 10 hours, London is 11 hours 40 minutes (including a connection).

TELEPHONE :

IDD available. Country code: 297. Outgoing international code: 00. Payphones, from which international calls can be made, are located all over the island. Call the old lady and tell her you're playing in a highly competitive basket weaving competition and can't be interrupted for the next week.

Cellphones:

These can be hired from SETAR (tel: 586 7138) (www.setar.au)
A deposit and proof of identity are required. Setel NV operates GSM 900 coverage across the entire Netherlands Antilles.
Internet: Public access is available at the Internet cafe in Oranjestad.
(www.cybercafe.aw)

MONEY MATTERS :

The Aruban florin is the official currency, which is divided into 100 cents. Silver coins are in denominations of 5, 10, 25 and 50 cents, one florin, 2 1/2 florins and 5 florins. Current exchange rates are AF 1.77 to the U.S. Dollar and AF. .34 to the Canadian Dollar.

ATM machines: Travelers with ATM cards bearing the CIRRUS or Plus System network logos can withdraw cash in Aruban florins. In the Wyndam hotel you can get dollars at the ATM machine. Avoid the casino ATM, huge fees. Many places will take US bills higher than $20 due to currency fraud.

RECOMMENDED RESTAURANTS :

Since this info can change weekly, we can't recommend enough the "**Zagat Survey**." Pick up their travel book, or signup online. Worldwide reviews, menus, and pricing. **(www.zagat.com)**

HOTELS :

Rooms are subject to 5% government room tax and hotels also add 16.6% service charge, the greedy bastards.

Holiday Inn
(www.excelsiorcasino.com)
(800) HOLIDAY Toll Free Hotel Reservations

Aruba Marriott Resort
(www.marriott.com/epp/default.asp?MarshaCode=AUAAR)
(888) 236-2427 Hotel Reservations

Hyatt Regency Aruba Resort
(www.aruba.hyatt.com)
(800) 233-1234 Toll Free Reservations

Wyndham Aruba Beach Resort & Casino
toll-free at 877-999-3223
(www.wyndham.com/hotels/AUAPB/main.wnt)

There are apartment complexes and a list is available through the Aruba
Tourism Authority offices.
(www.aruba.com)

THE GAME PLAN :
The layout and business approach here is almost the same as
Curacao. On the other side of the island from the hotels is a club district of
31 bars called **San Nicolas.** The club owners import 150-200 Columbian
girls to work in their bars. The girls send photos along with a health
certificate from home, and the clubs pick and choose the best ones. Upon
arrival, the girls receive another health check, and then rent rooms at the
clubs for $30 a day. The girls do quite well under this arrangement
compared to poverty-stricken Columbia, and the clubs foot the bill for their
airfare, as well as health check ups. While working on the island, the girls
require weekly screenings, and they have only 90-day visas and then they
can't return for a year…all approved by the local government. New meat
every week. Turnkey sex tourism boys, and there are some extremely high
caliber ladies to be found here…a buffet of Latin American coochie.
Taxis are a rare find out here at night, and charge exorbitant rates,
so rent yourself a jeep for a few days while on the island. The clubs utilize
an in-house arrangement for sessions, either in small cottages behind the
bars, or the upstairs rooms. The bar gets $10 per girl, which includes a few
lady drinks, and a condom. The girls run $35 a session. The whole
arrangement is low key, there's no crime, and the island is beautiful. The
girls speak Spanish only. Some of the most popular clubs you should visit
are **Chesterfield, Papa Ciga, Kiss Me Night Club, Ron & Menta Bar,
Caribbean Club, China Clipper Bar, Minchies, Copacabana Bar,** and

111

the **Bongo Bar.** Frankly the names are unimportant, it's a strip of clubs…that's all you need to remember. Many times the bartender is the owner, so buddy up and ask for a chica recommendation from him.

The pack of nightclubs make up an entire area of town, so the best bet is to grab a beer or ten and walk around and take your time picking. Pop in one bar, pop out….the *diamond in the rough* decision will quickly become the half dozen diamonds in the rough. Some of the bars are open at 12 noon, and close at 12 midnights. Others open at 8pm and close at 2am or later, depending on the existing crowd. Some are open 7 days a week, some are closed on Sunday. Girls may be allowed to be taken out of the bars, but the bar fine is high. The professional approach is to take her for an in house test drive, get her phone number, and then pick her up the next day for a romp at your beach hotel during her off hours. Find a cutie that works at the bars that close at 12, and pull her back to your hotel beach. Apologize to her that you're a little stressed out from all the paperwork maintaining your billion-dollar trust fund.

For day time action, rent a car and have your chica take you on a tour of the island, the girls love to take a break away from the club cruising during the day in convertible jeeps. Rentals are available at the hotel and are surprisingly cheap in comparison to the rapist cab rates.

You also have the option of escort services on the island, there are several found in the classifieds of the local newspaper. The cost is $100 in your hotel room, or if the wife is sleeping, $120 including a ride to a room elsewhere.

(www.arubaescort.com)

VACATION STUFF :
And now for the cover story for the old lady.

GOLF COURSES :

Tierra del Sol.
Robert Trent Jones II world-class course is located on the northwest section of the island. The 18-hole, par-71 course is laid out amongst beautiful rugged terrain, home to wildlife and wild animals. Reservations are needed, and can be arranged at your hotel.

Aruba Golf Club.
Southwest part of the island, this is a beer drinking 9-hole course.

Miniature Golf

Adventure golf is advertised as the world's largest miniature golf course, surrounded by endless waterfalls, played throughout the night.

OCEAN FISHING :

The Caribbean is home to some of the best Big Game Sport fishing, and Aruba is no exception. Offering some of the best weather you can ask for while trolling for your trophy fish battle, you can come here for the challenge year round. Various species of fish are waiting for your line such as: **White and Blue Marlin, Sailfish, Sharks, Mahi Mahi, Barracuda, Wahoo, Amberjack, Kingfish, Bonito, Black and Yellow fin Tuna** and many more! Prices range from US$ 220 to US$ 350 for a half-day charter, or US $400 to US $600 for a full day.

Local restaurants will cook your catch for a reasonable fee.. Half day or full day tours can be arranged at the hotels. The Seaport Marina at Oranjestad Harbor is home base for sport fishing activity.

(www.teasercharters.com) ... (www.aruba-mahimahi.com)

DIVING AND SNORKELING :

Aruba has over 40 dive sites with up 100 feet of visibility. A very healthy selection of marine life is clearly visible, including barracuda, manta rays and the green moray. Water temperatures average 82°F, and divers with Open Water Certification can visit World War II wrecks, wall diving, reef diving, and many coral formations. Resort Certification Scuba Diving Course is available for beginners. Some of the best snorkeling spots are off the beaches of **Boca Grandi** and **Baby Beach**, though snorkeling is possible in many other places. Gear can be hired from water sports centers at hotels, which organize combined sailing and snorkeling day trips. Rent some whores and let them experiment on your trouser snorkel in the hotel Jacuzzi.

SAILING :

Smooth constant winds are perfect for sailing conditions. You can rent catamaran, trimaran, as well as Sunfish or the Minifish.

WINDSURFING :

Tons of rental equipment and guides. Prime locations on island for the advanced users. In June, Aruba has the Hi-Winds Amateur World Challenge windsurfing tournament. This 10-day competition has worldwide pros.

TENNIS & SQUASH :

The all-inclusive clubs have tennis. The fanciest location to play is the Aruba Racquet Club, Aruba's first world-class tennis center, and is located at Rooi Santo 21 in the Palm Beach area. 8 well lit courts, swimming pool, gym, bar and restaurant.

UNDERWATER TOURS :

Seaworld Explorer
Great glass bottom views from this boat, with morning and afternoon rides that visit boat wrecks, **Antilla** and **Arashi** and the coral reef.
Atlantis Submarine
Explore the Caribbean at 150 feet below surface on board the 46 passenger state-of-the-art Atlantis Submarine. To get there you take a catamaran ride from downtown Oranjestad to the dive site, then you switch to the sub and head underwater.

CASINOS :

There are eleven Casinos located in the major hotels. In addition to **blackjack, poker, craps, roulette, baccarat**, and hundreds of ringing slot machines, Aruba's casinos offer **Caribbean Stud Poker**, invented in 1988 in Aruba and currently skyrocketing in popularity all over the world. In Caribbean Stud Poker, as in blackjack, each player vies only with the dealer. Unlike blackjack, however, Caribbean Stud Poker offers players the thrill of a progressive jackpot that can reach into the hundreds of thousands in U.S. dollars.

Wyndham Aruba Beach Resort & Casino
The 12,000 square foot casino features 310 slots and twenty table games. The property has seven restaurants and a hotel with 510 rooms.
Address:
J. E. Irausquin Boulevard 77, Palm Beach, Aruba
Phone: 297-586-4466, toll-free at 877-999-3223
(www.wyndham.com/hotels/AUAPB/main.wnt)
Slot Machines - 317 total Progressive Slots- 5 cents to $25.
Table Games
American Roulette- 5 tables- USD 2.00 to USD 25 bets
Blackjack- 16 tables- USD 5.00 to USD 1,000 bets
Caribbean Stud Poker- 4 tables
Craps- 2 tables- USD 5.00 to USD 500 bets
Mini-Baccarat- 2 tables- USD 10 to USD 1,000 bets
Roulette- 6 tables

Aruba Marriott Resort & Stellaris Casino
The 10,700 square foot casino features 300 slots. The property has seven restaurants and a hotel with 413 rooms.
L.G. Smith Boulevard # 101, Palm Beach, Aruba
Phone: 297-586-9000 Fax: 297-586-0649
International Toll-Free: 1-800-223-6388
(888) 236-2427 Hotel Reservations
(www.marriott.com/epp/default.asp?MarshaCode=AUAAR)
Total Slots - 300.
Table Games
Baccarat ,Blackjack ,Caribbean Stud Poker, Craps, Roulette

Hyatt Regency Aruba Resort and Copa Cabana Casino
The 11,000 square foot casino features 304 slots and twenty-three table games. The property has nine restaurants and two hotels with 738 rooms. Address:
J. E. Irausquin Boulevard 85, Palm Beach, Aruba
(800) 233-1234 Toll Free Reservations
(www.aruba.hyatt.com)

Holiday Inn SunSpree Aruba Resort & Excelsior Casino
The 12,000 square foot casino features 257 slots and sixteen table games. The property has three restaurants and a hotel with 600 rooms. Address:
J. E. Irausquin Boulevard 230, Palm Beach, Aruba
 (800) HOLIDAY Toll Free Hotel Reservations
(www.excelsiorcasino.com)

Pattaya, Thailand

About :

Pattaya is located just north of the equator, bordered by Cambodia, Burma and Laos. Pattaya remains one of the most popular holiday destinations in Thailand. Tourists can windsurf, water ski, swim, sunbathe, snorkel, sail, or take trips to offshore coral islands. Pattaya's main beach is at Jomtien, which runs for a distance of about 5 kilometres. Among the other superb sites to be visited are the Nong Nooch Tropical Garden, and the Pattaya Park Tower hotel & Water Park. A curving 4 km beach on the Gulf of Thailand, South Pattaya is the hub of Pattaya nightlife with shops, department stores, boutiques, beauty salons, supermarkets, bars, discotheques, restaurants and nightclubs.

Much of its Pattaya's success lies in its reputation for offering vibrant entertainment in a laid-back resort ambiance, with its infamous nightlife of **Go-Go bars** and **Beer Gardens** galore. As far as Go-Go bars go, all roads lead to **Walking Street** in South Pattaya, as well as having good quality seafood at a reasonable price this area.

Pattaya has become a Mecca for single men seeking paid companionship of young Thai girls. The town is infamous for the quality of good looking inexpensive women, whom excluding Brazilians, are quite possible the most enthusiastic and best performing women in the sack. Recently, the city has made efforts to change its image with the addition of more legitimate attractions like golf, horse riding, water-parks, convention centers and grand botanical gardens. There is a bit of everything for everyone in Pattaya now. That's incredibly interesting guys...
We'll settle for choreographed nude line dances
and $50 orgies in our $25 hotel suite.

Climate :

Pattaya lies within the humid tropics and remains hot throughout the year. There are three seasons: the cool season from November to February, the hot season from April to May and the rainy season from June to October. The best time for visiting is between November and February. During these months, it is not too hot and dry. From March to May the country is hot and humid. Tropical with three distinct seasons. Temperatures range from 77 to 95 degrees year round.

ENTRY REQUIREMENTS :

Principal airports are Bangkok, Phuket, Chiang Mai, Hat Yai, U-Taphao (Pattaya).

Airport tax: International 500 baht; domestic 20 baht.

Visa Requirements: None required for most visitors, for visits of less than 30 days if traveling for pleasure. Visits longer than 30 days require a visa.

Airport check-in times: International – 2 hours. Domestic - 45 min

Electricity: 220 volts, 50 cycles. Many hotels have 100-volt outlets for electrical devices.

Time: GMT + 6hours. YYC 1800 = Bangkok 0600 the following day.

GETTING TO PATTAYA :

Pattaya does not have a commercial airport. The closest airport is in U-Tapo, which is a half hour drive from Pattaya. At the moment, there are no scheduled flights between U-Tapo and Bangkok. Fly to Bangkok Airport. From Bangkok it takes 2 hours by Bus to get to Pattaya. Use the air-conditioned buses. Bangkok Ekamai Bus Terminal has coaches leaving every 30 minutes from 5.30 am to 9.00 pm at a nominal fare of 90 Baht. The trip is a comfortable 2-hour ride and the bus terminal in Pattaya has plenty of waiting Song Thaews for transfers to the hotels. It is similar from Pattaya to Bangkok; from the bus station a bus leaves every hour or so. You don't need to buy a ticket in advance, you can easily get one at the bus station for about 70/80 baht. Taxi from B to P should run you 300 baht. Airport limo site. (**www.thaiair.com/thailand/limousine/fares.htm#Schedule**)

Train :

There are two trains daily between Bangkok and Pattaya. Other parts of Thailand can also be reached from Pattaya via train. The train trip actually takes longer than the bus trip, but the comfort and lack of traffic makes the trip more relaxing.

MONEY MATTERS :

Currency:

The baht is divided into 100 satang.

Notes: 10, 20, 50, 100, 500, 1000 baht.

Coins: 25, 50 satang; 1, 2, 5, 10 baht.

For today's exchange rate, go to here:

(**www.oanda.com**)

ATM Machines

Available at most banks and shopping centers throughout the city. Thai Baht only. ATMs generally have Thai and English language displays and will accept most internationally recognized foreign cards. Many ATM's will also accept cards under the CIRRUS, Maestro, VISA or MasterCard system.

Travelers Cheques / Credit Cards

Most traveler's checks can be cashed at banks. Take your passport or ID. MasterCard and VISA are widely accepted by major banks, restaurants and shops. AMEX, Diners and tend to be accepted only at up to market rates. Credit cards have been known to have large extra charges added here, use your ATM card.

Helpful Tips :

The temperature and humidity here is stifling, bring sunscreen and sunglasses everywhere you go. Slam bottles of water down like it's last call. **AVOID** getting drinks with ice as the source is questionable, meaning your shorts will all have racing stripes quickly. The only acceptable ice is the type with holes through them. When you're eating out in the evenings, watch out for mosquitoes. Ask the waiter to put a mosquito coil under the table to discourage them. Wearing pale colored slacks and mosquito repellant will also keep them at bay.

DO'S AND DON'TS :

DO as many hot young Thai women as you can. Rinse and repeat.

FLATTERY will get you everywhere, no matter how phony it is. In other words, speak like a stripper. Lie.

DON'T let a girl convince you to shower before her. She'll be in your suitcase shopping and gone before you finish.

DO AVOID shady people trying to be your friend and show you the ropes. You'll wake up 3 days later naked in the woods, brain dead and broke.

DON'T display public affection. No holding hands or kissing, it's just not done here. But, negotiating gangbangs in public is customary.

DON'T invest in a business - especially a bar. You'll likely be OUT of business very quickly. Don't expect any sympathy; expect to be laughed at behind your back.

DON'T ruin your trip by doing the same girl numerous times. She will claim ownership of you, and start whining about how she needs money for buffalo in hospital. Move on quickly and enjoy the variety the city has to offer. Avoid the parasites. It costs a fortune to get here, why put up with a girl telling what you can and cannot do.

DON'T signal waiters with the hand, palm downwards, fingers straight and waving rapidly. Don't snap your fingers or clap, or point your foot towards them.

DO SHAVE every day. Thai Girls are not fond of facial hair. Of course, a lot of them have bushes like the Brazilian rain forest and they think that's normal. Make them shave it before paying them. Goes both ways sista.

DON'T brag about the superiority of the US. That is bad. Bragging bout her Thai pussy is good.

BUDDHA
Buddhism is sacred here. No taking pictures standing in front of statues, the utmost respect in temples. Shorts are not allowed, don't parade around drunk and loud. You'll be escorted away. Look but don't touch.

DO LEARN some, any of their language is a plus. At the very least, the number system, which is actually quite easy. Speaking awful Thai is worse than no Thai. Speak slow, distinct English and some dirty Thai words at the minimum.

DO WEAR flashy gold. Not the real stuff, get the knock off Rolex in the Patpong are for $10. Gold is a big status symbol in BKK. As if you don't get enough attention here, this will increase it even more.

DO keep your feet to yourself. They have this strange custom surrounding pointing feet, use of feet. Never point towards anyone, don't flop them on chairs, never step on a Thai, over a Thai, or over a Thai's food.

DO get a price up front.
If a girl says no price and says whatever you pay me is fine, expect a huge argument in the morning, no matter what you pay her.

ELECTRICITY :

Voltage is 220 Volt AC with flat 2 pin plugs. You can buy an adapter for shavers, laptop computers, mobile chargers, etc., on arrival at most department stores.

Most hotels now have Internet either from the room by laptop, or from their business center. Charges vary from around 100 Baht for the first 15 minutes with lower charges afterwards. Additional surcharges times apply, so check first. There are also Internet cafes in most shopping areas which are expensive.

CRIME AND SCAMS :

Thailand is the land of bartering for everything, and there's plenty of it, as they also specialize in selling knock off versions of Rolexes and everything else. Take care bringing the goods back home, their illegal…pack in bag securely.

Stay on top of the currency exchanges, watch for bogus folded bills, etc…pay in their money for everything. The cabbies will constantly try to take to a buddy's store to get a commission. Give a specific street address when you tell your destination. Don't say this store, or this mall, etc. If they try to scam you and play the no English game, tell them "tourist police." Suddenly their memory gets much better.

Be aware that a lot of the girls here haven't been girls their whole lives. "Ladyboys", or transvestites, whether pre- or post surgery are commonly found walking the streets looking for the naïve. We're talking a complete sex change. Just look for the giveaway signs..they are taller, w/big feet and big hands. They thrive on fooling you.

Map of Pattaya :

(www.pattaya-maps.com)

(www.pattayaplaza.com/maps/map_pattaya.htm)

RECOMMENDED RESTAURANTS :

Since this info can change weekly, we can't recommend enough the "**Zagat Survey**." Pick up their travel book, or signup online. Worldwide reviews, menus, and pricing.

(www.zagat.com)

HOTELS :

There are literally hundreds of accommodation choices in and around Pattaya. Two major chains, **Marriott Hotels** and **The Hard Rock Hotel** are here along with the big Thai Group, **Dusit Thani Resort.** If you plan on visiting Bangkok on your trip, consider the **Dynasty Inn**. They have nice hotels in both cities and a free shuttle for travel from one to the other. Nice rooms, nice pool, $25 a night including breakfast. Situated in the heart of Pattaya and within short walking distance of Pattaya beach, shopping complex and other entertainment attractions. The hotel can be accessed from both Beach Road and Pattaya 2nd Road.

Make sure you check out the room in advance. Make sure the AC works without a noisy fan, check shower hot water, street noise, cable box working, inquire about guests and a safe. If the room is no good, ask to see another. If they so no guests, say your girlfriend is coming in tomorrow and you want a double.

(www.dynastyinn.com)

Here's a couple clean Cheap Charlie ones in a great location.
AA Residence
Located half way down Soi 13 off Beach Road.
aaresidence@yahoo.com (038) 423403, 410565
109/20 MOO 10 SOI 13 Beach Road

Siam Sawasdee
Located on the Corner of Soi Buakao and Soi Honey
Phone : (038) 720329
(www.sawasdee-hotels.com)

A.A. Pattaya Hotel
Phone: (038) 428-656, 420-894
Located on Corner Beach and Soi13, 182-182/2 Soi 13 Beach Road.
750 Baht including breakfast

Because it is impossible to give details on all the hotels here, see the below link to find one that meets your needs. As a general rule you can get a clean room in a good area with air conditioning for around 1000 baht ($25). The 5 star hotels are less guest friendly and have rooms starting from around 2500 baht. If on a budget, small clean rooms can be had for as little as 195B.

(**www.pattayacity.com/pattaya/hotels.html**)

121

THE GAME PLAN :

When it comes to nightlife, South Pattaya is home to dozens of **Discos**, hundreds of **Go Go Bars**, hundreds of **Karaoke Bars**, and literally **thousands** of pubs and cafes, **Massage Parlors, Beer Bars**, and **Blow Job Bars**. Starting from Soi Pattayaland 2 and extending south to Soi 18, this is a huge bimbo area, with many side streets (sois) and much to do and see. The action takes place in the Sois, and along Beach and Second Road, as well as Beach Road from South Pattaya Road to Soi 18. At night, the area is closed to traffic and metamorphoses into **The Famous Walking Street**. The streets become energetic, chaotic, noisy and full of happy sleazy young girls. There's are always some bizarre sights that will amaze you, nothing like the occasional nude fire eating show while throwing back your sixteenth beer. Nothing like a hot date with a girl named Poo.

While strolling down Walking Street, there are plenty of great steak, seafood, and barbecue joints. The food is hot and spicy, so make sure you have a dozen beers nearby. **Lobster Pot** was one of the favorites of our crew. Also, on Saturdays, the Swiss Bar has an all you can eat Pig roast for 200 baht. ($5).

Again, concentrate on Walking Street and the side roads along Beach Road. Flashing red lights and seedy ambiance everywhere.

YES!! Home at last.

There are countless go go bars all in a row. For the latest and greatest, you must see **Club Electric Blue**. It has 4 stages, with seating on 3 levels. The highest level rotates around above you, on the other levels there are sensuous girl girl acts galore. The beers are cheap and there's an American style restaurant here as well. Some real stunners make this their home on any given night.

The red zone is one long strip, so you can sample many bars in an evening. Some other popular clubs are **Livingdolls 2, The Freelancer Bar, Happy-a-GoGo, Marine Disco, Carousel, Bubbles,** and **Peppermint Plaza.** The names of the clubs change regularly, but the look and feel is always the same. Besides the go go bars, there are literally hundreds of small open air Beer Bars around the town, featuring a wide variety of music, staffed with tons of girls available for dates for a small bar fine. Expect the girls to pull you in off the street and make you buy them drinks, as they get a commission on each one. Not to worry, everything is dirt-cheap and the experience is well worth it. They will leave short-time or long-time, the cost of her date is up to you.

Me so horny, me wuv you wong time.

As far as pricing goes, here's a rough guide.
Short time (ST) refers to 90-120 minutes, or 2 rounds with a girl, whichever comes first.
Long Time (LT) means over night.

Along Beach Road or Soi 6, the ST rate is 500 baht, bar girls 500-800ST, 1000 LT. Freelancers are 1000 Baht, Go Go girls 1000-1500 ST, 1500-2000 LT.

Bar Fines are an additional required cost for the house, the price you pay to take the dancer out of the club, in a Go Go bar it's a 500 baht bar fine, some bars are charging 700-1000 baht bar fines. In a beer bar expect around 200-250 baht.
There are the infamous **Blow Job Bars** as well, where you stroll on in and for $10 can be serviced in private or literally right at the bar. Tilt back your beer and bark out instructions, she can't understand you anyway. Now that's service. *Don't hit your head on the bar getting up honey* . The phrase Blow Job has a slang in Thai, it is called "**Smoke**", as in "You smoke?"…answer: "Yes, Me like smoke you long time!"

Thai Soapy Massages :
The other kind of Massage is the "sensual" kind. These places are usually very up-market establishments with plush furnishings. For soapy body massages, you can definitely have a great experience in Pattaya. Here's the lowdown. On entering, you will see an area behind glass, with tiered seating and between 10 and 100 girls seated here, waiting for you. The famous "fish bowl". The girls sit there all orderly in bleachers like a prom dance, with numbers on their chest as identity. Take your time, sometimes at first glance it looks like they haven't clean out the tank in quite a while, there's a lot of bottom feeders. There's a lot activity here, girls pop in and out, and in any minute some cute little hottie will pop on in and sit down in the bowl. Get your fishing pole ready, soon it will be time to answer the call of the gods of testosterone.
Most parlors have a lounge area by the fishbowl, where you can have a drink and choose your masseuse at leisure. Take your time, pick one you really want bad, and don't just settle. Pick out your girl, pay and move to a room. You hop in the hot tub and get a sudsy bath, then onto the massage mat. Best done in a sandwich, i.e., 2 girls. Request the body massage. Then it's onto the bed for the last part of your date. The whole thing is around 90 minutes, with the taxi fare of 1300-2500 baht.

The best known parlors in Pattaya include **Sabai Dee, Sabai Land** and **Sabai Room**, all on Second Road near Big C. Sabai by the way is the Thai word for comfortable. Others of note include **Susie Massage** in Soi 4, **Diamond Massage** in Soi Diamond, Walking Street and **Heaven** on Sukhumvit Rd near Central Pattaya Rd. The way the places operate is they a house fee of 400 baht for the massage, and the goodies are negotiated directly with the girl. They tend to ask for 1500 baht but can be negotiated down to 1000 baht.

Aside from the bars, the **Excite Discotheque** is the most talked about club in town, with a good mix of sophisticated tourist and local clientele. The crowd at **Hollywood Disco** has more locals and the party can get rowdy at times with occasional fights. **The Hard Rock Café** has a daily live band, and on weekends foam parties that offer 'bubbles of fun". If you're into live music, there's a great house band at the **Climax Beer Bar**, not to mention 20-30 hot little ladies.

(http://www.pattaya-at-night.com/gogo.htm)

Club Websites :
(www.clubelectricblue.com)
(www.thedollhouseagogo.com)
(www.livingdollspattaya.com)
(www.mistysagogo.com)
(www.spicygirls.org)
(www.classroom1.com)
(www.tahitianqueen.com)

An up-to-date listing of Pattaya Go Go bars :
(www.bahtbus.com/bars/index.html)
(www.pattayagogoguide.com/gogolist.html)

For massage parlors with photos of buildings :
(www.bahtbus.com/massage/index.html)
Download a copy of this map
(www.pattaya-at-night.com/postcard/pictures/pattaya-map.jpg)

Thailand escort site :
(www.escortsinthailand.com)

VACATION STUFF :
Tell the old crone you flew 20 hours to take your childhood seashell collection to a new level. Make her bow to you at the airport when you return.

GOLF COURSES :
There are 18 golf courses throughout Pattaya.

Laem Chabang International Country Club
The crème de la crème, only 30 minutes out of town. Designed by the legendary Jack Nicklaus, the course is one of the best in Thailand with 27 holes against a mountainous backdrop and plenty of water and sand hazards to challenge any golf enthusiast.

Siam Country Club
Another old favorite is the over 30 year old Siam Country Club, just 20 minutes from central Pattaya. The 18-hole fairways are lined with big mature trees and there are plans to upgrade the greens. 865 Rama 1 Rd, Patumwan, Bangkok 10330
Thailand Tel. 215-3334 (**www.siamcountryclub.com**)

Phoenix Golf and Country Club
The scenic 27-hole course never ceases to dazzle golfers with its dramatic sea views at the last 9 holes of the Ocean course. The 10-year-old course is not for the faint-hearted and promises some exciting and extraordinary holes. Note that it is worth trying to tee off on weekdays to avoid the avid golfers coming from Bangkok.
106/8 Moo 4, Beung, Sriracha, Chonburi 20230, Thailand
Tel: 0-3837-2273   info@laemchabanggolf.com
(www.laemchabanggolf.com/golf.html)
(www.pattayainfo.com/golfcourses.html)
(www.thailandgolfholidays.com)
(www.golforient.com/index.html)

OCEAN FISHING :
Thailand takes great pride in it's deep-sea sport fishing. In fact, the most expensive rods in the world are made in Chiangmai, Thailand, which is also the home of 10 trout fly companies. In Pattaya, there are plenty of trophy catches to be made, featuring **sailfish, marlin, Mahi Mahi, Dorado, tuna**, and other species. Shallow island reefs are home to many species of light-tackle game fish including **sea bass, barracuda, giant trevally, queenfish,**

and **mangrove jack**. Pelagic species like **black marlin** and **sailfish**, as well as **king mackerel** and **tiger sharks** are found in Blue water. Late November is a good time to go after marlin, tuna and any number of other fighting fish. Larger **black marlin**, up to 300kg, also found are **yellowfin tuna** (20kg), **Wahoo** (40kg) and numerous **barracuda, Dorado** and **skipjack tuna**. Sharks like **tiger, hammerhead, bull** and the occasional **Mako shark** take the bait during day or night-fishing trips.

Here are some sites to arrange your trip.

(www.asiatradingonline.com/pattayafishing.htm)

(www.asiatradingonline.com/fishing.htm)

CASINOS :
Gambling is illegal in Thailand. Guess they have high standards here. Of course, girls shooting darts 10 feet from their pussies and popping balloons are perfectly acceptable behavior.

DIVING AND SNORKELING :
There are several pristine islands with incredible coral reefs. The most popular is **Koh Larn**, about 8 kilometres away or 45 minutes by boat. The island is host to many white sandy beaches, the most tranquil being the 700-metre Laem Thian beach in the south-western side followed by the lively 750-metre Ta Waen Beach in the north. In addition to the usual water activities like **parasailing** and **jet-skiing**, glass bottom boats reveal bejeweled treasures of colorful corals.

The adjacent rocky island of Ko Krok has a small beach and is one of the best spots for snorkeling. There is a string of islands about 20-30 kilometres away or 2 hours by boat from Pattaya known as the "Far Islands." They have untouched beaches and extraordinary dive sites. The islands include Koh Rin, Koh Man Wichai, Koh Keung Badaan, Koh Hu Chang and Koh Pai. The Mermaid Dive Centre offers trips to explore the underwater landscape and a chance to catch a glimpse of barracudas, tunas, stingrays and moray eels.

Shipwreck Dives take adventurers to the final resting place of ships like The Hardeep, which is a cargo ship that sunk during World War II. Other wrecks include the Petchburi Bremen, an old freighter and now a hiding place for groupers and barracudas.

BUENOS AIRES, ARGENTINA

ABOUT :
Argentina is the world's eighth largest country, covering almost the entire southern half of South America. **Buenos Aires**, a buzzing metropolis of three million people, is located in the north, and is the most European of all Latin American cities. With its wide boulevards, stunning gardens and parks, grandiose buildings and varied culture and nightlife, the city is reminiscent of Paris or Barcelona. The Porteños ('people of the port'), as the residents of Buenos Aires are called, seem more European too – but this is rational as in reality most descended from Europe, predominately Italian immigrants who settled here in the 19th century. Their unique culture followed them from overseas, as well as their fabulous cuisines. As far as culture, the city is home to countless art galleries, theatres and museums, as well as fine restaurants.

For the visitor from abroad, there has never been a better time to visit Buenos Aires. Devaluation has made it an incredibly cheap city to explore and enjoy. For exotic travel, you'll find beautiful waterfalls, nestled amongst some of the world's tallest mountains. Normally cuisine is not mentioned in this book, but BA has some of the best food in the world, particularly their meats and Italian food. Make sure you eat at least once at Cabana Las Lillas, which will serve you the juiciest tasting steak of your life for a little over $10. There's a buffet of hot Blonde meat strolling around in that area as well. **Recolecta**, your home base, is extremely convenient, with everything close by in walking distance, the strip clubs, discos, bars, cafes, restaurants, stores, subway, and the hotel of your choice.

Buenos Aires is a busy capitalist trade center, but it's kept squeaky clean and cosmopolitan. The official language is Spanish. The women tend to be gorgeous statuesque blondes, who take pride in living life in a sophisticated fashion. This is true of the girls you'll be chasing as well. If you're the type that dresses up in Gen X garb and gets shitfaced and loud, you will attract no one, no matter how much money you have. Well, that's not true, all women are whores for the big bucks, but it certainly won't help your chances. Think big city Europe and you'll have a feel for the town and women.

For daytime eye candy, BA has an abundance, since it's considered the shopping capital of South America. Two of the most exclusive malls are Galerias Pacifico, Calle Florida and Calle Córdoba, and Patio Bullrich, Avenida del Libertador 750 and Posadas 1245, which are overflowing with supermodel blondes checking out the latest boutiques of Argentine fashions and international labels. The main drag for upscale stores and leather goods (their specialty) is Calle Florida, located in the city center.

COUNTRY DIALING CODE : 54.

TIME ZONE : GMT - 3

ELECTRICITY : 220 volts AC, 50Hz; two-round-pin plugs are standard.

LOCAL NEWSPAPERS :

(www.lanacion.com.ar/suples/vialibre/0345/)

(www.laguia.clarin.com)

CLIMATE :

Spring is September to November, fall is March to May. Winter is 35 degrees daytime to 55 at night. Average January temp. is 84°F, and the average July Temp. is 57°F

GETTING THERE :

Buenos Aires's airport Aeropuerto Internacional Ministro Pistarni is referred to as Ezeiza, located some 35km (22 miles) west of Buenos Aires. Argentina's major airline is Aerolineas Argentinas (tel: (011) 4340 7800; website: **(www.aerolineas.com.ar)**

Getting to BA, there's a shuttle bus service for $12 which runs every 30 minutes. The local bus 86 to the city center is much cheaper at $1.35 (coins only), but it takes up to two hours. Taxis set you back $25+ for the 30-minute journey to the city center. Use one of the official taxi firms located at the airport.

FLIGHT TIMES TO BUENOS AIRES :

From New York is 11 hours; from Los Angeles is 16 hours; London is 13 hours, and from Toronto is 13 hours.

ENTRY REQUIREMENTS :

A valid passport and a visa if needed (check this with your consular authorities or our diplomatic authorities). Passengers from not bordering nations with Argentina don't pay customer tax on personal effects and new products for a value under $300. If this goods were bought in a free shop you have additional $300.

DEPARTURE TAX :

A tax of $7.50 for domestic flights (payable in Pesos only) or US$30.50 for international flights, due on departure.

TELEPHONE INFO :
USA calls to Buenos Aires:
011-54-11-xxxx-xxxx (xxxx-xxxx is the local number in Buenos Aires).
USA call to Buenos Aires cell phone: 011-54-911-xxxx-xxxx
Companies with cheap calling cards:

Blackstone
(www.blackstoneonline.com)

BestPriceTelecom
(www.bptelecom.com)

MONEY MATTERS :
The official currency is the peso. There are notes of 2, 5, 10, 20, 50 and 100 pesos, coins of 1, 2 and 5 pesos and 1, 5, 10, 25 and 50 cents. Currently around 3 pesos to 1 dollar.
For today's exchange rate, go to here:
(http://www.oanda.com)

RECOMMENDED RESTAURANTS :
Since this info can change weekly, we can't recommend enough the "**Zagat Survey**." Pick up their travel book, or signup online. Worldwide reviews, menus, and pricing. **(www.zagat.com)**

CRIME :
Taxis are known thieves down here. When you choose one, visibly write down the cab number while he is watching. Typical scam is they take your money, say it's bad currency…and while you're not watching, they very quickly do a bait and switch slight of hand, fold the bills in half and hand them back to you with WAY less money.

HOTELS :
There is a huge concentration of hotels in the center of the city, but depending on your needs, you may want to consider staying in a fully furnished apartment for the same price or less. Cook your own meals and save your money for the putas. Here's a link to very reasonable apartments right in the heart of the action, the Recolecta area. Around $40 a night. Hotels will run you $120 a night.

(www.alojargentina.com.ar/apartmentsRECOLETA.html)

129

THE GAME PLAN :

Instead of a full-blown brothel or terma scene like in Rio, in Buenos Aires it's more like just going out to regular nightclubs, called **Boliches**. Here, to pull a girl out requires not much more than buying a mandatory expensive drink or two, negotiating your price, and then going back to your place for a 2 hour date. If you're American, don't expect the oh my God rock star treatment you get elsewhere in the world. You are visiting one of the wealthiest South American cities, so your money doesn't impress them as much.

The main target rich environment is called Recolecta, near the Recolecta cemetery. Definitely stay in this area if you can. This hot trendy area has parks, fancy open-air cafes and restaurants, museums, high-level shopping malls, gourmet restaurants, five stars hotels, and a cinema theater complex. Cost for a date ranges from $60-120. Some of the prettiest women in this sport you'll ever find. Blonde classy European style. Pay for dates when you're done, not before.

The main clubs to hit are **Madahos, Black, Hooks, Shampoo, Playwoman, and Cocodrillo**. These are very high-class dance clubs, with the occasional strip club atmosphere thrown in. Black has the hottest girls usually. *Caution #1*, you can drop a lot of money clubbing long before you find the one you want. The cover charges are high, $ 8-10, and the girls work you hard for drinks. Make sure you have a good feel of a club before going in. Ask around, look who's going in and out, etc. *Caution#2*, when you go in, *stand at the bar*. Otherwise, the second you sit down, girls whom you may not want will plop their asses down and work you for a $10-20 drink. Stand at the bar, take your time, narrow in on a hot chica who shows a real interest in you. Work her, own her, and then rent her. Who's yo daddy?

At the more popular clubs, you're required to purchase for your girl an exit drink or two for the club fee. Pricing can be steep, at Hooks for example, the men's drink is $12 pesos, $24 pesos for the woman. Find out in advance chic drink prices and exit fees, don't get taken. In some places, the girl won't even talk to you or *about her price* until you have bought her a drink first. This can be an expensive route if she follows up with a huge requested price. Try to find a girl who will talk and give you the scoop without being required to buy drinks first. Look for the part time girls, and skip the pros. As far as pricing, there's huge variation. They of course will go for the jugular and try for $150-$200 US dollars. You, of course, will only discuss money in pesos. "this ain't the United States, cuantos pesos, senorita?" The hottest ones will cost you $100 US, others from $50 +.

What makes BA unique is the unbelievable high quality of the escort women. There are hundreds of girls in the links we provide you below who are 9's and perhaps 10's. Don't drop a lot in the clubs settling for a girl if you can do much better for about the same price using an escort service. Try to go to as many clubs as you can until you find the latest trendy place that has a lot of new girls on the scene. The pricing will be half of the established clubs. Locals are very much an option in this city. If you're staying here for a little while, a good technique is going to the top places, pick out the hottest one, buy her a drink and get her phone number. Go out the next day for lunch. Daytime "nooners" are half price and you may get a part time girlfriend out of it. However, if she isn't smothering you when you first meet her, pick another.

The other choice is freelancer clubs, which eliminates the bar drinks and exit fees. Check out Newports and Affaires, located next to the corner of Junin and Vicente Lopez. The same non-strip club setup can be found on Suipacha Street next to Paraguay Street at the clubs Ness, and Cattos. Remember, negotiate in pesos.

DAYTIME CAFES :
Café' Excedra : at intersection of Pellegrini and Cordoba.
Café Orleans : on Cordoba at the corner of San Martin.
Estilo Nuevo Boliche : at Figueroa Alcorta and La Pampa.

BOITES :
(www.blackbuenosaires.com/home.htm)   (Black)
(www.madahos.com/home.html)
(www.trampitas.com/night.html)

ESCORT SITES
(www.area-vip.com)
(www.sensualbaires.com)
(www.trampitas.com/escortsvip22.htm)
(www.platynum.com.ar)

VACATION STUFF :
Argentina is an 11-hour flight from the US, so far away that you really don't need a cover story. Take the red eye flights and wake up in the morning hitting the ground running.

GOLF COURSES :

The best golf courses to play in the BA area would be the **Jockey Club** in San Isidro (combine a visit to the San Isidro town), the **Buenos Aires Golf Club**, the **Olivos Golf Club** further north and either **Pilar Golf Club** or **Martindale C.C.** in the Pilar area (35 miles north). These are the 5 top golf courses in the country. Even though they are private, they are open to public one day in the week. Usually Wednesdays or Thursdays. Don't expect to play there on weekends if a member does not accompany you. Fees are amazingly low and may vary from USD $8-15.

(www.aag.org.ar)

OCEAN FISHING :

There are more than 3500 KM of coasts over the Atlantic Ocean. Plentiful rivers such as the Paraná, Uruguay, Salado, De la Plata, Pilcomayo, Bermejo, Colorado, and Negro, among others. Endless lakes, rivers, and mountain streams. We normally prefer the quickie deep-sea marlin fishing escapades, which don't seem available here. However, check out here for what's available.

(www.argentinaturistica.com/2pesca.htm)

CASINOS :

Casino Buenos Aires is located on a Mississippi style boat and offers black jack, roulette, poker and slot machines. The minimum age is 18 years and dress is smart-casual. Located in Puerto Madero, Buenos Aires, Argentina and is open daily 24 hours. The casino features 644 slots and ninety-five table games.

Address:
Elvira Rawson de Dellephiane s/n Darsena Sur, Puerto Madero, BA
Telephone
+54 11 4363-3100 General Information
Slot Machines - Total Slots - 644 machines
Table Games - 95 total
American Roulette- 1 table- 25 to 300 bets
Blackjack- 3 tables- 100 to 10000 bets
Punto Banco- 1 table- 100 to 10000 be

Madrid, Spain

About :

The capital city and epicenter of everything Spanish, **Madrid** is a city that never sleeps. Regular sightseeing is passé in Madrid if you are not an avid art lover. They showcase some of the best European art in their hosts of museums. But, more than that, Madrid is a party city, a place with a passionate nightlife where no one seems to sleep before dawn. In fact, many people consider Madrid not one but two cities, one in day and another in the night and perhaps you will have enough time to enjoy both. Don't forget to savor the world famous Spanish delicacies in some of the finest restaurants in Europe.

Madrid is a city of captivating back streets, beautiful parks, atmospheric cafés and lively nightlife. Begin your explorations in the old part of the city - the area between Paseo del Prado and Palacio Real. Stroll through the Puerta del Sol - the old city gate - to the impressive Plaza Mayor, the real heart of Madrid. The surrounding streets play host to a lively mix of restaurants, cafés and bars. Don't miss the **Museo del Prado** - one of the world's greatest art galleries. It features some of the best Spanish, Flemish and Italian art of the 15th to 19th centuries with Goya, Velazquez and El Greco well represented. Check out the Museo de la Escultura Abstracta for a good collection of abstracts by Miro and Chillida and the Centro de Arte Reina Sofia for an excellent collection of 20th century art, which includes Picasso's Guernica.

If you plan on doing any traveling, some of the most exclusive tourist beaches in the world are straight east, the islands in the Mediterranean Sea off Spain's Eastern shore. The five islands are **Mallorca, Menorca, Ibiza, Formentera** and **Carbrera**. Due to their climate, beaches and tourist installations, they are some of the most prestigious and attractive places to "get away from it all" in the entire Mediterranean.

South of here is the Canary Islands, volcanic in origin, are situated over 1,000 kilometers from the Iberian Peninsula, off the coast of North Africa. They have an exceptional year-round climate with superb beaches where you can enjoy the sun, sea and beaches at any time of the year. Popular resorts include the town of Puerto de la Cruz, in the south of Tenerife and Puerto Del Carmen in Lanzarote. The spectacular, rolling sand dunes of Maspalomas in Gran Canaria are a must see for any beach lover. For your Spain vacation, we recommend two cities; first visit Madrid, and then fly to Malaga, a beautiful fishing town on the southwest Mediterranean water. Keep in mind, some of the most famous islands and resort areas are an hour east of you. (see above).

CLIMATE :

The best time for travel to Madrid is from June to September, Madrid has extreme summer temperatures (100+), while winter months are below freezing and bitter, with February being the coldest. It stays in the 80's thru most of October.

ENTRY REQUIREMENTS :

A valid passport is required for entry. Barajas International Airport is situated at a distance of 13 km northeast of the city center and connected to almost all the major destinations in Europe and North America. Regular buses would shuttle you to the city center from the airport.

MONEY MATTERS :

The currency in Spain is the peseta (pta). Coins are available in values of 1, 5, 10, 25, 50, 100, 200, 500 ptas. The one pta. coin, worth less than 1 US cent, comes in three sizes. While any of the others (5, 25, 50 and 200ptas) come in two sizes. This can be rather confusing, particularly as many vending machines only accept the older (larger) version of the coins. Notes come in denominations of 1000, 2000, 5000, 10 000 ptas; these are colored green, red, purple and blue respectively.

Exchange :

There should be no problem finding a place to change money in Madrid, in almost all banks, 'cajas' or in the many exchange houses in the tourist areas, which have the advantage of longer opening hours (some are open 24 hours a day). Credit cards are widely accepted in Madrid, except in tapas bars, cheap restaurants and low-budget hotels. VISA is the most widely accepted card, but AMEX and Master Card (Access) are also accepted.

American Express
Plaza de las Cortés, 2
Tel: 91/322-5500

For today's exchange rate, go to here:
(http://www.oanda.com)

RECOMMENDED RESTAURANTS :

Since this info can change weekly, we can't recommend enough the "**Zagat Survey**." Pick up their travel book, or signup online. Worldwide reviews, menus, and pricing. **(www.zagat.com)**

Hotels :

There are hotels everywhere downtown, ranges from $ 50 - 300. Holiday has 4 locations, including this spot at 55 Euro including breakfast.

Plaza Carlos Trias Bertran,
4 MADRID, 28020 SPAIN 34-91-4568000
Downtown: MADRID 3.5 KM/ 2.17 MI
Holiday Inn   (**www.holidayinns.com**)

All major chains are represented there. Here's the national websites, as well as a Madrid hotel directory.

Hyatt   (**www.hyatt.com**)
Marriott   (**www.marriott.com**)
Radisson   (**www.radisson.com**)
Wyndham   (**www.wyndham.com**)
Madrid   (**www.madridshotels.com**)

The Game Plan :

Brothels
In Madrid, there is a great setup for getting the coochie in a place called **Flowers Park**. You stroll into the main bar area and discover wall to wall hotties, some 60-75 girls of all sizes, shapes, and colors, mainly from Eastern Europe and South America. Located next door for your shopping convenience is a short time hotel. Pricing for your pending date..girls ask for 100 euros, offer 60-70 Euro. This will get you 30 minutes, or for the heavy hitter upgrade, 200 Euro gets you one hour in an upgraded room with a Jacuzzi and champagne.

Flowers Park is situated next to the Las Matas train station, and from the Principe Pio train station in Madrid, it'll take you around 20-30 minutes to get here from downtown. If driving, look for Salida 28 off of the A-6. The caliber of women is absolutely top notch, and the service is the same. Certainly gold plated prices, but in Europe this is considered reasonable.

For your next stop, check out **Sana Azul**, found next to the Gran Via train stop in Madrid. There are also a lot of girls strolling around looking for dates near the Plaza Puerto del Sol in town, as well as the same Gran Via train stop.

135

Malaga

Outside of Madrid, for more action, head on down to the Costa del Sol of southern Spain. Set up your new home in the waterfront town of Malaga, where you'll be traveling to clubs in the town of Torremolino. Stop #1 is very well known, about a 15 Euro cab ride, located west off of M-340 at salida 214. **Estark 92** features an even better setup than Flowers Park in Madrid, with a bar full of 50 outrageous looking South American girls and a hotel *right above the bar*. Dates are much cheaper here, at the rate of 50-70 Euro for 30 minutes. No cover charge, beers are 6 euro. These are some experienced and hot women, they come complete with sex toys, and will wear naughty outfits if you want. The club, as an added bonus, switches the girls who work at the club every two weeks with new girls, which eliminates the occasional hassling from previous girls who suddenly think they're your girlfriend. Geez, pay them once for sex and they think they own you. What is this, America?

While in Malaga, the other big brothel to hit is called the **Scandalo Club** on the Guadalorce industrial estate. The owner actually has 5 locations spread around Spain. Same setup as **Estark 92** , with around 50 great looking South American and E. Europe girls. Pricing again is 70 Euro ½ hour, 120 Euro for a full hour date. Before entering Scandalo, stroll around the streets for a bit. There are dozens of young Nigerian sistas walking the pavements. It seems they've been told there is a sword swallowing competition to be held, and they would love to practice their craft on you, for about 10-20 Euro.

The fanciest place in Malaga is called **Club le Cocdor**, found a few kilometers from Torremolinas. The setup is quite impressive, it's a huge exquisite Mediterranean Estate with a hotel room feel, complete with whirlpool. Cover charge here is $13 Euro, which includes a drink. The girls are a large international assortment and are lounging about in high back chairs. Each girl is just dying to hear all about your job at McDonald's in Detroit, in fact they'll all sleep with you for 120 Euro while you're telling this fascinating life story. Make sure you speak in English, because no one else here does, and don't forget to staple a Benjamin to your forehead. Be forewarned, the girl drinks they try and force on you here are $25-30 bucks, politely decline.

Prostitution is 100% legal in Spain, but pimps are illegal.
Great minds at work here.

136

Nightclubs

For local nightlife, Madrid offers a diverse choice of flamenco, salsa, jazz, rock, World Music and cantautores – Spanish singer-songwriters. Visit **The Café de la Palma**, **Calle la Palma 62**, for cantautores, as well as flamenco and Cuban music acts. Latino music lovers flock to **La Negra Tomasa,** Calle Cádiz 9, for live music nightly from 2100. Moby Dick, Avenida de Brasil 5, in the Castellana district, plays live pop and rock on weekdays and hosts DJs (reggae and rap) at weekends. The crowd is made up of both locals and touristas. At **Café Populart**, Calle Huertas 22, you get a mix of everything, from live jazz to swing, salsa, blues, gospel, African and reggae. There are two shows nightly, at 2300 and 0030. The **Irish Rover** pub, Avenida de Brasil 7, imports Irish, folk and country music. International acts play regularly at the **Café Central**, Plaza del Angel 10, Madrid's top jazz venue. Pop stars and the best salsa bands perform at **La Riviera**, Paseo Bajo de la Virgen del Puerto.

(www.gomadrid.com/madrid-maps.html)

CASINOS :

All told there are 32 Casinos in Spain, we're list the main casinos in Madrid and Malaga, as they're the best cities women.

Casino Gran Madrid is in Madrid, Madrid, Comunidad de, Spain and is open 4pm-5am. The 110,000 square foot casino features 174 slots and twenty table games. The property has one restaurant.
The website is **(**www.casinogranmadrid.es**)**
Autovia A6 (Madrid-La-Coruna) KM.29 Torrelodones
Madrid, Madrid, Comunidad de 28250
Telephones +34 902 303 500 General Information
Total Slots - 170 Slot Machines
Table Games - 20 total
American Roulette- 10 tables- ESP 500 to ESP 10,000 bets
Baccart, Baccarat -Chemin de Fer,
Blackjack- 10 tables- ESP 1,000/2,000 to ESP 50,000/100,000 bets
Stud Poker, Omaha Poker and Texas Hold'em Poker.
Features
Bar (4 Gran Casino Bars)
Dress Code (Jacket, except in summer)
Entrance Fee (ESP 500)
ID/Passport Required
Language Spoken (Spanish)

137

Casino Marbella is in Malaga, Andalucia, Spain and is open 8pm-4am weekdays, 8pm-5am weekends. The 12,912 square foot casino features thirty-two slots and twenty-three table games, and a hotel with 416 rooms. The website is **(www.casinomarbella.com)**

Total Slots - 32 machines
Table Games - 23 total
Blackjack- 10 tables- ESP 1,000 to ESP 100,000 bets
Caribbean Stud Poker-2 tables-ESP1,000 -ESP 25,000 bets
Electronic Horse Racing- 1 table- ESP 100 to ESP 600 bets
English Roulette- 6 tables- ESP 500 to ESP 20,000 bets
French Roulette- 3 tables- ESP 500 to ESP 15,000 bets
Punto Banco- 1 table- ESP 2,000 to ESP 100,000 bets
Features
Beach (Beach Club)
Entrance Fee (ESP 500)
Gym
ID/Passport Required
Language Spoken (Spanish)

VACATION STUFF :
And now for the cover story for the old lady.

RUNNING WITH THE BULLS :
Every year from July 7th-14th thousands pack into Pamplona to start Spain's most famous bull-running fiesta to honor Navarre capital's patron saint, San Fermin. Spain stages more than 3,000 fiestas (festivals) each year but the 7 days of bull running are the favorite in terms of spectacle and excitement.

After the daybreak of July 7th, runners gather at the bottom of Santo Domingo, which is the starting line. They crowd together and sing to the image of San Fermin, which is placed in a niche on a wall. The song goes: "A San Fermín pedimos, por ser nuestro patrón, nos guíe en el encierro dándonos su bendición" ("We ask San Fermín, as our Patron, to guide us through the Bull Run and give us his blessing.")Then, as a rocket goes off, a number of fighting bulls are let out onto the streets. A second rocket is then let off to make sure everyone knows the bulls are loose in the street. The bulls run along the narrow street 825 meters (half a mile) to a bullring. The runners dash along in front of the bulls, aiming to feel the breath of the bull on their backs, getting as close as possible - all whilst trying to avoid getting gored by their sharp horns. The supposed way to do this is to start off slowly when the bulls are quite a distance behind. Then as they get nearer start running like hell! You can then go near them for a short time, as near as you are prepared to risk it, and then quickly get out of the way. Runners look for a gap in the fence to slip through or jump over, or a space against the wall of the street. It's a lot like running in front of American housewives at an all-you-can-eat buffet.

When the bulls finally reach the end of the street, they go into pens and are kept until later that day they are killed in a bullfight. Every year a few drunks get gored by the bulls, it seems for some reason they forget that a 1500 pound animal that can run twice as fast as a human may present a challenge when he wants to pass you.

The technique we recommend is to view the action from above the streets, leaning out of a 2nd floor window. Below you on her knees should be a hot little Madrid Chica about to be gored by you. In honor of the bulls, sing some drunken gibberish songs during the action.

Bullfighting :
If you've never been to a bullfight, this is the world's headquarters for the infamous Bull Run sport. Enjoy the passion and intensity of a bullfight in Plaza de Toros Monumental de las Ventas, the world's largest bullring. Or head to the nearest brothel and enjoy the passion and intensity there.. drink heavily, and wear a pair of bullhorns for the finale.

Museums :
Alright, I know you're laughing, a museum list. Don't worry, so are we, and we're typing this bilge. Unfortunately, there's not a heck of a lot of titty bars and sports stuff to do in between lays in Madrid. So get yourself a cultured bimbo from the brothel and do a little touring. Maybe take some public exhibitionist photos of her while standing next to some Picassos.

Museo del Prado
Second most important art museum in Europe after the Louvre, however to the layman is remains unknown. If they want more attention, they should set up a display of Ibiza topless beaches, otherwise, quit your whining. Some 7,000 works hang on the walls of this museum, containing some of the masterpieces by Angelico, El Greco, José de Ribera, Rubens, and the Spanish master Velázquez.

Centro de Arte Reina Sofia
Packed with works of 20th century painters of Spain like Picasso, Miró, Dalí, and Gris, this modern art gallery of Madrid should be on essentials list. The best of the pack is Guernica of Picasso, an eloquent and massive black and white commentary on horrors of war.

Palacio Real (Royal Palace)

The construction of this 2000-room palace began in 1734 outfitted in barouque and rococo styles. Not all the rooms are open to the public viewing though the royal family is not staying in the palace anymore.

Thyssen Bornemisza Museum

This is the newest art museum in Madrid situated directly across the road from Prado. This is a unique museum that contains works of Ghirlandaio, Caravaggio, Tintoretto, Memling, Rembrandt, El Greco, Goya, Monet, Manet, Picasso, Hopper, Mondrian, de Kooning, Degas, Dürer, Velázquez, and Dalí.

Museo Lázaro Galdiano

Set up in a 19th century mansion by Senor Lázaro Galdiano the museum houses objects of decorative and fine arts. There are royal daggers and swords, pocket watches, medieval armour, Roman bronzes, and crystal and enamels from Limoges. Paintings by Velázquez, Goya, Bosch, El Greco, and Ribera can also be seen.

FESTIVALS AND EXHIBITIONS :

The entire city of Madrid goes crazy during carnivale in February/March, Fiesta de la Comunidad de Madrid in May, and Fiesta de San Isidro also in May. June and July are the months when the city celebrates most of the holidays and many establishments would be closed during this time.

GOLF COURSES :

Club de Campo Villa de Madrid

A par 72 with 27 holes. , Telephone: (91) 357-2132
2 km north of Madrid this course, Javier Arana, opened in 1984.
(www.clubvillademadrid.com)

Golf de la Moraleja

Holes: 18 , par 72…Metres: 5923
Telephone: (91) 650-0700
Designed by Nicklaus and located 8.5 km from Madrid on Burgos Road.

Real Automovil Club de Espana

Holes: 18 , Par: 72…..Telephone: (91) 616-2382
A Putnam design with 18 holes (nine with par 3s) on the banks of a small river.

Golf Herreria Golf Club
Holes: 18, Par 72.
Metres: 6050
Telephone: (91) 890-5111, Fax: (91) 890-7154
A side attraction to this course is the historical El Escorial built by King
Phillip II in the 16th century.
(www.herreria.com)

Real Club de la Puerta de Hierro
Holes: 36
Par: 72
Telephone: (91) 216-1745
This course, designed by Simpson and John Harris, is located on the
northern edge of Madrid.

DEEP SEA FISHING :

Yes, there is plenty of big game sport fishing east of Madrid a few hours
away. The Atlantic and Mediterranean shorelines are ideal, with most
marinas set up for a perfect day of open sea fishing. **Swordfish** fishing here
is most spectacular, it is immortalized in several feature films. From July to
September swordfish are found off the coasts of Almería, Granada and
Málaga, and in the Bay of Cádiz. There is also **tunny** fishing in the open
sea. The tunny swim so near the surface in the summer that they become
visible. The tunny fishing grounds are Barbate, Zahara or Conil in Cádiz,
and Isla Cristina in Huelva. On the Atlantic coast, expect to catch **mackerel,
big-toothed pampano, blue fish, sea bass** and **spotted bass, corvina,
gilthead, grouper** and some 150 types of **shark**. True enthusiasts will
compete for various trophies awarded by competitions organized throughout
the summer. Amateurs can also try their luck as well, inquire at your local
marina. You can also get in some whale watching down off the straits of
Gibraltar. If you can't make there, visit the Denny's all-you-can eat-buffets
when you return home.

The Bay and Straits of Gibraltar have a large population of Whales
and Dolphins. The Mysticeti are the family of whales here and they are the
largest, in some cases growing to 120ft long and weighing up to 190 tons -
particularly impressive when you consider that a Boeing B747 airliner
weighs 150 tons.

Imagine how many beers that is. Imagine how many beers you will
have to drink to even consider leaving Madrid's hot brothels and traveling
hundreds of miles for the hopes of seeing a friggin' whale.

141

CARACAS, VENEZUELA

ABOUT :

Venezuela is bounded by the Caribbean, Brazil, Colombia, and the Atlantic Ocean. Venezuela offers the tourist a great variety of landscapes – tropical beaches, enormous rivers, forests, jungle, waterfalls, great mountains, and arguably some of the most beautiful women in the world. Nestling in a long narrow valley, **Caracas**, the capital, is typical of the 'new Venezuela', despite being one of the oldest established cities in the country (founded in 1567). The area has numerous pristine beaches and resorts ranging from the comparatively luxurious to the unashamedly opulent, which stretch along the coastline.

One of the most popular destinations for water-based activities is the **Isla de Margarita**, which lies some 25 miles off the mainland, with access twice daily by ferry. This is a picture perfect Caribbean location and climate, with some 105 miles of white, sandy beach shoreline, and home to fabulous **swimming, surfing, snorkeling** and **diving enthusiasts**. The busy season is December 15th thru the end of January. The island is packed with Venezuelan Amazonians on vacation, looking to party and work on their tan. Venezuelans as a whole are some of the most intelligent and sophisticated of the South American women. You'll discover the country is more appropriate and enjoyable picking up a part-time girlfriend for your vacation than the purchased quickie. The language spoken here is Spanish.

If you're the adventurer type, we'd recommend you get your butt over to **Merida**. Venezuela is home to the **Andes Mountains**, as in 15,000 feet high. Merida is a regional tourist hub for serious trekkers, as well as home to a large local university full of stunning looking young women who love, but never get to meet Americans. To say you will be in high demand is an understatement. The Mérida region is also noted for its Hi Wire Cable Car, (teleferico), the world's longest and highest. It runs for 7.9 miles from Mérida to the top of Pico Espejo (15,629ft), and provides easy access to starting points for mountain treks. Another popular trekking destination is **Guyana**, home to the country's most famous natural attraction – Angel Falls, the world's highest waterfall (with an uninterrupted drop of 807m/2647ft, which is about 16 times the height of Niagara Falls).

CLIMATE:

The climate varies according to altitude. Lowland areas have a tropical climate. The dry season is from December to April and the rainy season from May to December. The best time to visit is between January and April.

ENTRY REQUIREMENTS :
Visa required if not entering the country by air. Passport is required and must be valid for at least six months (if entering with a visa) or for the duration of stay (if entering with a Tourist Entry Card). There's have been reports of people traveling from Isle of Margarita back to Venezuela and scammers trying to charge a $30 entry fee. There is no entry fee. There is however a $36 exit fee from the Isla.

MONEY MATTERS :

Currency : Bolívar (Bs) = 100 céntimos. Notes are in denominations of Bs50,000, 20,000, 10,000, 5000, 2000, 1000, 500, 100, 50, 20, 10 and 5. Coins are in denominations of Bs500, 100, 50, 25, 5, 2 and 1, and 50, 20, 10 and 5 céntimos. The import and export of local and foreign currency is unlimited. Pay for everything there in Bolivars, it goes a lot further.

Currency Exchange : Banks will change cheques and cash, and cambios will change cash only; as will hotels, although often at a less favorable rate.

Credit & debit cards: Visa, American Express and MasterCard.

For today's conversion price, go here:
(www.oanda.com)

RECOMMENDED RESTAURANTS :
Since this info can change weekly, we can't recommend enough the "**Zagat Survey.**" Pick up their travel book, or signup online. Worldwide reviews, menus, and pricing.

(www.zagat.com)

CRIME AND SCAMS :
There's a large black market for dollar to Bolivars conversion. If you have a local guide, inquire about the black market for currency changing. Although the dollar is trading at a fixed rate of 1600 Bolivars, on the black market it trades for 2100-2500. Do not consider this unless you are 100% confident with whom you are dealing with, as they can exchange your dollars for fake play money and you'd never know.

There are some taxi scams here similar to Russia where they set you up for dangerous situations, and the rate and/or route is a joke. Utilize the Black SUV taxis from the airport to your hotel. A fixed rate of $12.

143

HOTELS :

This is an upscale city with all the major hotels represented, most people stay at the Marriott or Hilton for location and convenience.

Hilton Caracas
Avenida Libertador-Sur 25,
Caracas, 1010-A
The 796-room Hilton Caracas is positioned in the heart of the financial and cultural districts of the city, next to the metro station and 25km to the international airport.
(www.hilton.com)

Jw Marriott Caracas
Av Venezuela Con Calle Mohedan
Caracas, Venezuela
866-667-9330
(www.marriott.com)

and for cheap rooms with girls waiting in the hotel bar...

Hotel Embassy
Av Las Acacias Sur
Urb. San Antonio - Sabana Grande
Caracas, Venezuela
(582) 782.78.21

On the Isle of Margarita, here's a list of hotels in the beach area.

Hotel Tanausu
Final Av. de La Atlántida,
Catia La Mar
Price: (US$24 - US$30)
Phone : 212-312-6518

Casatrudel:
$29 a night (min. 3 days), they offer charter fishing as well as quick access to clubs. Dan & Trudy O'Brien, Playa El Agua, Isla Margarita, Venezuela, E-Mail: obrien@casatrudel.com
TEL ++58-295-249-0558 **(www.casatrudel.com/ctenglish.htm)**

144

Hotel La Parada
Av. Principal de la Atlántida, Catia la Mar
Price: Bs.40.000 (US$29.00)
Phone: 212-351-2148

Hotel IL Prezzano
Av. Principal de Playa Grande, Catia la Mar.
Price: Bs. 37.000 (US$23.00)
Phone: 212-351-2626

Hotel Olé Caribe
Macuto, NEW - 5 star - English spoken
Price: US$120 + tax of 17% , reservas@hotelolecaribe.com
(www.hotelolecaribe.com/home.htm)
Phone: 0212-331-1133 (ext. 1010) Arelys Rivas

Best Western Puerto Viejo
Av. Principal de Puerto Viejo,Catia la Mar. Five star
Price: US$129.28 (incl. tax) 2 persons 1st or 2nd Floor
Phone: 212-352-4044

THE GAME PLAN :

Caracas resembles Buenos Aires in that the best technique may be the escorts, although the pricing is way cheaper here, around $40. There are hardcore brothels, as well as rent-a-ladies in hotel lobbies as well to be had, escort services galore, and local discos and malls.

Brothels

For you hardcore shoppers, head on down to the Chacaito Plaza, just a few blocks down from the Marriott. Look for local theater in the Sabana Grande area, it's the only one, next to the subway stop in Chacaito. Next door is an office building, the nameplate on the building says **Edificio Avalon**. There are some guards at the door. Stroll on in past them and go up to the second floor. This is a three-story brothel filled with chicas, and not the only one in the area.

Edificio Volta is the most known one, with others just a block away. These are in house full service location. Just walk in and they are all lined up in a row, pick your meal and dive in. The quality is naturally going to be lower than the strip clubs, but then again so is the price. *Take your time* and find yourself the diamond in the rough. Pricing starts at just $15.

145

Strip Clubs

For strip clubs there are a few favorite choices where they have rooms in the back. **Club Angelus**, located in the Altamira area in a shopping strip mall. It's an upscale in house strip club with 30 girls roaming around hopping in your lap. Lap dances are 10K, to take them in the back is 150K Bolivars. Also go **to El Saxo** in Sabana Grande. A good daytime places is **Club Noche de Ronda** (100K). Located in Chacaito, el Centro Commercial. This is in a mall, and it's somewhat difficult to describe the path, as it's disguised to hide its identity. Go downstairs in the mall and have someone point you the way. Pretend you're the Grand Pimp Daddy and someone stole yo' bitches and there's hell to pay. Closing time is midnight, and you don't want to be in this area at that time. Now, having told you all this, we prefer safety and convenience to seedy and mysterious.

Hotel Lounges

There is a much easier method to getting some classy looking women. For the pros and non-pros in bars/hotels, head to the area called Las Mercedes, Casanova Avenue in Sabana Grande. Girls will come up to you and try to get you to buy an exorbitant priced drink which you'll pass on, and you can either take her upstairs (after paying the club exit fee) and her negotiated fee, or just pay the exit fee and take her back to your hotel and settle up there. Some of the club names are **Onix, El Tiburon, the Rose,** and **Morrisons**. This is not a cheap route, $100 and up, but you can pick and chose as you please, and there are some you would mortgage the house for. As always, any cabbie or your hotel concierge will know the location of these.

The downtown Caracas Hilton has call girls roaming all over the hotel, appropriately dressed for a Hilton, but blatantly giving you the up and down *let's go* look. You can find them by the pool, the bar, or just hanging around the elevators in the lobby. The hotel really doesn't put up any effort to stop the transaction, but you may have to grease a palm or two to take her to your room without a healthy guest fee. Pricing for an hour is 60K-120K, depending on your ability of negotiating.

Escort Services

There is an amazing crop of hotties on the escort sites listed at the end of this chapter, and the pricing is quite reasonable considering the quality. Make sure you look at the Spanish version of the web sites, the pricing is a lot cheaper. The same girl advertised on the English site is 20% higher. Make it very clear in your phone call that the photo is actually her and a

146

recent one at that, and that if anyone else shows up you will say no. The girls advertising in the local paper are also an inexpensive route, from $30-55, but no photos here.

Discos

For local discos packed with semi-pros and locals, head to the Las Meredes area. Studio 54 is always hopping, you can try Alcatraz, also La Gartos, and for the hot young college girls, go to Club U. In Caracas, most of the clubs are located in somewhat seedy areas, make sure you watch your back and take cabs.

Locals

For local non-pro girls, or just full-blown eye candy, you have to visit Centro Sambil, also called the **Mall de Caracas**. This place is massive, it's the largest commercial and recreational center in South America. Chicas, chicas, and more chicas.

For beaches and sport fishing, there are two locations you should travel to. From Caracas, hop a quick flight to Barcelona on Aeropostal Air. It runs $125 roundtrip, then take a 15-minute cab to Puerto la Cruz. This is a beautiful Caribbean beach town, nestled amongst some 30 different islands. Mild temperatures, crystal clear water, beaches packed with gorgeous Venezuelan women. It's also a great spot for sport fishing. Stay at the popular Hotel Rasil, which has a hopping disco on the ground floor and is full of chicas, and there's no guest charge for your chicas. It's located one a road full of clubs to sample from.

Isla of Margarita

The other favorite stop is a two-hour ferry ride to **the Isle of Margarita**. Granted this is more of a tourist spot with tourist pricing, but it is one of the prettier places on earth, and the same can be said for the women on the island. For the women, head out to Playa El Agua to a place called **Woody's,** on Avenida 4 de Mayo. This is the strip club row, others to see here are **Goldfingers** (owned by a Canadian) also go to **Fat Boys** if it is still in business under that name. You can find it on the right hand side across the street from Goldfingers. There's a fair amount of expat Americans living down here doing offshore gambling businesses.

For local discos, the mainstay is **Senor Frogs**, which is the same setup as the one in Cancun. No cover, merengue all night, and a drunk fest until 6am. Plenty of pros stick out like a sore thumb.

Newspaper Escort Ads
El Universal (http.clasifacados.eluniveral.com) $30-55.

Escort Sites

(www.sexycaracas.com)

(www.jardinerotico.com)

(www.800chicas.com)

(www.cupos.com)
Remember, the prices are cheaper on the Spanish version website, quote that one when negotiating.

VACATION STUFF :
For the cover story, tell the old lady you'll flew to the Amazon Jungle to enhance your childhood rock collection.

GOLF COURSES :
Caracas has no public golf courses, the only way to play a round is to have the concierge at a five-star hotel make arrangements for you at a private club. Keep in mind that you must be a handicapped golfer with a membership card from your home club or golf association. Even then, prices are high, and you're usually limited to weekday play at non-peak hours. Screw the bastards, sleep with their daughters and then head to the Isle of Margarita. They have golf, great Big Game Sportfishing, and maybe some of their other daughters to bang as well.

On the Isle of Margarita is the brand new 5 Star **Hesperia Isla Casino and Beach Resort.** The course has 18 holes with a Par 70, Pro-shop and bar. The hotel has a total of 312 spacious deluxe rooms.

CASINOS :
On the Isle of Margarita is the brand new 5 Star **Hesperia Isla Casino and Beach Resort.** It is located just 30 minutes from the airport and offers shuttle transport into the town of Porlamar. This is a complete island resort, with activities including Windsurfing, Scuba diving, Sailing, Jet-skiing, Water-skiing, and a Gym on site.

OCEAN FISHING :
Venezuela is one of the most frequented destinations for Big Game Sport Fishing in the world. This activity may be practiced all through the year, and it represents a great challenge for every fishing aficionado. Expect an

148

abundance of species such as **Blue Marlin, White Marlin, Sail Fish, Wahoo, Tuna, Barracuda**, making this area a true fisherman's paradise. Fishing zones are only a 30 minutes off shore cruising at normal speed.

"El Placer" (the pleasure) is a sport fishing paradise. This superb fishing area is approximately 40 miles off the Venezuelan coast. Here the underwater formations give shelter to the little fish, which attract the bigger fish, which in turn attract the really big trophy fish. Here's a highly recommended crew with a great track record.
$ 550+ for a day. +58 414 2877554

(**www.venezuela-fishing**)
Yachts@explorepartners.com

If you're planning fishing from Caracas, stay at **the Hotel Ole Caribe**. This brand new 5-star hotel is convenient to Caracas International Airport and Caraballeda Marina, where your fishing boat is waiting for you. Located in the best and most privileged area of Macuto, in front of the Caribbean Sea, at 15 min. from the International Airport of Maiquetía and at 40 min. from Caracas. $120 for 2 a night.

Puerto Viejo Airport Inn (Best Western Property for $100-120)
Av. Ppal, Catia La Mar, Venezuela
Toll free reservations: 0800 100 2244
(http://bestwestern.worldexecutive.com/index.shtml)

The fishing from the Isle of Margarita is just 18 miles offshore. Average daily charter rate is around $ 500 for 5 people. The best seasons for fishing are Jan-early April. Margarita is also a "DUTY FREE ZONE" so some things with traditionally high taxes are very low priced. In other words, expect to get bloody shitfaced for pennies. For example, a case of 36 Polar beers is $ 3… a 750 ml. bottle of Cacique rum costs $2. Together with a 2 liter bottle of Coke at under 60 cents, ice for 75 cents, and you could have a quite a party for $10. A $ 20 party could put you in black out zone. Add in a $ 40 escort or three and you have a complete family pack evening for a song. Venezuela lays claim to some of the best freshwater fishing in the world. **Peacock bass, piranha, tarpon, giant catfish, payara, aymara** to name a few. Payara are big fanged monster looking predators that congregate in swirling rushing currents below falls and rapids in South America's tropical, fast water rivers. Using their great hunting speed and power, payara strike a bait with amazing force and immediately take-off on peeling, breathtaking runs punctuated by wild, acrobatic leaps. If you want some World Class fishing experiences, you'll find them here in Venezuela.

149

Here's a few links with all the info to chase these freshwater beasts on a fishing tour of the Amazon jungle.

(**www.acuteangling.com/index.htm**)   (**www.payara-fishing.com**)

MOUNTAIN CLIMBING :

Most serious trekkers head up to the **Venezuelan Andes**, which stretches some 250 miles from Táchira on the Colombian border northeastwards. It offers everything from snow-capped peaks to lush rainforests. The most popular area for mountain trekking and rock climbing is the **Sierra Nevada de Mérida**, where several of the country's highest peaks (such as the Pico Bolívar or the Pico Humboldt) and the magnificent Parque Nacional Sierra Nevada are located. Experienced guides, who are strongly recommended for mountaineering, and equipment can be hired in Mérida, the regional tourist hub.

Other popular trekking destinations in the area include Los Nevados, (reached via an easy trek along a beautiful mountain track); Pico El Aguila (accessible from Valera, which can be reached on a bus ride from Mérida along Venezuela's highest road); and the Sierra de la Culata (particularly known for its desert-like landscapes). The Mérida region is also noted for its cable car (teleferico), the world's longest and highest, which runs for 12.6km (7.9 miles) from Mérida to the top of Pico Espejo (4765m/15,629ft), and provides easy access to starting points for mountain treks. Another popular trekking destination is Guyana, in the southeast, a region dotted with Venezuela's characteristic tepuis (flat-topped mountains with vertical flanks) and home to the country's most famous natural attraction – Angel Falls (called Salto Angel in Spanish), the world's highest waterfall (with an uninterrupted drop of 807m/2647ft, which is about 16 times the height of Niagara Falls). Access to the falls is fairly difficult (there is no road link) and involves a flight to Canaima (the main tourist base, some 50km/31.5 miles northwest of the falls), followed by either another scenic flight in a light aircraft, or a motorized canoe trip to the foot of Angel Falls (which only operates from June to November, the rainy season, and takes approximately two days).

Local Newspapers :
(www.venezuelapost.com)
(www.eud.com)
(www.el-nacional.com)

Cali, Columbia

About :

Located on the northwest tip of South America, between Venezuela, Brazil, and Panama, Columbia is the fourth-largest country in South America, and the only one with coasts on both the Pacific and Caribbean. The country is filled with dramatically beautiful rainforests, mountains and beaches, wild and exotic plants, trees, animals, and dark haired tight bootie Calenas. The official language is Spanish.

Cali has a population of 2.3 million, situated in southwestern Colombia on the Cali River. The city was established in 1536 by Sebastian de Benalcazar, and is a major industrial and commercial centre. The city is famous for its gorgeous women and delicious food, like pandebono, empanada and exotic fruits like chontaduro and borojó. It is well known throughout Colombia and many parts of South America as a major center of salsa dancing. Located 3° north of the Equator, the weather in Cali is very tropical, with hot, sunny days punctuated by intense storms.

If it is beaches and warm Caribbean waters you are after, not far from Cartagena, home to crystal clear waters and magnificent reefs. There is abundant marine life, perfect for snorkeling and scuba diving alike. The busiest season is Dec-Feb, when Columbians take their vacations. Hotels can fill up so plan ahead. Also, make sure you don't go on one of Cali's 3-day weekend events. Everyone leaves town.

Climate :

Both mountainous and spotted with the rainforest, the temperature varies very little year round, since it's so close to the equator. Rainfall is moderate and the mean annual temperature varies between 19°C and 24°C, depending on the elevation.

Entry Requirements :

U.S. Passport must be valid 3 months beyond intended stay, tickets and Documents for return or onward travel. No visa is required for your stay up to three months. Departure tax is $23. For business travel, you need to get a visa and contact the embassy.

Here's the url: (**www.traveldocs.com/co/embassy.htm**)

U.S. visa requirements (**http://usembassy.state.gov/colombia/**)
or Colombian visa information that is available through any of the Colombian consulates around the US and the world.
(**www.colombiaemb.org/consulados_visas.htm**)

AIRLINES :

Colombia's national airline is Avianca (AV). British Airways and Avianca each operate flights, Monday to Saturday, to Bogotá. During the summer season, British Airways only operate flights Wednesday, Friday and Sunday. Other airlines flying to Colombia include American Airlines, Air France, Continental Airlines and Iberia. However, as with Avianca, some may not fly directly there but with other airlines as part of a Code Share agreement.

Most visitors fly to Colombia's major international airport in Bogotá; the other international airports include Cartagena and San Andrés. Approximate flight times: From London to Bogotá is 11 hours 45 minutes, from Los Angeles is 10 hours 30 minutes, from New York is 6 hours 30 minutes. Cali (CLO) is 10 miles from the city.

All air tickets purchased in Colombia for destinations outside the country are liable to a total tax of 15 per cent on one-way tickets and 7.5 per cent on return tickets.

RECOMMENDED RESTAURANTS :

Since this info can change weekly, we can't recommend enough the "**Zagat Survey**." Pick up their travel book, or signup online. Worldwide reviews, menus, and pricing.

(www.zagat.com)

TIPPING :

Taxi drivers expect 10 per cent tips. Porters at airports and hotels are usually given c. pesos500 per item. Restaurants and bars usually add a 10 per cent service charge to the bill or suggest a 10 per cent tip. Maids and clerks in hotels are also tipped.

CRIME :

The facts are important to remember, Cali, maintains the second highest murder rate in Latin America, it is the home to one of the most powerful drug trafficking rings in Colombia and remains rife with narcotics-related violence. It is also in a region where guerrilla and right-wing paramilitary forces have become increasingly active in recent years. Pickpockets and purse-snatchers prowl downtown and armed assaults on both pedestrians and vehicles pose a high threat at night.

Security in Cali is an everyday common sight. Police and security are ever present. Armed security guards are at offices, malls, restaurants, and retail stores. Do not be put off by this, it's a natural occurrence in Cali.

Armed police with machine guns searching cars for drugs is common.

Ironically, people in Columbia think of America as the most violent place in the world. Use your head, do not travel out of the city, if you venture out in the countryside and you may not return. It is safe walking during the day. The city itself is very modern, enjoys capitalist endeavors, and has beautiful malls to visit. Do not accept rides from strangers, including girls. They can be in cahoots with the cabbie. You choose all cabs during interactions not her. At night, use taxis exclusively.

Make sure when you're chatting up a girl you ask her if she has a boyfriend. You may be hitting on some drug lord's girl. Also, never take open drinks from strangers. They have some mind eraser, as in total mind eraser drug they put in your drink where you'll forget everything. Don't make yourself an obvious drunk gringo, blend in. Try to limit your trips to a week or else. If you stay a month, the bad guys may spot your daily pattern and you're a sitting duck. Stay in the areas we recommend, your whole trip will be in a few block radius, so you should be fine.

Only get in the yellow marked taxis.

MONEY MATTERS :
Currency: Peso (**$**), around 2800 to the dollar. ATM's often give better exchange rate than the banks, but there's a daily limit.

For today's exchange rate, go to here:

(http://www.oanda.com)

HOTELS :
Mucho Hotel listings

(www.cotelco.org/hoteles_afiliados/valle_cauca.htm)

Hotel Casa del Portal
Avenida Sexta A.,(4 blocks from Chippi Chappe mall)
Avenida 8 Norte 10 - 104 -
Email: hotelportal@colnet.com.co
Phone: (57+2) 661 6214 -

Hotel Don Jaime
Avenida 6 N # 15-25
092.6672828 -6614598
mailto:hoteldonjaime@telesat.com.co
Middle of the action, good one.

Hostal San Fernando
Calle 3, 27-87
Phone: +57 (2) 556-4818
Prices: $25 US and up
(**www.calihotel.com**)
calihotel@hotmail.com
Located in a safe residential area. Very secure, good ac, hot water, Jacuzzi, Tennis, pool. Taxi service $7 an hour, $18 to airport. English speaking dudes. Cash Only, no CC, 011 (572) 556 4818.

Hotel Intercontinental Cali
Avenida Colombia No. 2-72
PO Box 7457
CALI, COLOMBIA
Tel: 0057-2-8823225
Email: cali@interconti.com
By far the classiest hotel in the area, however a large guest visitor charge.

Hotel Casa del Alférez
(Avenida 9N 9-24 Juanambú, phone 661 8111).

THE GAME PLAN :
Columbia is one of the poorest stops on our recommended World Sex Tour. Average monthly income here is $500, which includes doctors. For vacation prices, you can't beat it. Meals from $3, gourmet is $10. Hotels for $30, 3 bedroom apartments for $60 with balconies. As a whole, Cali is not renowned for pay for play. However, for sexy part time girlfriends and ease of meeting young ones and getting dates, it may be one of the best. There's not a hell of a lot to do here, since you have to be careful of the potential drug lord situation. Best plan is to spend several days here, then visit Cartagena (see our chapter on it). Cartagena is a beach town and has more sport activity possibilities. Cartagena is more pay for play, Cali is more for girlfriends. If you want to marry and bring one back, this is the best city in the world. They're very open to dating, and definitely not sharks.

Avenida Sexta is the center for restaurants, shopping, clubs and discoteca in Cali. Here you'll find some of the sweetest and sexiest girls in the world, similar to Brazil. It is very easy to get dates with most girls, but they have a lot of pride, so treat them with respect. Screw over one and the word will spread real fast.

The two main malls in town are **ChipeChapi** and **Uni Centro**. Girls love to shop and meet guys there. They have these "beer stands" where they hang out and wait for you. Particularly at nighttime you will find the local friendly chicas. Even the ones with dates will stare down any gringo. Small note, don't dress like a slob Gringo. (No tennis shoes or t-shirts). According to the girls there, a man's shoes are important. Skip the air Nikes, backwards caps, and tank tops.

The "**Reggae and Pop**" is the most popular stand in both malls, packed most any night. (The malls have fast Internet access available). The sights in here are extraordinary. If you're on a long vacation, you'll want to be able to give your phone # out to arrange dates. You can buy a cell phone in the ChipeChapi mall at the phone stores. Bell South has one there for example. They sell pre-paid calling cards as well. Phones are around $50, calls are 1000p a minute.

But almost all of us are on a short vacation, so a sure thing is the next best thing. For the paid dates, there are "houses" on practically every block, with 5-20 girls inside dying to meet you. These are for the quickies only, the girls don't leave. The layout on the inside is nothing to be desired, but you'll love the approach. Like a beauty pageant, in the casas the girls come out and parade by you, shake your hand, and then stand in line or leave the room. Then the mamasan asks you to pick one you want. Bring a pen and paper, it gets hard to choose sometimes if they leave the room. The local paper is El Pais, for the addresses and # of the houses, check under the category Especeialistas. There's 80+ houses listed in Cali. Remember, *don't go on a holiday weekend,* the girls and their families leave town for Cartagena or elsewhere.

Kaliente
Calle 25 Norte No 2 Bis - 47 B. San Vicente,
(2) 653-6832. House live-in situations for the girls, and a lot of them are scorching hot. Some of the best in all of Cali, and the prices are *sky high* compared to other locations. Dates on the premises in the back rooms are 100,000k for an hour, 180K for 3 hours.

Floras Fresca
Calle 20N, No. 4N-16, very well known strip club with some wild acts and dances, a lot more expensive but worth going at least once. Use this place for entertainment only. Expect to see 8's and 9's doing full-blown lesbian acts, 69, strap on humping..incredible.

Faraon and Faraon del Norte
(located next-door to each other)
Calle 2 #23-48
About 4 blocks past the Torre de Cali tower, (tallest building in Cali).
Faron has a 10K entry fee, del norte is 15K .

Both have the same prices for girls:
20 minutes for 30k pesos ($11)
30 minutes for 40k pesos ($14)
60 minutes for 50k pesos ($18)

> One $11 session will destroy any excitement you have for
> lap dances at titty bars back home.

Club Social Dinas
(Cra. 50 No. 10-31, tele- 553 5007)
20 minutes for $30k
30 minutes for $40k
60 minutes for $50k

Cambiadero De Aceite
(Calle 5 B3BIS No. 38-60, tele- 514 0355).
45k for 60 minutes

Venu's Club
Carrera 66 No.9-61, 330-1104

2 Norte #24N105
$27Kpesos for 30 minutes

2 Norte #23n23
30 minutes for $40k
60 minutes for $50k

El Eden
Calle 5, No. 63A-19,
551-1775

Hero's Club
Cra. 30 A N0. 7-73
557-4391

LOCAL DISCOS :
La Casa de las Cervesas
Avenida 4 and Calle 20 Norte
Mysti-K:
2 blks east of Av. Sexta on 25th

If you venture on down to south Cali, there are a ton of hot looking locals since the Universities are located there. The pay for play situation isn't near as good, but you can stumble on a few things. The Cristal Club on Calle 13 #72-75 is one good place. Also, if you're in for a change, there is a nude billiard bar, in which for a $1 cover you can play pool with a hot little nude calena. The location is Carrera 28 at #6-37, near Roosevelt Blvd.

Latina Dating/Marriage Agencies
(www.tlcworldwide.com/tlc_site/photos.htm)
(www.southamericanladies.com)
(www.colombiansweethearts.com)
(www.allcolombiangirls.com)

VACATION STUFF :
And now for the cover story for the old lady.

GOLF COURSES :
Club Campestre de Cali is a large sports complex located in south of the city of Santiago of Cali, set against the Commercial Center Unicentro, diagonal to Holguines Trade Center. The most prestigious Universities surround it. Tennis, polo, futbol, squash and spinning, all here as well as the golf course.

(www.campestrecali.com)

DIVING AND SNORKELING :
Off the Cartagena coastline, Columbia's favorite spot to snorkel and diving is off the Islas del Rosario, about 18 miles offshore from Cartagena, and off the Isla Barú, the south peninsula.

CASINO :
Cali Gran Casino is in Cali, Valle del Cauca, Colombia and is open 24 hours. The casino features 180 slots and eight table games.
Address: Avenida Estacion, #5 N 60, Cali, Valle del Cauca
+57 (2) 6689218 General Information
Slot Machines : Total Slots - 180 machines
Table Games - 8 total Blackjack, Roulette.

Cabo San Lucas, Mexico

About :
Los Cabos ("The Capes") is situated at the southernmost tip of the Baja California Peninsula, with the Pacific Ocean on its western coast and the Sea of Cortez to the east. The resort town of **Cabo San Lucas**, named for the slender cape extending eastward from Baja's southernmost tip, has transformed from a tiny quaint fishing village into a breathtaking tourist hot spot during the last forty years. Here the crystal clear azure waters of the Sea of Cortez softly splash onto stunning white sandy beaches, home to glittering resorts, hotels, and condominiums. The marina is full of some 300 super yachts for sport fishing and touring.

Cabo San Lucas has held onto its old world style and feel, and other than the resort areas, remains virtually unsettled and third world, with a population of only 28,000. However, take a trip to the resort areas and you'll find an extravagant 5 star golf and fishing vacation paradise with no peers, in one of the most beautiful places in the world. Cabo San Lucas is world recognized as the Marlin Capital of the World, as more large billfish are caught here than any other location. Each October, Cabo is home to a $1 million dollar biggest marlin competition. Due to the close proximity to the US, this is one of the best Vacations we can recommend as far as a Weekend Warrior Sportsman goes. The spectacular golf courses overlooking the Gulf combined with a potential 1000lb marlin catch are unsurpassed. For the sex tourism, it's not cheap, but there are some real diamonds here, dark exotic hard bodies from Amazonia who will make your toes curl.

Climate :
Mean temperature of 80 degrees F. (28 C.) with an average of 340 sunny days per year.

Money Matters :
US dollars for everything here, and lots of 'em.

Entry Requirements :
From the US, a certified birth certificate and driver's license is sufficient, but bring the passport anyway just in case. Fee included in airfare in most cases, no fee to return.

AIRPORT TAXIS :

Cabo taxi businesses are owned and operated by the government, including the airport cabs, so they won't negotiate…not even for reefer. Airport vans cost $14 each way to your hotel, but they will stop at everyone else's hotel first. It's a long haul of about 30 miles, and with stops can easily take an hour. Who needs to start a vacation with hassles? Your best bet is to grab a bunch of guys and pool together for a cab. Around $80 total to the center of Cabo, a direct shot. They will stop at the liquor store, on the way during the first few miles.

HOTELS :

Nothing is cheap here on the peninsula, and the hotel you choose depends on your game plan. Rooms run around $100-200+ a night if you're close to the action. There are some dumps away from the action for a lot less. If you're here for golf, there are 5 star hotels home to their own courses that are about 15 minutes away from downtown and the action. The courses are gorgeous, and the room rates are ugly.

If you're here for fish, booze, and chicas, there are a few top-notch hotels right on the beach to choose from. Resort development growth is continuing northward up the coast. Recommended is the beachfront Hotel Melia San Lucas. It is centrally located, walking distance from all the titty bars, clubs and brothels, and just 100 yards from the best beach bar in town for daytime action. Also, the fishing marina is minutes away by cab.

Melia San Lucas has a spectacular view, overlooking the Lands Ends rock formation, a new open-air all-suites resort that features a large, majestic freeform swimming pool, health club and spa.

Address: Playa El Medano S/n, Cabo San Lucas 23410
Toll free Reservations: 1-800-745-2226
Email: info@melia-los-cabos.com
(www.melia-los-cabos.com)

Hilton Los Cabos Beach & Golf Resort, located between the two towns of San José del Cabo and Cabo San Lucas where extensive golf layouts weave in and around sheltered coves and grand sweeps of beach. Cabo Real is one of the finest developments on lower Baja. The ocean front course, was the site of the 1996 – 1999 PGA Senior Slam, designed by Robert Trent Jones Jr., and the El Dorado Golf Course, a Jack Nicklaus creation. This beautiful resort is on an 11.3 acre stretch of ocean front land, approximately 30 minutes driving distance from the airport , 15 minutes from San José del Cabo and 15 minutes from Cabo San Lucas. 1-800-Hiltons
(www.hiltonloscabos.com)

Sheraton Hacienda del Mar Resort and Spa
Corredor Turistico KM 10, Lote D, Cabo Del Sol Cabo San Lucas, Baja California Sur 23410 Mexico
Phone (52)(624) 14 58000

Located on a private beach surrounded by 28 acres of quiet, private gardens, home to a Nicklaus designed ocean-lined course. The old-world hacienda architecture of the resort's deluxe guest rooms, fountains, cafés and shops evokes the rich history of the Baja region. In addition to an array of first-class services and amenities, the Sheraton features a selection of fine restaurants, private swimming pools and beaches, and a state-of-the-art fitness center.
(www.starwood.com/sheraton/index.html)
information@sheratonhaciendadelmar.com

The Westin Regina Golf and Beach Resort
Carretera Tran peninsular KM 22.5 San Jose Del Cabo, Baja California Sur 23400 Mexico
Phone (52)(624) 142 9000 Fax (52)(624) 142 9050

At the tip of the Baja peninsula, Beach Resort boasts a dramatic location at Land's End, where the Sea of Cortés meets the Pacific Ocean. Luxurious ocean view rooms, plenty of outdoor activities, a private beach and seven pools help you take advantage of the year-round sunshine and are just a few of the reasons it was recently named to Condé Nast Traveler's 2002 Gold List. Hailed as 'one of the best golf resorts' by Condé Nast Traveler's 2001 Top Golf Resorts readers' survey, The Westin Regina Golf and Beach Resort enables you to fill your days with golf and sun and relaxation, and your nights binge drinking, bogus fish stories and hookers.
(www.starwood.com/westin/index.html)

For a complete listing of hotels, go here:
(www.loscabos-tourism.com/cabo/cabohot.htm)

RECOMMENDED RESTAURANTS :
Since this info can change weekly, we can't recommend enough the "Zagat Survey." Pick up their travel book, or signup online. Worldwide reviews, menus, and pricing.
(www.zagat.com)

CRIME AND SCAMS :

The town is tiny and safe to walk at night, cabs are everywhere. Ironically, the biggest scams are the hotels themselves. If drinking at the pool bar, pay cash. Try to avoid charging anything to the room. They pad it like nobody's business. Also, be prepared for the arguments at checkout. Everyone incurs bogus room bar charges, unmade phone calls, etc. When you check in, inform the staff you will not be charging anything to the room, or using the room bar. Put in writing on the receipt if you can.

The beach is filled with touts(vendors) selling you overpriced crap. They are relentless. For fun, if you see something you like, offer 20%, a lot will take it. The jewelry guys have "special goods" for sale under the hidden level of their traveling suitcase if you want.

THE GAME PLAN :

Big league pricing in Cabo, even though the supply and demand doesn't support the concept. At 3am, most of the girls foolishly hold to their high prices and go home empty handed, rather than scoring with some mild negotiation. It's either some code of honor, or more likely a lack of IQ, and muchas tequilas.

Most of the strip clubs have back rooms, expect $100 for BJ, $150-200 for full contact fun. Don't stand around posing or contemplating whether you should go for a girl you really like. If you see a great one, make your move. Remember, Cabo's marina is full of multimillion-dollar yachts owned by guys from California with getaway homes down here. What we've seen too many times is out of nowhere a guy walks in, signals the manager, and in 5 minutes leaves with 2 or 3 of the hottest ones. Take action quickly.

The smartest move is to negotiate in the early am hours for a hotel room experience. The girls will leave the club with you. In each club it can be hit or miss, you'll find 10-20 girls in each, with Rating 4-6, but there are a few hot to trot lookers in each place. The girls are really dark and bronze, the Cuban look. At first you'll think they're sistas until you hear them speak. None of them speak any English.

The clubs pop up and go quickly, so the names here may change, but all are in the same central area, walking distance from each other. Main clubs are **Twenty 20, Mermaids/Splash, Placers, Lord Black, El Toro, Bolero,** and **Amnesia**. No real high pressure except for the lady drinks, which run a bit more at $6-8, which the girls make $2 off of each.

All the clubs have a cover charge, but there are street touts everywhere who will escort you to the club for a free entrance (a buck or two tip) You will never have to worry about finding the clubs, every fifty yards some guy will be offering you a walking escort to one. Normally these guys piss you off, but in this case they are valuable guides *and* you skip paying the cover charge. Ask him where the brothels are instead of strip clubs (**El Toro** for example), because you'll never be able to find them without a guide.

The hottest looking girls currently in Cabo work above the club **Mermaids** at the club called **Splash**. We're not sure why they consider them 2 clubs, it's the same location, just 2 stories. Splash is the upstairs, Mermaids downstairs. Splash is an all nude strip club, private dances are $20 behind a hidden bed sheet. Nothing rated X. They have 2 for 1 dances every hour, they're done out of view and are quite erotic. This place is a lot of fun and offers great eye candy, without the stupid prices or hassles. Negotiate for an after hours hotel room rate if you can.

There are only two bonafide brothels in plain view in Cabo. El Toro is located 100 yards from **Cabo Wabo**. Just ask any street dude to walk you there. **The Nowhere Bar** is the other. Don't worry about the names, there are no signs on the doors, just ask someone. El Toro has two pools tables in the back, a rough crowd of girls, but enough sexy chicas to make it an interesting evening. Some hold out for $100, others have brains and will settle for $50. This is a fun little dive for drink, music, billiards, and hummers. After all, your girl is just one more fish story on one can verify.

Twenty /20
Lazaro Cardenas y Francisco Villa (next to McDonalds)
Tel: (114) 35380
Really nice classy setup, but lately is friggin dead in there. In it's day it must have been something. Two floors, upstairs have the private dance rooms. Who knows, this could be the hot spot next week.

Mermaids/Splash
Lazaro Cardenas y Vicente Guerrero
All nude, all tease, all the time. Hottest girls in town, $20 dances.

Lord Black
Plaza Nautica
Tel: (114) 35415
Very classy, around 20 girls, rooms in back, mucho dinero.

EL Toro
16 De Septiembre Street, east of Morelos
The locals hang here, all cabbies know it, you can actually get decent pricing here under $100, just be patient and hold firm.

Bolero
Blvd. Marina (across from Plaza Bonita Mall)

For local action, there are a lot of clubs, but don't expect much to work with. The cruise ships will load the beach clubs in the daytime, but they generally pull out to sea around 6pm. The night clubs are full of Americans on vacations, mostly guys with their dates. The American chicks in packs are usually the ould mouth beer gut drunks. Who wants to leave the country and then end up with hometown hogs? Unfortunately there are almost no local chicas there. Frankly, the only jobs available for local girls in Cabo are waitresses or titty dancers.

What you're looking for are the groups of strippers who aren't working that night. They're easy to spot, they Spanish, dance sexy, smile non-stop, and don't weigh 200 lbs. Make your move quick, there are not a lot of them to go around. They're usually broke, so buy a bucket of beers and you're in.

Forget the infamous Cabo Wabo, it's a hopeless empty tourist trap full of American whales, and they wanted $5 to go in to view the cattle. Go to El Squid Row, it rocks till 4 am. Cheap buckets of beer and plenty of eye candy. Don't forget, the daytime beach bar near the end of the beach in Lands End is as good as anything else, start your day early.

El Squid Roe
Blvd. Marina (across from Plaza Bonita Mall)
Tel: (114) 30655 / Fax: (114) 31269
Hard Rock Cafe
Marina Blvd., Plaza Bonita Mall
Tel: (114) 33806 / Fax: (114) 33872

Nightclub Listings :
(www.loscabos-tourism.com/cabo/cabonig.htm)

The worst time to go for a chica vacation here is during the Bisbee Marlin tournament in the last week of October. The marinas are full of huge multimillion-dollar yachts, and this is when the big boys who own them come to town, i.e., the prices double and triple.

Vacation Stuff :
For the cover story for the old lady, tell her flew 2000 miles for a horticulture and yoga convention.

GOLF COURSES :

Los Cabos is considered one of the ultimate golf travel destinations. There are two Nicklaus designed courses, the new **El Dorado Golf Course**, and **Cabo del Sol Ocean Course**. Also here is a premier Robert Trent Jones designed course, the **Cabo Real Golf Course**. Others include the Pete Dye designed **Raven Cabo San Lucas Country Club**, as well as Tom Weiskopf's **Palmilla Golf Course**.

The courses will set you back around $150-250, and vary according to the season. Peak season is October to April. No need to worry if your game is a little off, there are plenty of titty bars in town where you can purchase a hole in one as well.

Cabo del Sol Los Cabos
Tel: (800) 386-2465
Public Course, 18 holes, par 72, 7,037 yards

Jack Nicklaus has designed a prime second course now in Los Cabos, dubbed the **Cabo del Sol**, the "Ocean Course". The course layout is straddling one mile of immaculate coastline and combines amazing mountain, desert and ocean views. Jack Nicklaus has called the holes 16, 17, and 18 as "the finest three finishing holes in all of golf." (he obviously hasn't read out chapter on Rio). Cabo del Sol, often referred to as the "Pebble Beach of Baja", was the site of the 1995 and 1998 Senior Slam PGA Tour event. Golf Magazine rates this course among the top 100 courses in the world. Greens fees $250 peak, $200 off, twilight rates are available.

Tournament (black) 7037 yards , Championship (gold) 6736 yards
Regular (blue) 6282 yards , Member (white) 5843 yards

Cabo Real Golf Course
From U.S. Tel: 01152 (114) 40040
Semi-private Course, 18 holes, par 72, 6,988 yards.

A Robert Trent Jones II masterpiece, layout is over 7,000 yards of lush landscape with every hole overlooking the Sea of Cortez. The first six holes navigate well up onto the mountainside, which follows up with the course cascading down to spectacular views with waterfront holes. This demanding course with endless fairways and sneaky traps, was home to the 1996 and 1999 PGA Senior Slam Tournament. Greens fees $200 Peak season, $150 off.

Tournament (black) 6988 yards
Championship (gold) 6690 yards
Regular (blue) 6333 yards ,
Men (white) 5920 yards

Cabo San Lucas Country Club
Tel: (877) 461-3667 Semi-private Course.
18 holes par 72, 7,277 yards.

An 18-hole Roy Dye designed championship course with some of the most spectacular ocean views seen anywhere. This challenging course is the only Cabo course with views of Land's End and the Pacific Ocean from each fairway. The fairways are lined with Palo Blanco trees and Cardon Cactus, as well as seven dazzling lakes. The course has five tee boxes for each hole and a 620-yard seventh hole - double dogleg around a lake.
Championship (gold) 7220 yards
Regular (blue) 6603 yards
Member (white) 6135 yards

El Dorado Golf Course
Ph: 01152(624) 1445451

This magnificent course, built from rugged desert terrain, features six ocean front holes and four lakes. Carved out of some of the most difficult terrain in Los Cabos, another Nicklaus design. Greens fees $250 peak season, $200 off.
Phone: (14) 45440
Tournament (black) 7050 yards, Championship (gold) 6593 yards
Regular (blue) 6240 yards, Member (white) 5771 yards

Pamilla Golf Club Los Cabos
From U.S. Tel: 01152 (114) 45245
Semi-private Course, 18 holes, par 72, 6,938 yards

Jack Nicklaus built his first Latin America course here in 1992. The course features 27 holes with spectacular views of the Sea of Cortez from nearly every hole, while nestled tightly in rugged desert mountain terrain. The course is divided into the Arroyo Nine, the Mountain Nine, and the Ocean nine. Five sets of staggered tee boxes ensure golfers, from beginners to professionals, an exciting game. The signature hole is a 440-yard, par four on the Mountain Nine course, which calls for a lengthy drive over two desert arroyos. This course was home for the 1997 Senior Slam, Senior PGA Golf event, and several other Pro-Am Tournaments. Greens fees $ 200 peak season, $150 off.
Tournament (black) 6939 yards, Championship (gold) 6572 yards
Regular (blue) 6130 yards, Member (white) 5673 yards

For complete listings of the Mexican Baja peninsula for golf courses,
(www.bajagolf.com)

OCEAN FISHING :

Recognized as the best location in the world for big game Marlin fishing, with some of the great billfish reaching over 1,000 pounds. Cabo is home to the huge angling competition called **Bisbee's Black & Blue Marlin Jackpot Tournament**, which occurs in late October. Total prize money is over $ 1 million, with first place in the $400,000 range for the biggest marlin. One week prior to the Bisbee is the Gold Cup Sports-fishing Tournament. The **marlin** types are blue and striped, also readily caught are **wahoo, sharks, yellow fin tuna, roosterfish, sailfish,** and **dorado**.

The marina is just a few miles from the major hotels, and you can arrange your charter the day before with little difficulty, except during special events. Day rates vary obviously, but expect to pay about $4-500 for a full day of fishing. Even if the fish aren't biting like you'd want, the views make it a great day on the water. It also helps if you bring an obscene amount of booze to guarantee your fun. Remember, the charters are BYOH, **bring your own hooker.** We can vouch that local strip club girls will be your all day boat sex assistant for about $200. They will assist in any and every pole problem each fisherman requires. Optimistically, we assume they smell better than the fish you'll be catching. Hopefully that's all you'll be catching.

Baja Raiders
Cabo's best Sportfishing and scuba diving charters.
Tel: 01152(114)77268 **(www.bajaraiders.com)**

Bisbee's Black & Blue Tournament
Tel: (949) 650-8006
(www.bisbees.com)

Cabo Connections
Tel: (114) 34466... **(www.caboconnections.com)**

Dorado's
Tel: (114) 31630

Earth, Sea, & Sky Tours
Tel: 800-PIK-CABO (800-745-2226)
or: (831) 475-4800

166

Los Cabos Fishing Center
Tel: (114) 33736

Ocean Lure Sportfishing
email: info@oceanlure.com
Tel: (714) 625-3455 , or toll free in U.S. at (800)441-8514
(www.oceanlure.com)

Picante Bluewater Sportfishing
Tel: (800) 260-1885
You'll fish these famous waters in the finest fleet of Cabo Yachts in the world. Because we are also a dealer for Cabo Yachts, our fleet is always upgraded with the latest high-performance models.
(www.picantesportfishing.com)

DIVING AND SNORKELING :

what you'll see :

At **Land's End** where the Pacific Ocean joins the Sea of Cortez, **Sea lions, turtles**, huge **Sea Bass** all loitering around for views of the topless beach. Marauding schools of game fish brought in by large schools of baitfish such as sardines and greenjacks. Pelagics such as **whale sharks** and **mantas** also spotted in this area...also **morays, octopus, tropicals**, etc.. Average depth of 60'.

Divers in Baja can explore shipwrecks, seamounts and an abundance of large sea life. Best visibility is during the summer months, and of course the water is warmest then, usually in the 80's. Varied schedules depending on dive, equipment, professional guide, tanks, and weights. Certification card required. Refreshments and boat transportation included. Approximate cost: $ 45 for one tank, $ 90 for two tanks.

Amigos Del Mar
P.O. Box 43
Cabo San Lucas, B.C.S. 23410
Tel: (800) 344-3349 **(www.amigosdelmar.com)**

Cabo Acuadeportes
Chileno Beach at Hotel Cabo San Lucas
Hacienda Hotel Beach
(114) 30117

Cabo Diving Services
Hotel Plaza Las Glorias
(114) 34302

Discover Baja
Ignacio Zaragosa L.4
(114) 32181
Land's End Divers
Hotel Plaza Las Glorias
(114) 34302

For the best snorkeling in all of Los Cabos, head out through the Cabo San Lucas Bay along the scenic coastline to Santa Maria Cove to the remote cove **the Playa del Amor** (Beach of Love). Approximate rental cost: $45 per person.

JET SKIS AND PARASAILING :
Available all along the beach. The jet skis run $40 per half hour.

Dominican Republic

About :

The Dominican Republic is in the heart of the Caribbean, located between the Caribbean Sea and the North Atlantic Ocean, east of Haiti. Discovered by Columbus in 1492, it features over 1,200 kilometers of coastline, and has become the largest Caribbean tourist destination for North Americans and Europeans. Gorgeous white sand beaches with azure waters, magnificent waterfalls and rivers, stunning mountain ranges and exotic wildlife are just part of the Dominican Republic's appeal. One night listening to the seductive beat of the Merengue, as well leering at the mesmerizing young booties shaking on the dance floor, and it can give the tamest tourist a sweaty brow and bulging crotch in minutes.

The island fulfills our sports requirements effortless, and definitely on the cheap. The north island has casinos and championship golf courses. The Robert Trent Jones in the **Playa Dorada complex** and the Playa Grande course are two of the best, and very affordable. The Playa Grande course has been compared to the Pebble Beach course for its beauty and challenging layout. The coast will fill your days with it's fabulous relaxing beaches, and diverse selection of activities, which including snorkeling, scuba, horseback riding, jeep and 4 wheel tours, sailing, white water rafting, casinos, dancing and dining.

Climate :

A tropical maritime; little seasonal temperature variation, between 65 and 81 degrees Fahrenheit; seasonal variation in rainfall. August is unbearably hot, so is the DR bootie. October to May is the rainy season of the north, and May to October in the south; buy an umbrella, these are monsoon rains lasting half a day sometimes.

Entry Requirements :

All visitors are required to have a valid passport, if you're stay exceeds 30 days. Your passport must be valid at least 6 months prior to entry. As soon as you arrive at the airport, you have to purchase a $10 tourist visa, good for 90 days, which is bought at the office to the right of the passports area. If you bring a lot of electronic toys, expect an extortion tax attempt. Bring some cheap perfume of something, if the customs inspector is female you can bribe her in exchange. Go to the local Dollar Store and buy some fake bling bling. Customs usually ignores you, but occasionally will rifle thru all your stuff. Tips for baggage carrying is $1 per. Grab some pesos here at the airport.

TAXIS :

Expect insane extortion rates for the first quote of $40-50 American.
Negotiate in pesos only, feel free to walk from one to another. Here's and approximate rate for fares from the airport.
To Boca Chica = 300 pesos (30 minute ride)
To Santo Domingo = 500 pesos
Santo Domingo to Boca Chica = 400 pesos
Cabbie will try and steer you to his favorite hotel to stay for a commission, tell him you have on already. Write down the name of your hotel and hand it to him so he doesn't get lost on the way. The most popular way to get around town in Boca Chica is the Motoconcho, or Motor-Taxi. These are 100-125cc motorcycles used for short distances, usually 8 blocks or less. The cost is fixed at D$10US$0.59) per person per stop.

Local Map :
(www.bocachicabeach.net/map.html)

MONEY MATTERS :

Credit cards and traveler's checks will get you by in Santo Domingo but aren't much use in rural areas. They love taxes down here…23% for a good night's sleep. Restaurant bills collect 8% VAT and a 10% service charge. The dollar is so strong down here right now at 40X 1 peso, few years ago it was 16X1. The only thing you should pay for in US dollars is the hotel. Pass on restaurants or anyone asking for dollars. The exchange rate fluctuates wildly, sometimes 25% from day to day. Be patient, change a few at the airport ATM, and ask the first American you find for the best spot.

For the current exchange rate:
(http://www.oanda.com)

CRIME :

This is not a place to have overnight guests. There are short time motels lining the street, use them and stay at an all-inclusive place with security. With a girl in your room, you need a third eye on the back of your head to keep track of all your stuff. The girls can be a little slippery down here. Rule of thumb is to buy a sledgehammer and some 2-inch thick bolts and anything over $5 in value should be imbedded into the floor. Even that just buys you time. If you go to your bathroom and piss longer than 30 seconds, one minute later you'll be chasing her down the street. Her arms will be full of your stuff, your boxers will be at your ankles, you dick is flopping, and the cops will be laughing at you.

If you think you can pick a trophy girl and want to risk an overnighter, you should purchase an acetylene torch and build a cage for your visitor while you're sleeping. Don't leave any toiletries in the bathrooms, and nothing on the bedroom desk.

RECOMMENDED RESTAURANTS :
Since this info can change weekly, we can't recommend enough the "Zagat Survey." Pick up their travel book, or signup online. Worldwide reviews, menus, and pricing. (www.zagat.com)

HOTELS :
Scattered about **Boca Chica** are numerous smaller hotels and guesthouses. There are many small hotels that dot the beach town, and it's just a short walk to the discos at night. Regardless of your taste in accommodation, you will find something to suit you. If you stay in Sousa, there are over 2000 rooms. For upscale, there are 3 huge all-inclusive resorts, which are from $100+ per night. Prices include the room, meals, drinks, and non-motorized water sports. The properties are located at each end of the beach and one in the middle... the Hamaca, the Don Juan, and Dominican Bay (formerly Boca Chica Resort).

The Hamaca Coral by Hilton is generally regarded as the best and most expensive property in Boca Chica. This is a large high-rise hotel with 623 rooms, with multiple restaurants, a disco, casino, multiple shops, two pools, and a private beach that is off-limits to anybody not staying at the hotel. It is a full-service all-inclusive fortress and usually recommend this hotel to first-time visitors to Boca Chica. Generally $100-150 a night, fluctuates by season. A very popular disco at night, $10 gets you all you can drink.
(www.hilton.com)

Hoteur Dominican Bay Resort is the only one of the 3 big ones not located directly on the beach, however they do have their own private section on the beach that is connected to the main property via a private walkway and bridge. It is the most affordable of the 3 big all-inclusive hotels. The resort has at least one super-giant pool,
and offers an outstanding value for those that prefer an all-inclusive resort at an affordable price. $40-60
809-412-2001

The Don Juan is the oldest and smallest of the all-inclusive hotels. The best location, layout, and gardens, right on the beach in the center. There are no buildings over 4 stories tall, but there are no elevators either. Request a room on one of the lower floors if stairs are a problem. Contact them directly ($100-130 per person per night per person.). 809-687-9157

Most of the night life in Boca Chica takes place on Calle Duarte, which is the street that runs parallel to the beach, 1 block in. Which places are popular change from season to season, but one thing is for sure, night life in Boca Chica has two phases, 7-11pm and 11pm to 4am. From 7-11pm, Calle Duarte gets blocked off at both ends and becomes pedestrian only. Most of the restaurants are completely open on one side and extend their service into the sidewalk and street. By midnight, the restaurants close and people head out to the discos.

There are a number of cheaper Gentleman's hotels in Sosua, definitely on the cheap side. These are truly all inclusive, as they include women supplied by the hotel management. Most every guest is a gringo.

Sousa Palace
$45, Hotel manager is a Pimp Daddy, has a black book for of local girls for dates on site. Gringo hotel.
(http://sosuapalace.com/)

Blue Dolphin
Located on the main street, Pedro Clisanti, in the middle of town.
$45, girls on site. (http://www.a3tnet.com/p4.htm)

Hotel Plaza Europa
Sosúa, DomRep , Tel: 1 809 571 3335 or 571 3479
$30. Guest friendly.

Caribe Campo Hotels
150 clean rooms, 2 pools. $25

For Apartments: (www.dominican-real-estate.com)

THE GAME PLAN :
Boca Chica is a tiny beachfront city that derives its income solely from tourism. Parallel to the beach is the main street, which runs barely a mile. It's lined with bars, local shops, tourist crap, and hundreds of women. You literally just have to walk the strip and you'll be propositioned relentlessly. A lot of the girls cruise up and down on little motorcycles looked for men. There are short time motels right on the strip for $10, the girls are around

$25, with no time limit. Be real careful for theft if you bring one back to the hotel, particularly the hardcore disco pros at night. Avoid overnight guests like the plague. Check ID's on the girls, they start real young here. There have been some political crackdowns as of late, in the evening the women will only be pros. The cops are arresting locals who loiter after 11pm.

In the daytime stroll around the beach and be patient, you'll find dozens and dozens of local young girls who can't wait to hear all about your life in the local Motel 6....more like Motel 1/6th. Daytime pricing is 500 pesos. Since they speak no English, you can really dazzle them with the tales of how you made your first billion. The women are very dark skinned, and the range in talent is considerable. For the most part though, they are extremely nice to the local Gringo, and will flash you, grab your crotch, and compete in numbers for the chance to have you. Negotiate all terms up front no matter what. For a more adventurous technique, rent a car a drive around the outskirts of town. To find a cute available local girl is like shooting fish in a barrel.

At nighttime, the easiest route is to grab a seat at one of the outdoor cafes and watch the strutting chicas go by until you see one that must be conquered. As simple as that. If you want to dance, you'll find clubs and freelancers all over town. Try **La Noria** and **Zanzibar**, and **Casa de Modelos**. There are about 40 girls looking to date you for around 1200-1500 pesos for overnight. Also **Remington Palace** and the **Cosmos disco**. The **4 Roses** and **the Sexy Lady** are a few other popular spots. The best beach bar is **La Isla Bonita**. This town is so poor its 4th world country, don't get your sightseeing expectations high. The names of the clubs will change frequently. What you want to do is go to as many as you can the first day until you run into a pack of gringos. There are a number of bars owned by younger Americans who've moved down here. The country is a very popular hangout for the quick 3-day getaway from Miami. There will be plenty of pros there who've been dozens of times you can show you the latest hot spots.

Currently, one of the more popular approaches and setups here are the all-inclusive places. They house maybe 30 rooms, most are gringos, and the daily buffet arranged by the hotel is prime dark meat, hold the vegetables. Located in Sosua, gringos in numbers visit the spots **the Palace, Blackbeards** and the **Blue Dolphin**. The Palace is very small, with just 20 rooms, so remember to plan ahead and leave a deposit in advance. The hotel manager is a pimp daddy who provides a steady flow of young hoes who pop in and out and in and out during the day. Dates are around 800 pesos. Outside of here the rate is a lot less, you pay for convenience and quality here. Make sure you negotiate/pay in pesos, not dollars. It's a much better value. (**www.sosuapalace.com**)

For hot looking locals, **High Caribbean** is a great spot. If you've ever been to Rio de Janiero, it's layout and atmosphere is like a mini Help Disco. Cover is $3, girls are $25-40. Talent is somewhat lacking, but their desire is not. Drink heavily, pull a few out, and take no pictures. Who's gonna know you're telling a fish story back home anyway with no evidence. Wrap that bad boy in stainless steel in this town. Make hydrogen peroxide your best friend.

Other clubs the girls frequent for gringos are the **Latino Club** and **Crystals**. Another comical event to do is the Dominican car wash bar. Ask around to find the right one to go to. Here's the plan, you get your car washed, drink and eat, and get a girl while your there. If you don't have a car, walk there, drink, eat, and then have her wash you and do her. Hell, pull up in a taxi, make her wash it, then clean you up in the back seat with that high powered vacuum suction mouth of hers. There are non-pro young girls everywhere walking the streets since cars are beyond their pocketbook. Trust me, the minute they see yo' happy ass Gringo face they turn pro in a second. Just be patient and you'll find some impossibly ripe teen hard bodies strolling around.

For you golfers, the town to stay in is **Puerto Plata**, about 25 minutes from the airport , and maybe 25 minute north from Sosua. This is the home of the several casinos as well as great golf courses. The fantastic Playa Grande course, compared to Pebble Beach in California, is about 30 minutes down the road. It is best to fly into Puerto Plata's Gregorio Luperon International Airport. If you fly into Santo Domingo's Las Americas International Airport, you will be about a 3-hour bus ride to Nagua, from which you will have to take a minibus or cab to get to your hotel. Caribbean Village at Playa Grande and the Bahía Principe are the two big hotels in the area.

The inexpensive Robert Trent Jones course in Puerto Plata, which is just 20 minutes from Sousa north up on the coast. To get women to escort you here will take about a minute to find during a drive across from the course complex. Point and click. ST dates are the time period of choice.

Here's a convenient local map to print out.
(www.selectcaribbean.com/pics/maps/sosuamap.jpg)

Local Nightlife Link :
(http://www.bocachicabeach.net/)

CASINOS :

These of course of stripped down dumps, but you can still blow all your money there.

The Hamaca Coral by Hilton

Right on the beach in Boca. Caribbean poker is available.

Playa Chiquita Resort & Casino is in Sosua, Dominican Republic . The property has a hotel with ninety rooms.
Playa Chiquita Resort & Casino Address
Isabel Iaq Catolica 165
Sosua, Dominican Republic
Toll Free - (800) 922-4272
Baccarat , Blackjack, Craps, Roulette

ATTRACTIONS :

And now for the cover story for the old lady.

The biggest attraction in Boca Chica is the beach. Each hotels offers array of water sports and beach activities to keep you occupied. As far as high culture, there are no theaters, galleries or movie houses. We recommend practicing your bongo technique on the tight booties you find on every corner. The big hotels have shows and discos, and there are many public discos throughout the town. Plus the Hamaca Hotel has a casino open to the public. Most visitors to Boca Chica spend their days either on the beach or going on excursions to see the rest of the country.

Excursions

Jeep Safaris
Santo Domingo (Full day and Half day tours)
Saona and Catalina Island tours
Horse Ranch tours
White Water Rafting, Jarabacoa

The Hamac hotel rents single-speed bikes with chain brakes. There are bike tours every morning, with a guide who takes you to local places of interest. Get to the bike rack a little early to ensure getting a bike with fully inflated tires and meaningful tire tread. Be alert as mopeds and motorcycles zip by at breakneck speeds on the narrow streets of Boca Chica. The roads, though paved, are interrupted by killer speed bumps and deep storm channels from rain run-off. You don't want to ride into them.

OTHER THINGS TO DO :

Ride a horse, go snorkeling, ride a banana boat, take an excursion to a nearby island, rent out a sailboat, paddle-boat, kayak, windsurf, go scuba diving, walk out to the reef, go fishing, dance Meringue, learn to salsa dance, rent a jet ski, do some water skiing, gamble in the casino, sip espresso while people watching at a sidewalk café, or travel an hour and see everything that Santo Domingo has to offer. Dine on great fresh seafood, rent a motorcycle and hit the dirt trails, drink from a pineapple or coconut , get a massage on the beach or get your hair braided, buy some of the local music to take home, buy some fresh mangos at the local fruit market. Have a four-girl orgy for under $100 dollars.

GOLF COURSES :

Casa de Campo is a 7,000-acre enclave with top facilities for exotic golf courses, tennis, as well as polo. A 183-slip marina offers deep-sea fishing, snorkeling and sailing excursions. The stable always has 100 horses in residence for trail rides, polo or lessons. Also, there's the beach, and swimming pools at every turn, and shopping.

Casa de Campo
The buzz is all about Pete Dye's fourth and newest course at this outstanding, multi-faceted resort. Opened April 21, 2003, Dye Fore joins the **Teeth of Dog** (ranked 35th in the world), the Links Course, and the private La Romano Country Club. Dye Fore has nine dramatic cliff top holes; Teeth of the Dog has 7 spectacular Oceanside holes. 800-877-3643

Guavaberry Country Club
Ph:800 847 0291. Located at the Coral Resort, this Gary Player-designed track is one of the region's newest and most challenging. After a healthy round, strolling around in the streets across from the complex, are scores of young Amazonians who will fondle your club and let you go for a hole in one for around $15.

Playa Dorada Resort
Flat, conditioned course with exceptional greens surrounding the Playa Dorada resort complex. This par 72, 18-hole course serves the 14 resorts within Playa Dorada, where there are approximately 4000 hotel rooms, three casinos, numerous restaurants, bars, shopping, discotheques, and various other sports.

Playa Dorada Golf Club, designed by Robert Trent Jones, is located in the beautiful Playa Dorada Project in Puerto Plata, Dominican Republic, where there are approximately 4,000 hotel rooms, three casinos, numerous restaurants, discotheques, bars, shopping and various other sports. Surrounded by crystal clear beaches and 14 hotels of maximum quality and comfort, this championship golf course has 18 holes with a yardage of 6990, and par 72. Located on the North Coast of the Dominican Republic, a mere 15 min from Puerto Plata International Airport. Greens fees are $28, mandatory caddy is $9. Cart is $23.

(www.playa-dorada-golf.com)

Playa Grande Golf Course
Km. 9 Carretera Río San Juan-Cabrera, María Trinidad Sánchez province, about an hour's drive from Sosua, in Puerto Plata.
Tel: 809 582-0860, ext, 27. Fax (809) 248-5314 Built in '98, called The "Pebble Beach" of the Caribbean, with 10 holes interacting with the Atlantic Ocean. Pros and occasional golfers alike praise this course for its breathtaking Atlantic views. Blue 7,046 yards, white tees are 5,917 yards. A round is $67, carts are $23, and clubs are $10.

OCEAN FISHING :
Excellent saltwater fishing here. Offshore, the Mona Passage, Caribbean Sea, and Atlantic Ocean offer opportunities for anglers to catch **marlin, sailfish, tuna, wahoo, dolphin, kingfish, red snapper, grouper,** and more. The towns along the beaches of the Dominican Republic offer access to outfitters whose captains consistently provide their customers with exciting offshore action for **marlin, sailfish, tuna, wahoo, dolphin, kingfish, red snapper,** and **grouper**.

DIVING AND SNORKELING :
Many of the all-inclusive hotels offer lessons and certification. The north coast features dives amongst shipwrecks, the south is more pleasant due to the warmer water. Barahon and Cabo Rojo are two of the more popular spots.

TENNIS & SQUASH :
Most of the major hotels have courts, many flock to the resort Casa de Campo for tournaments.

Tijuana, Mexico

About :

Renowned as "the world's most visited border city", **Tijuana** invites you to discover and enjoy its extensive variety of attractions and activities. Home to a magic cultural entertainment, as well as world-class restaurants, nightclub shows and discotheques to such tourist attractions as bull fights, golf courses, museums. That's at least what you'll tell the old lady, for us it's home to a surprisingly exotic **Red Light District**, with hundreds of gorgeous girls looking to show tourists a close up view of their *crotch tacos*.

Tijuana is an easy daytrip from San Diego, California. From downtown SD there is an $ 8 trolley to the border, and from there you can take either a bus or a cab. At a cost of $13 total for the trip, there is no excuse not to pop on down when in SD. The red light district is called **La Coahuiiila**, located in the city of Tijuana in the Zona Norte. The zone itself isn't exactly upscale, but the caliber of some of the girls here is often stunning. Many girls are downright exotic, having flow up from Buenos Aires, Venezuela and southern Mexico looking for healthy gringo dollars. The pricing is $20-30 in the street area, to $50-60 in the clubs. It's truly a compassionate humanitarian gesture of yours to invest your hard earned US dollars to help the struggling Mexican economy.

(www. seetijuana.com)

Climate :

Mexico is hot and humid along the coasts, but inland, at higher elevations such as Guadalajara or Mexico City, the climate is much drier and hotter. The hot, wet season is May to October, with the hottest and wettest months falling between June and September over most of the country. December to February is generally the coolest months, when north winds can make inland northern Mexico decidedly chilly, with temperatures sometimes approaching freezing.

Entry Requirements :

From the US, no visa is required, a passport is recommended. Also make sure when you enter you have a desperate desire to screw like the energizer bunny non-stop for 48 hours.

178

DEPARTURE TAX :
Border exit fee varies, usually around $10. Maximum of one free bottle of tequila allowed, duty tax on more.

MONEY MATTERS :
U.S. currency is King. Change some into pesos in America for a better rate. Spend them, their kind of worthless back home. Also bring some 1's, 5's, and a few 10's of both pesos and US dollars. People pretend they don't have change for larger bills. People don't want $100 bills, they think they're counterfeit.

For the current exchange rate:
(http://www.oanda.com)

TIPPING :
Change your money to pesos. If you pay in American dollars, ask the waiters for your change in US dollars. Naturally, in the spirit of Mexico, all the waiters will all try to rip you off. Do you really want the going exchange rate as per Pedro? They hold up a tray with your change on it, you won't be able to see the coins. Grab the paper, say keep the rest senor. As a token of your appreciation, hand out your ex-wife's business cards to all the waiters …."for a good time, call collect 24 hours a day."

HOW TO GET THERE :
Tijuana is just south of San Ysidro, California. From downtown Los Angeles or from Los Angeles International Airport (LAX), you can drive to TJ in about three hours (depending on traffic) by going south on I-405 to I-5. From San Diego, you can drive the approximately 25 miles in about 30 minutes on I-5. Take the exit that says last exit, or specifically "Camino de la Plaza - Last USA Exit and Parking". Go down the ramp, thru the first 4-way intersection, $7 lots are on the right. Put all valuables in the trunk, as in bud six packs, joints, hustler mags, knives, guns, maybe throw in the wedding ring, and family photos as well. Leave the lot, go right towards the dead end looking street to the walking pedestrian turnstiles. Searching is rare at customs. Take a $5 cab, tell him to take you to Adelitas Bar (AB) in Tijuana. Don't tell him you think tacos sucks, Mexican tequila is piss water, or that he smells like a street bum. Bring exact change.

For you professionals, from San Diego take the trolley to the border and then the bus or taxi from there. Total cost is under $10 each way. Expect to negotiate you taxi rate if it's a non metered taxi.

We recommend weekends, and getting there about 9pm latest for the best selection. For extended stays we also suggest you stay just north of the border, but there's plenty of hotels in the RLD if you prefer. If you are using the trolley, be aware that the northbound trolley service is not available after 1:00 a.m., except for occasional trips on the weekends. Take a cab is you miss it, about $20 to San Diego from Chula Vista. If you drive your car or a rental, your insurance is not valid in Mexico…you have to buy special insurance. Not worth it, there's no secure parking in TJ anyway.

WHAT TO WEAR :
Your favorite binge drinking and orgy T-shirt. Maybe break out the old dependable "College" shirt from Animal House days.

CRIME AND SCAMS :
As soon as you cross the border, take a cab. Stop walking, there are street thugs waiting for drunk idiots looking to save cab fare. (it's only $5.) Once in Tijuana, there are pickpockets galore. If you're the kind of guy who walks around with a huge wallet in the back packet, stay home. No wallets down here. Streets are full of the usual hustlers and pickpockets, and since it's Mexico, the cops can be thieves as well. DO NOT bring a camera to the zone, picture taking will get you arrested or paying off a cop.

RECOMMENDED RESTAURANTS :
Since this info on the best restaurants can change weekly, we can't recommend enough the "**Zagat Survey**." Pick up their travel book, or signup online. Worldwide reviews, menus, and pricing.

(www. zagat.com)

HOTELS :
Most people return to the US since it's so close, but there are plenty of major hotels here.

Hotel El Conquistador
Boulevard Agua Caliente #1777, Tijuana, MX
Located in the Heart of Tijuana just minutes from Caliente Racetrack, the Jai Alai Palace, Tijuana Country Club Golf Course and the Spectacular Pageant of the Bullfight Ring. Also home to your famous cockfights with the local chicas. "Ay, que grande, papasito."

La Villa de Zaragoza Hotel,
1120 Avenida Madero, between 7th and 8th Streets. (Behind the jai alai emporium, which should be on most maps.) Rooms are $35-40 per night, the staff speaks English.011 52-66-851-832
(http://members.aol.com/hotellavilla/)

Upscale can be had in the center of the RLD zone as well for $100.
Residence Inn By Marriott Real del Mar
KM 19.5 Tijuana-Ensenada Toll Road
Tijuana, MX (www. marriott.com)

The Hotel Real del Rio
Jose Ma. Velasco #1409 A, Tijuana, Mexico
Located in the heart of the district, near the most popular entertainment sites, 5 minutes away from the International Border and 15 minutes from the Airport. There are 103 rooms with either one king or two double beds.

THE GAME PLAN :

The red light district is called **La Coahuiiila**, located in the city of Tijuana in the zona norte. Like all districts, the names of the clubs will change, but the layout remains the same. Avoid the strip clubs down here. The clubs you're visiting resembling a disco, with DJ or a band. The girls are fairly easy to spot. Look for the ones who make eye and hand contact with your crotch, should take about 3 seconds. Be patient, and find something worth remembering. There are short time hourly motels in the area.

Now, like any RLD, there are outstanding clubs in a safe area, and numerous more in seedy and rougher areas. You should confine your search to the two best clubs, Adelita's, and the Chicago Club. Strolling around aimlessly and drunk will open up the door to potential trouble. As always, you will be approached by local scammers who have the inside scoop on where to go. These would be the Mexican guys with tequila-stained shirts and puke on their breath, looking like outcasts from the Three Amigos. Ignore all offers, no need to make this complicated and dangerous. If you're bored, tell him you're Billy the Kid's great grandson and you're interested in a standoff.

Adelita's
The Adelita Bar is on the south side of Calle Coahilla, which is the street that runs parallel to Calle Primera (first Street). A dance floor setup, with

181

the music being tejano. The girl's are found lined up in the bar area, with the best in the back right section.

Adelita's has an incredible display on some nights, literally some 8's and 9's. Dates here are around $ 40-60. This will get you 30 minutes give or take, in the short time room upstairs, which will cost an additional $11. Be very clear in your negotiations what you want. Most girls will try to speed you up so as to return downstairs. They clubs prefer the in-house set up, if you want to take them to your hotel, the bar fines are pretty steep, in the $80-100 range plus the cost of the girl.

Chicago Bar

The Chicago Club is located on the east side of Avenida Constitucion, half a block north of Calle Coahilla. The setup is also a disco, with the music being mostly techno. Short time hotel next door, girls ask for a little more here, in the $60-80 range, just negotiate like a prick and you'll knock of 20 at a minimum. Expensive lady drinks here, $ 8.

Bounce from one club to the other until you find the lucky winner. When you're done, get a $ 5 cab and go to the border, do not attempt to walk out of the zone to the border.

Bad Areas :

The intersection of Avenida Revolution and Calle Coahilla, ¼ mile east of Adelita Bar…next to the Alaska Motel. Another is one block east and one block south of the Adelita Bar. Also one block west of Adelita's near the New York Club. The modus operandi of crime are street thugs sneaking up behind you for muggings, similar to Help disco are in Rio. Recommended is walking in the streets under lights, they jump out from behind cars.

The other well know clubs in the zone are **Chavelas, CC, Déjà Vu, Hong Kong, La Tropa, Madonnas, Mermaids, Miami**, and **Tropical**. The club names can change with the wind, or depending on who's greasing palms and who isn't. There's a different setup in each, most you just stroll in a pick out you girl for an nearby rendezvous. Déjà Vu has a $40 cover which includes an hour date.

Be aware there are numerous drink hustler chicks in the clubs. The easiest method to avoid them is for you to stand. If you're inclined to sit at tables, they'll appear out of nowhere at your table, and an $8 drink arrives seconds later, which you're now expected to buy. (the girls make a few bucks for each of these).

For the cheap Charlie route, there are literally hundreds of street girls loitering around looking for $20-30 dates in their private love shacks nearby. While this is hardly a romantic encounter, and is not exactly high class, some of these girls can be stunning. Expect a buffet of attempted up sells for clothes off, positions, grunting, farting, you name it.

Prostitution is illegal in Mexico, but the Zona is a tolerated area. However, cops are still crooked as hell, and will look for a way to temporarily arrest any drunk and disorderly Gringo. If you get in a fight, or pee in public, you're either going to jail or paying off a cop not to. They periodically storm into a club and search everyone for guns and proper paperwork. Be prepared, it's legal for them to do this.

VACATION STUFF :
And now for the cover story for the old lady.

Bullfighting :
(*Corridas de Toros*) Toreo de Tijuana at Agua Caliente
011-52 (66) 86-1510 Plaza Monumental at Playa de Tijuana

GOLF COURSES :
Baja Mar
Using the natural environment as an advantage, the rugged Baja coastline provides an unforgettable setting for Baja mar's Scottish links style golf course. You'll be using some unnatural silicone environment in the red zone immediately follow the round. The challenging 6,968 yard layout is rated 74, with a slope of 137 from the back tees and is truly a memorable experience. Located an easy 50-mile drive south of the San Diego/Tijuana border on the toll road. Tel: (800) 225-2418

Club Campestre Golf Resort Tijuana
(Executive Course-Tijuana)
Domicilio Conocido, Tijuana
From U.S. Tel: 01152 (562) 45450

183

Club Campestre Golf Resort Tijuana
(Executive Course-Tijuana)
Domicilio Conocido, Tijuana
From U.S. Tel: 01152 (562) 45450

Real del Mar
Tel: (800) 662-6180
Public Course, 18 holes, par 72, 6,400 yards
A breathtaking view with the Los Coronados Mountains that perfectly frame the lush green fairways and rugged canyon walls. Carved out of the Christy canyons, this spectacular course is located just 12 miles south of the international border. The unparalleled site provides natural slopes and curves on every fairway throughout this challenging 18-hole course, which is accentuated with 7 lakes and 51 bunkers.

Tijuana Country Club
Agua Caliente Blvd. Tel: (011-52664) 681-7859
(http://golf.baja.com/images/courses/tjcc/info.html)

Club Campestre Tijuana
One of the most beautiful golf courses of Mexico, great views and challenges for amateur and professional golf players. That's just the hookers, the course is real nice too.
For further info on all the courses, visit the below site.
(www. bajagolf.com)

GREYHOUND RACING :
Hipodromo Caliente
Agua Caliente at Tapachula 12027, downtown
011-52 (66) 81-7811

OCEAN FISHING :
Most of the fishing around the nearby Coronado Islands is booked through fishing companies in the United States.
Cortez Yacht Charters (619) 469-4255.
Located in San Diego. Fishing packages to Coronado Islands, Guadeloupe Island, short and long trips.
Fisherman's Landing (619) 221-8500.
2838 Garrison Street, San Diego, California 92106.
Fleet of over a dozen privately owned, fishing vessels 57 to 124 ft.
H & M Landing (619) 222-1144.
Sports fishing charters to the Coronado Islands and local Mexican waters.
(www. bajafishing.com/charters.html)

St. Maarten

About :

St. Maarten is the smallest island in the world ever to have been partitioned between two different nations, the French and the Dutch in the Lesser Antilles of Eastern Caribbean have shared St. Martin/St. Maarten for almost 350 years. The border is almost imperceptible. and people cross back and forth without ever realizing they are entering a new country. The only marker is a monument between Union Road and Bellevue.

Located midway through the chain of islands in the Caribbean, just as the Antilles begin to curve to the south, with balmy weather, sun drenched powder white beaches, modern resorts, gourmet dining, dazzling casinos, and the best duty-free shopping in the Eastern Caribbean, people find it easy to worship this heavenly island paradise. The Population is 27,000 and made up of a mix of Dutch Europeans and Spanish descent. The official language is French, though most speak English as well. In addition, a significant number of the tourists speak a heavily slurred dialect of an undetermined origin.

Climate :

St. Maarten is sunny and warm year-round, averaging 82 degrees Fahrenheit in summer and just 2 degrees cooler in winter. The island is buffeted by cooling trade winds that keep things temperate all year long. Average annual rainfall comes to about 45 inches, most of which occurs around late summer and early fall. St Maarten is the land of perpetual summer, and the beach life is perfect 24/7 year round. Mid-December to mid-April the busiest season. The Venezuelan goddesses that you'll be meeting in the brothels are unusually damp during both the wet season and dry season, although this may be more indicative of the tourist cash you are packing, than what your trousers are packing.

Entry Requirements :

From the US, no visa or passport is required. Judging from the security personnel here, no IQ is required either. Arriving at Juliana Airport, US & Canadian citizens can stay up to three months. Others need a valid passport. If entering on the French side: EU citizens need an official identity card, valid passport or French *carte de séjour* (visitor card); US & Canadian nationals can stay up to two weeks (maximum three months, on request) without a passport if they have the same documentation required for the Dutch side. Citizens of most other countries need both a valid passport and a visa.

MONEY MATTERS :

As U.S. dollars are widely accepted on both the Dutch and the French sides, visitors do not need to exchange their U.S. money for a visit to the island. Official currency of the Dutch side is the Netherlands Antilles florin or guilder (NAF). Official currency of the French side is the Euro. Nearly all prices are listed in U.S. dollars as well as the local currency, so there's no need for calculating exchange rates. Hookers phone numbers written in lipstick on napkins are not considered currency on either the French or Dutch side.

TIPPING :

Most hotels and restaurants add between 10 percent and 15 percent to the bill as a service charge. Tip more if your waitress is topless. If she's under the table devouring your banana for dessert, be a good sport and give her a healthy cream topping for a tip.

Taxi drivers expect 50 cents or $1 for short runs and more for an extended narrated tour. As always, inquire if he knows any young horny local chicas looking for hedonistic drunk studs.

TIME ZONE :

St. Maarten is on Atlantic Standard Time year-round. During the fall and winter, noon in New York equals 1 p.m. on the island. During daylight savings time in the U.S., the hour is the same in NY as it is on the island.

ELECTRICITY :

Hotels are US wired: 110 volts, 60 cycles. On the French side, all run on 220 volts, 60 cycles so a converter and adaptor plugs are needed for travel appliances. If you yell at the French appliances, they will surrender immediately and cease to operate until further instruction.

TELEPHONE :

When dialing the Dutch side from the U.S., dial the international access code 011, the country code 599 and the local number. Special codes are required from one side to the other, though only a local number is required when calling the same side.

CAR RENTALS :

Available for around $150 a week, and cell phones run around $2 a day with a $20 calling card purchase.

RECOMMENDED RESTAURANTS :

Since this info on the best restaurants can change weekly, we can't recommend enough the "**Zagat Survey**." Pick up their travel book, or signup online. Worldwide reviews, menus, and pricing.

(www. zagat.com)

HOTELS :

The hotels on the French side of the island are much more expensive, and the people generally smell a lot, are anti-American, and have the spine of a napkin. The Dutch side hotels are the closest to the fun. Check out the Holland House Beach Hotel in central Philipsburg. Since St. Maarten is a tiny island, none of the hotels are too far from the action.

Holland House Beach Hotel
Front Street, Philipsburg
Phone: ++ (599) 542-2550
(www.hhbh.com)

Club Sunterra Flamingo Beach
Pelican, on the Beach
Phone: ++ (599) 544-3737
(www.sunterra.com)

Great Bay Beach Hotel
Front Street, Philipsburg
Phone: ++ (599) 542-2446
(www.greatbayhotel.com)

Divi Little Bay Beach Resort
Little Bay Road, Philipsburg
Phone: ++ (599) 542-2333
(www.diviresorts.com)

Hotel Beach Plaza
Baie de Marigot, Saint Martin
Phone: ++ (590) 878700
(www.hotelbeachplazasxm.com)

The Game Plan :

The main area to be in is **Philipsburg** on the Dutch side. Not exactly a red light district per se, but a central location where there's a great line up of bars and line up of women. The best place is **Seaman's** club, featuring women from Venezuela and Columbia. This is a clean well-organized in house strip club/brothel, with an attractive fleet of 20-25 girls, very young professionals..it's a fun bar to hang out in with a dance floor. Drinks are $3, and the session rooms are out back where the girls live. Only Spanish is spoken, dates from $35-50 here as well as throughout the area. Other strip clubs located here in the home base are **Defiance** (30 girls), **Casa Blanca** (35 girls) and **Le Pitie Chatue.** At Chatue you have pool tables, as a side show the girls tend to get smashed drunk and dance in unison on the bar, and as opposed to the out back location, the girls will leave with you. Try not to dance with the girls on the bar, impersonating Chris Farley will not improve your chances. Hard currency accomplishes that.

For English speaking girls there are **Cats** and **Strawberrys**, featuring Jamaican or Trinidadian girls. Cats opens after midnight, has special shows like bondage and stupid crap like that. Do we really look like butch dykes. Take a hint girls, see the kneepads, be the kneepads. These places are strip clubs with lap dances available as well as private sessions behind doors.

Near the airport is **The Platinum Club**, which is more like your upscale strip club at home. Here they feature a high dollar extravagant layout filled with stunning European girls. There's a $10 cover. Unfortunately, it's a strip bar with teasing only. I mean really. What is this, friggin' Disneyland? Someone needs to score here guys, we're not all wingmen. Platinum is centrally located near hotels, restaurants, bars, nightclubs, casinos and some of the best beaches the Caribbean has to offer. Get some dances, get some numbers for daytime dates, and move on.

(www.theplatinumroom.com)

Vacation Stuff :

And now for the cover story for the old lady.

Golf Courses :

The one 18-hole golf course on the island is located on the Dutch side of St. Maarten nearby at Mullet Bay. The course is open to all visitors; call ahead to reserve a slot.

Ocean Fishing :

The offshore waters offer a wide and challenging variety of game fish including marlin, tuna, dolphin fish, barracuda, and kingfish. The Anglers Big Fishing Tournament occurs at the end of March and the Blue Marlin Fishing Tournament takes place here every year in the month of June. Boats can be chartered at reasonable rates all year long, although some of the fish are only in season in these waters from December through March. Charters typically include bait, tackle, and some form of refreshment. The best fishing grounds are conveniently near the island, meaning less time spent traveling and more time fishing.

Diving and Snorkeling :

Visibility in the waters around the island typically extends for about 100 feet and sometimes can even reach up to 200 feet. The coral reefs offer a wide variety of sea life, and just off the coast of St. Maarten in the Great Bay lies the wreck of an English battleship dating back to 1801. Dive operators may be found at many of the major resorts and hotels as well as at a number of independent shops around the island. Instruction from beginners to advanced is readily available, and certified divers should remember to bring their licenses as well as their diving logs. Equipment may be rented easily, and snorkeling is especially inexpensive.

Blue Ocean
Tel: 0590 87 89 73   (**www.blueocean.ws**)

Club Neptune
Tel: 0690 50 98 51   e-mail : neptune-dive@wanadoo.fr

Octoplus
Tel: 0590 87 20 62   (**www.octoplus-dive.com**)

Scuba Fun Caraibes
Tel: 0590 87 36 13
(**www.scubafun.com**)
contact@scubafun.com

Water sports :

Windsurfing, water-skiing, parasailing, and jet skiing are activities that are regularly offered at the more popular beaches and in the inland lagoons. Rental and instruction tend to be fairly inexpensive

189

SAILING :

St. Maarten is the Caribbean's leading sailing venues, playing host each year to the St. Maarten Heineken Regatta and offering plenty of stunning anchorages. Fully equipped marinas welcome visiting boats and rent everything from speedboats to canoes. Day trips can also be arranged for deep-sea fishing or for visits to nearby islands. In March, participants from Europe, the United States, and the Caribbean visit St. Maarten to compete in one of the world's biggest sailing events - the St. Maarten Heineken Regatta.

(**www.heinekenregatta.com**)

The event has come to symbolize the island's prominence as a sailing venue, and St. Maarten is one of the few places in the world where the average person can sail on a world-class racing boat.

HIKING :

There are 25 miles of clearly defined footpaths running through the mountains and along the shore, revealing some truly spectacular panoramas.

TENNIS & SQUASH :

Tennis remains one of the favorite pastimes in St. Martin, and there are more than 70 courts over the whole island. Most of the major hotels usually have both tennis and squash courts available, as well as fitness centers. Pros are available for instruction. Proper attire required.

CASINOS :

French St. Maarten does not have any casinos; however, just a short ride away, are eight casinos on the Dutch side. Most hotels provide round-trip transportation to the casinos. Here's the scoop on some of the bigger ones.

Pelican Resort Club and Hollywood Casino is in Philipsburg, St. Maarten, and is open 2pm-3am daily. The 7,000 square foot casino features 120 slots and sixteen table games. The property has three restaurants and a hotel with 514 rooms. (**www.pelicanresort.com**)

Address:

Billy Flly Road 37, Simpson Bay, Philipsburg, Sint Maarten

Telephones: +599-54-44463 General Information

Slot Machines: 120 machines

Table Games - 16 total

Blackjack- USD 5.00 to USD 500 bets

Caribbean Stud Poker- USD 5.00 to USD 500 bets

Craps- USD 5.00 to USD 500 bets

Roulette

Let it Ride- USD 5.00 to USD

190

Great Bay Beach Hotel and Golden Casino
open daily 7am-4am. The property has three restaurants and a hotel with 285 rooms. The website is (**www.greatbayhotel.com**)
Address:
19 Little Bay Road
Philipsburg, Saint Maarten
Toll Free - (800) 223-0757
Slot Machines - 150 total
Table Games - 10 total
Blackjack, 4 tables , Caribbean Stud Poker , Roulette

Tropicana Casino
34 Welfare Road
Cole Bay, Saint Maarten, Netherlands Antilles
General Information - +599-54-45654

Casino Jump Up
Emmaplein 1
Philipsburg, Sint Maarten
General Information - +599-54-20862
Toll Free - +599-54-20974
(**www.jumpupcasino.com**)

Diamond Casino
Frontstreet 1
Philipsburg, St. Maarten
General Information - +599-54-32523
(**www.diamondcasinosxm.com**)

Full tourist information packages can be requested from:
St. Maarten Tourist Office
675 Third Avenue, Suite 1086
New York, NY 10017
Phone: 1-212-953-2084 Toll free: 1-800-786-2278

Local tourism sites:
(**www. st-maarten.com**)
(**www.st-martin.org**)

Cebu, Philippines

About :

The Philippines is an archipelago nation made up of 7,107 islands spanning 1,840 kilometers north to south. It is part of the East Indies, a vast island group lying south and east of mainland Asia, with Taiwan at its northernmost coast and Borneo on the south. The three main Philippine island groups are Luzon, the Visayas and Mindanao.

The **Island of Cebu**, with its hundreds of white-sand beaches, is located south of Manila and boasts of some of the most magnificent shorelines in the Philippines. Cebu is an exquisite tropical island paradise, with pristine beaches, calm weather, crystal clean water, and immaculate resorts right on the beach, packed with all the water sports you can handle. Cebu is the oldest city in the Philippines, usually called the "Queen City of the South."

Cebu is now a huge tourist attraction with its unusual sea-valley-and-mountain location. Likewise, recent indications show that Cebu has become the country's most favorite tourist destination, due to a buffet of hot horny Filipinas who drop their panties in a moment's notice. English is the most widely spoken second language. Located a whopping 15 hours from Los Angeles, and to New York, 20 hours and 20 minutes.

Climate :

Cebu Island is blessed with year-round pleasant, tropical weather. The Philippines is tropical with just two seasons--hot and dry from November to June, and rainy from July to October. Casual attire for men collared T-shirts worn over slacks.

Entry Requirements :

If you are coming from America, Asia or Europe with a valid passport, and either a return ticket or a ticket to another destination outside the Philippines you may enter without a formal visa and stay for 21 days. If you wish to stay longer you must obtain a Visa Extension either before your trip from a Philippine Consulate or Embassy. Or locally at the Bureau of Immigration.

Airlines :

The Philippines' national airline is Philippine Airlines (PR). Other airlines serving the Philippines include Air France, British Airways, Cathay Pacific, Gulf Air, Kuwait Airways, Northwest Airways, Royal Brunei Airlines, Silk Air, Qatar Airways, Singapore Airlines and Malaysia Airlines.

APPROXIMATE FLIGHT TIMES :
From Manila to London is 20 hours; to Paris is 16 hours 30 minutes; to Los Angeles is 14 hours 25 minutes; to New York is 17 hours 30 minutes; to Singapore is 3 hours 40 minutes; to Hong Kong is 2 hours 35 minutes; to Bangkok is 2 hours 30 minutes; to Tokyo is 4 hours 50 minutes and to Sydney is 8 hours.

FROM THE AIRPORT :
From Cebu Airport – The city is some 40 minutes away, although a limo is only 200P($5), tickets for which can be found in the baggage claim area…then head to the arrival area…a few hundred-yard walk thru the terminal. Taxis can be a rip off, when they're honest, they are about the same price as the limo.

COUNTRY DIALING CODE: 63.
TIMEZONE: GMT plus 8 hours.

MONEY MATTERS :
The currency in the Philippines is the Peso (PhP) and the Centavo. 100 centavos = P1. Coin denominations are: 1, 5, 10, and 25 centavos, P1, and P5. Bill denominations are : 10, 20, 50, 100, 500 and 1, 000 pesos.

American Express , is located at Ayala Shopping Centre. Phone 231.6747 For security reasons, say you're going to Quantas Airlines at Ayala to the cabbie.

For today's peso conversion price, go here:
(http://www.oanda.com)

Foreign currency may be exchanged at your hotel, and in most of the large department stores, banks and authorized money changing shops. Exchanging money anywhere else is illegal and the laws are strictly enforced. Most large stores, restaurants , hotels and resorts accept major credit cards including American Express , Visas and MasterCard. Travelers checks preferably American Express are accepted at hotels and large department stores. Personal checks drawn on foreign banks are generally not accepted.

RECOMMENDED RESTAURANTS :
Since this info can change weekly, we can't recommend enough the "**Zagat Survey.**" Pick up their travel book, or signup online. Worldwide reviews, menus, and pricing. (**www.zagat.com**)

HOTELS :

Alegre Beach Resort
Calumboyan, Sogod, Cebu...
Tel. No. 254-9800 "AAA" $165

Perched above Cebu's most spectacular white sand beach, the Alegre Beach Resort offers its guests friendly, unobtrusive service in an idyllic tropical location. Upon arrival, the reception area offers uninterrupted views over the spacious pools to the surrounding islands beyond.

A five star resort, close to the charming town of Sogod on the northeastern coast of Cebu. Alegre's cottages are set in lush tropical grounds many of which offer ocean views and private gardens. The resort boasts a coconut grove, and three private beach coves, all of which have white sand. Complimentary roundtrip land transfers and scheduled city shuttle service.

Badian Island Beach Hotel
Badian, Cebu
Tel no. 475-1102 "AAA" $120
At Badian Island Beach Hotel you can savor the beauty of a Tiny Pacific Island basking in the tropical blue sea of the Philippine archipelago. Located in the Badian Bay at the sunset coast of Cebu, the guest will be warmly welcomed at the airport and accompanied to the hotel by our staff. Boat transfers to West Coral Beach for snorkeling and swimming, windsurfing, Tennis, Table Tennis, Paddleboats, Badminton, Volleyball, Billiard, and Darts. Evening entertainment.

Maribago Bluewater Beach Resort
Buyong Maribago, Mactan Island..Tel. No. 232-5411 "AAA" $100
Maribago Bluewater Beach Resort offers the best of Cebu for an ideal balance of creature comforts and nature's wonders. Located 15 minutes away from the Mactan Cebu Airport, Maribago takes pride as the island's prized beach. All the diverse pleasures of island living are at your doorstep; scuba diving, snorkeling, beach combing, swimming or just simply lazing under the tropical sun.

Cebu City Marriott
Cardinal Rosales Avenue
Cebu City, 6000
Cebu, Philippines
Phone: 63 32-2326100

(www.marriott.com)
Located minutes from downtown and the convention center, as well as the beautiful Ayala Shopping Center. Here you'll find 303 Rooms, 22 Suites. Outdoor pool, Health club, Sauna, Jogging, Tennis (1 km) Golfing: Alta Vista Golf Course (18 holes; 6102 yards; 72 par; 2.5 km away), Cebu Country Club (18 holes; 6500 yards; 72 par; 1 km away.

Waterfront Cebu City Hotel
1 Waterfront Drive, Off Salinas Drive, Lahug, Cebu, Philippine. $65.
+(848) 827 5839
Email: reservation@sino.net.
This is a centrally located Vegas like hotel with some great nightclubs on the premises and in the immediate area.

For a list of lesser expensive hotels, see here:

(www.resortsphilippines.com/cebu.html)

GETTING AROUND :

Buses : On an air-conditioned bus a short ride costs PhP 8.00, adding PhP 2.00 for every succeeding kilometer. The regular bus' minimum fare is PhP 3.00, with an additional PhP1.00 for every succeeding kilometer. Just tell the conductor where you are going and he will tell you how much it costs. Keep your bus receipt, as it is your proof of payment.

Jeepneys : jeepneys travel most of the secondary roads and even a few major thoroughfares. They're as much fun to ride on as they are to look at and you have to try one. Call out "bayad" (bah-yhad) and pay the driver. When you are ready to get off, call out "para" (pah-rah); wait till he slows down and jump.

The LRT : It's the fastest, cheapest way to go. The PhP 10.00-worth token takes you from Monumento (the northern end of Edsa) to Baclaran, traveling first along Rizal Avenue and then Taft Avenue. Many of the tourist maps have the route of the LRT marked.

Taxis: Air-conditioned taxis cost PhP20.00 on the meter and an additional PhP 1.00 is added for every succeeding 200 meters. to the final cost. Taxis are always lined up at the major hotels and tourist restaurants and can be hailed on the street. Unless you are taking a long trip or the traffic is unusually horrible, most taxi rides should be well under P100. At least a 10% tip is expected.

CRIME AND SCAMS :

If you take a taxi, make sure the driver turns on the meter. If he gives you a story that it is broken, get out and take another taxi. Always get the price up front. Jeepneys have been known to have theft in broad daylight; the passenger next to you pulls a gun. If you're not comfortable with your passenger, get off and take a cab alone.

ATMS in daylight are very much subject to high street crime in the Philippines. Some restaurants try to sweet talk you into their specialty meal and get you to order without an upfront price, and then they hit you with a $60-75 bill.

In clubs, the dancers will sit on your lap with a full drink, then miraculously a few more drinks appear rapidly without you ever ordering them. If you refuse to pay for them, huge bouncers who demand you pay for the drinks when you try to leave surround you. So, if a girl sits on your lap with a drink, politely ask her to leave or just stand up and go to bar area. One more option is to just sit there, look at her cross-eyed and continually fart and belch until she runs. **Pay cash** for your drinks in the bar, no tabs.

THE GAME PLAN :

Filipinas in Cebu are an exotic combo of both oriental and Spanish looks, with tight little bodies in beautiful dark bronze skin. While intelligent, confident and friendly, the residents are famously poor and are dealt a lousy hand in life. There are many local girls desperate for an American boyfriend or husband. Very often the locals are more than happy to go out for short time dates, just as long as you keep the payment terminology is expressed in the terms *helping her out*, or simply saying you'd like her company and *will take care of her*. They still have a lot of pride. It's probably the best situation, because they're sweet and often squeaky-clean honeys, and for the most part honest…well as honest as you can expect of a woman. The average monthly salary in the Philippines is $80 American. Hell, my bar tab last night was higher than that.

Thus, try the local's route before anything else, starting at **The Ayala Shopping Mall,** where there are a lot of pubs, with favorites being **Mi Vida, Brix,** and **Ratsky.** Mi Vida, located on the first floor, is the place to go on weekends after 10:30pm. The place is packed with pros, semi pros, and amateurs all looking for fun.

For daytime action, stop at any coffee clutch spot in the Mall. Freelancers will approach you. Make eye contact, buy her a coffee, and ask for an afternoon guide/date. If you prefer non-pros, stay at the Marriott, it's right there, and hit the mall in the days. Most every girl will be your girlfriend for as long as you want, from one hour to a week…just let her know that *you will take care of her.*

If you're into gambling, the waterfront airport and waterfront city are both casino hotels full of plenty of women lingering and available to console the gamblers.

On to the Cebu go go bars. In Cebu, you won't find the huge amount of clubs in a sectioned off red light district like in Angeles City or Thailand, but they are there. First up is the **Viking Bar,** located across and down the street from Iglesia Cristo Church on Mango Avenue. Opposite of the Viking Bar is the **Club Circus Disco,** (not a go go bar), which is packed with freelancers looked to wub you wong time. Wednesday is packed for ladies night, overnight dates run $20-30.

Next-door is strip club row, with **Exotica, Dimples, Cities, La Dolce Vita, Misty's** and **Papillon.** Uptown you will find the **Silver Dollar Bar,** located on Osmena Blvd.; any taxi will know where it is. **Firehouse** is found off of Jones Avenue. **St Moritz** is found off of Gorordo Avenue, a long running club well known as well.

Most go go bars have topless billiards available. All clubs have similar pricing; your beers are 35P before 9pm, 40-100P later on, with ladies drinks around 150P. Bar fine around 700P and girls is 1000-1500P. Sometimes the mamasan wants full payment for both Upfront, make sure you clear this up before leaving with your Asian flower and she later requests an additional gift.

Show Places: For experiencing something different and very upscale, show places are unique to Cebu City, and not found in Angeles City. It resembles a walkway fashion show, except at the end the models get completely naked or close to it. The prices for the girls quadruple to 4000P, with no real reason considering the quality of women, but it's fun to watch once anyway. The two more well known ones are side by side; **Thunderdome** and **Volvo,** located on F Ramos Street, across from the Holiday Plaza Hotel. Watch the lady drink scams here.

Next up, it's time to get down and dirty boys. Not far from Sanciangko-Palaez Streets are the **Jonquerra Brothels**. Here you'll find hysterical little Bamboo huts and shacks filled with short time Filipinas. This is the home of the cheap, really cheap, and unbelievably cheap young girls. It caters to the broke locals, but when you stroll on in you're a heavy hitter with a $20 bill and will be given the red carpet treatment. Find yourself a pimp on Palaez Street near the Mercedes Hotel, and have him escort you to Jonquerra. With a pimp, you won't have a mad dash from all the other pimps trying to throw their girls at you, you're at least guaranteed a quiet initial entrance.

Take your seat, and your guide will then bring his girls to you. You get to pick and choose to your liking, sort of like a waiter with wine; only you're not interested in aged goods. Take your time and choose your wine whenever you damn well feel like it. Maybe assume some preposterous tilted aristocratic head position and make small mysterious hand moments when you reject one. This area can have some scary sights initially, but a winner will soon appear. Best Showtime for the pickings is early evening, around 8 pm.

Regular ST price for Jonquerra is P500. The girl gets to split this massive sum ($10) with the house. When you're finished, have the pimp escort you out and tip him in case you fell like repeating later on.

Massage Parlors: of course are another avenue to explore, although don't expect them to equal the Thailand soapy massages. There are a few dedicated places to go, and many of the hotels will offer in house sessions as well.

For stand alone, try **Great Hearts Health Service Massage**, located on the Ground Floor of the Fuente Pension House on J. Lorrente Street. Massage is 250P, with extra bj service for 500P to full service rates of 1000-1500P. The oldest downtown hot spot is called **Finland**, down on Palaez Street. **Bodyflex Massage** can be found in the Cityview Pension House, with comparable rates. P600 for the massage. And P1000 for the extras. **Caesar's Palace** is situated in Mandaue near Innodata. One of the more plush locations, with large beds, hot bath and wall-to-wall mirrors. Room price is a bit higher at P1000, with full service another 1000-1500P. **Mogambo Falls**, located in the Plantation Bay Resort in Mactan is a gorgeous upper scale hotel with an on site spa, outdoor hot Jacuzzi, a salt water Jacuzzi, and swimming pool. Open daily from 10am to 11pm, the entrance fee is 300P for use of the above, and full service including massage is around 1750P. (**www.plantationbay.com**)

Freelancers are easily available as well at the many discos. There are lots of touts/pimps/girls working the Streets and a basic ST (Short time) can be negotiated from P500 up to P1500 for all night. For the truly hardcore territory, there are plenty of streetwalkers; this is not recommended unless you're double wrapping that bad boy. Women are so available and so cheap that you may want to pass on this; it's worth spending an extra $5 and still being able to stand up and pee in the morning without shooting blood and unidentified yellow stuff.

VACATION STUFF :
Now for the cover story for the old lady, tell her you flew 20 hours to collect some seashells.

CASINOS :
Waterfront Cebu City Hotel Casino
#1 Salinas Drive, Lahug, Cebu City, Philippines
Tel (63-32) 232 6888 Fax No (63-32) 232-6880
(www.waterfronthotels.net/cebu_main.html)

Everything about Waterfront Cebu City Hotel is grand. A sprawling hotel that's a testament to the relentless pursuit of perfection. There are 12 specialty restaurants and theme bars offering international cuisine, and plenty of choices of buffets.

Table Games
Baccarat, Big and Small, Blackjack, Craps, Pai Gow Poker, Stud Poker

Waterfront Airport Hotel & Casino
1 Airport Road, Lapu-Lapu City, Cebu
+63 (32) 340-4888 General Information
(www.waterfronthotels.net/mactan_main.html)

Situated in the historical island of Mactan Cebu, next to the Mactan Cebu International Airport. Just 15 minutes from pristine white beaches, 10 minutes away from the shopping center. It contains 167 deluxe rooms with a spectacular view of the islands.
Table Games
Baccarat, Big and Small, Blackjack, Craps, Pai Gow Poker, Roulette

GOLF COURSES :

Golf is very popular in the Philippines, and home to over 50 golf courses. Because the golf courses were build early last century, the Philippines have some of the oldest fairways in all of Asia.

With designs by Robert Trent Jones, Arnold Palmer, Bernhard Langer and Jack Nicklaus, you'll find some of best courses in the world.

Golf is not expensive in the Philippines. You pay for a green fee something between $10 and $70 per day, depending on location and the time of the week you play. Many fairways are located in the mountains or at the coast. The friendly climate, the fantastic views, the mountain or sea breezes, gentle people, all these things make the game an unforgettable experience. You're really enjoy the fulfilling foursomes you'll be having in Philippines, not to mention you may be playing golf too.

If you are mostly interested in playing Golf and like to stay at a superb beach resort with Spanish ambience, check out new Golf resort Casa del Mar.

Casa del Mar is located in the northwest part of the beautiful island of Cebu, in the charming town of San Remigio, just a 2 hour drive from the Mactan International airport. The resort hotel features condominium style suites, all air-conditioned and facing the sea. Each suite features elegant furnishings including beautifully pattered Italian tile floors. The long natural white sand beach is the place to spend a few hours relaxing or just watching the romantic sunsets.

For some exercise try a round of golf at the **Verdemar Golf Club,** with its challenging Par 6 and great sea views. Meals are also part of the experience here with a large selection of local and international dishes prepared by French and local chefs. There are many other activities including the Del Mar Dive Center, windsurfer, hobbie cats and inside games such as Billiards and Videoke.

DIVING AND SNORKELING :
Cebu is wildly popular for its fantastic diving grounds evidenced by the proliferation of resorts, which offer luxurious accommodations, excellent dive facilities, and the services of competent dive masters and dive guides.

For a complete listing of Philippines courses go here:
(www.worldgolf.com/courses/philgcs.html)

The dive spots around Cebu, Bohol and Negros belong to the best the Philippines have to offer. Some islands are famous for big fish like thresher sharks, manta rays and, if you are lucky, whale sharks. Others offer fantastic coral gardens, steep, often overhanging walls and cliffs, teeming with reef fish.   For the full-blown 3-day dive adventure, visit this site for the dive safari travel plans.

(www.cebu-travel.com/Safaris.htm)

ADVENTURE SPORTS :
Cebu is great for extreme sports as well, as you're set up for many potential events on the island, including **rappelling** over series of waterfalls, some overhanging and as high as 30 meters. Try the mountain biking, horseback riding or **volcano trekking**.

(www.action-philippines.com)

FINAL THOUGHTS

There is an intoxicating allure to the women you'll meet when traveling, but just like you wouldn't fly off to Disneyland expecting the Little Mermaid to fall in love with you, don't expect the girls to provide any more than a highly entertaining experience. This is what they do for a living, and they are probably better at it than any women on earth. Don't make it more complicated than that.

There are acquired skills that will become natural once you have a few trips under your belt. As the saying goes, treat a lady like a whore and a whore like a lady. Everyone in town knows the girls' career, so having a real boyfriend is next to impossible. When the vacation is over, we get to return home to our safe rewarding lives. By default, most of us have won life's lottery just by our location of birth. The girls however wake up every day in some real hellholes and bad situations that they can't control. Giving them a little romancing makes you a fantasy client, and is as close as some girls get to experience a Cinderella romance. They'll love you every minute for it. It's a real treat to see the sparkle in their eyes, the sexy strut in their step, and the constant public groping of your crotch. For once you're treated with an appreciation for your efforts, and the result is guaranteed. As a whole, just keep it fun and stress free, and don't get caught up in any soap operas. You're the boss.

When we look back in life, the career and expensive toys we collect will be a distant memory. What means the most are the risks you took…its the thrill of the chase, the conquests, and the experiences you look fondly back on. When you're lying on the hospital bed with the flat line approaching fast, make sure you can close your eyes and laugh about the impulsive and reckless adventures you've indulged in. You want to be able to picture some gorgeous women you've enjoyed over the years…to remember how you felt the first time you laid eyes on her. How she giggled and batted her eyes at you, how great she smelled, how smooth her skin felt, and the lust in her eyes as she mounted you like a rodeo bull on speed. You want to leave with a smile on your face, knowing that you were spontaneous, you took chances, and it was all real. You enjoyed the good life, and no one can ever take that away from you.

You lived the fantasy.